Henrietta Maria

ABOUT THE AUTHOR

Dominic Pearce studied Classics at New College, Oxford, before pursuing a career in financial analysis, which took him to Japan, Spain and Austria – countries where the modern world succeeds a rich historic tradition. Since then he has undertaken historical and cultural research on the seventeenth century in particular, and also on the practice of art. He has published a study of drawing in collaboration with Francis Hoyland called *Greek Light*. *Henrietta Maria* is his first biography. He lives in London.

Henrietta Maria

The Betrayed Queen

Dominic Pearce

AMBERLEY

This book was written in memory of my father,
the son of a French mother

First published 2015
This edition published 2018

Amberley Publishing
The Hill, Stroud
Gloucestershire, GL5 4EP

www.amberley-books.com

Copyright © Dominic Pearce, 2015, 2017

The right of Dominic Pearce to be identified as
the Author of this work has been asserted in
accordance with the Copyrights, Designs and
Patents Act 1988.

ISBN 978 1 4456 7726 2 (paperback)
ISBN 978 1 4456 4555 1 (ebook)

British Library Cataloguing in Publication Data.
A catalogue record for this book is available
from the British Library.

Typesetting and Origination by Amberley
Publishing
Printed in the UK.

CONTENTS

NOTE ON DATES AND NAMES

Dates

In the seventeenth century two calendars operated in Europe, ten days apart. In the Catholic countries the Gregorian calendar was used (introduced in 1582), but Britain used the older Julian calendar. As an example, 22 June in Paris was 12 June in London.

In my narrative the difference between the calendars is not critical for events. I therefore leave all dates in their local calendar, rather than clutter the text with annotations.

I date the beginning of the year 1 January, as we do today.

Kingdoms

Charles I ruled three kingdoms: England, Scotland and Ireland. He liked the title King of Great Britain, although there was no political union of the realms until the Commonwealth, and later, more permanently, under Queen Anne. However, contemporaries also referred to him (and his wife) as King (and Queen) of England. I use both titles.

Parliaments

In the seventeenth century, the English Parliament was an elected body, summoned and dismissed by the sovereign at his/her will. It controlled the supply of money to the sovereign additional to his personal revenues. There was only one Parliament, seated at Westminster.

The job of the French 'parlements' was to act as a law court of last resort. All members were lawyers. They were not elected, but inherited their places. They had no financial role and no financial veto. There were a number of parlements in France. Of these the Parlement de Paris was the most important.

Names

For flavour, I have kept most French titles in French – for instance 'Duchesse de Chevreuse' rather than 'Duchess of Chevreuse'. Kings and queens I leave in English as international figures. Other countries come into the narrative, but the events of Henrietta Maria's life mainly took place in France and England.

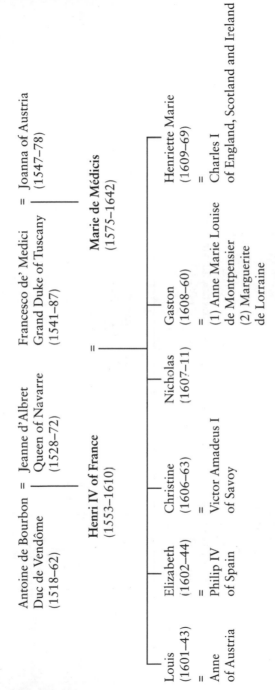

Antoine de Bourbon = Jeanne d'Albret
Duc de Vendôme   Queen of Navarre
(1518–62)   (1528–72)

Francesco de' Medici = Joanna of Austria
Grand Duke of Tuscany (1547–78)
(1541–87)

Henri IV of France
(1553–1610)

=

Marie de Médicis
(1575–1642)

Louis
(1601–43)
=
Anne
of Austria

Elizabeth
(1602–44)
=
Philip IV
of Spain

Christine
(1606–63)
=
Victor Amadeus I
of Savoy

Nicholas
(1607–11)

Gaston
(1608–60)
=
(1) Anne Marie Louise
de Montpensier
(2) Marguerite
de Lorraine

Henriette Marie
(1609–69)
=
Charles I
of England, Scotland and Ireland

House of Bourbon

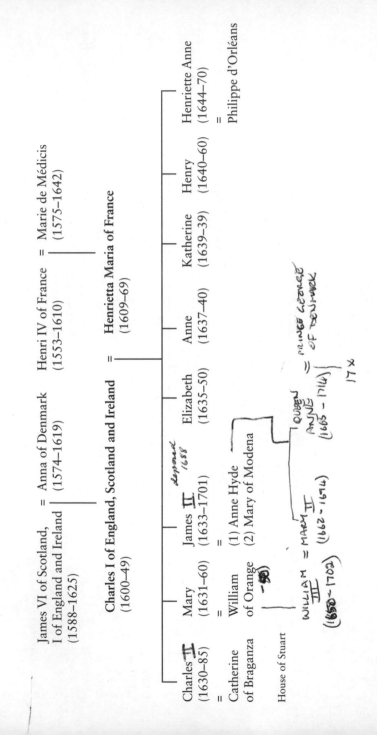

PART ONE

BOURBONS AND STUARTS

But how deceptive are the hopes of men, and how little safety is
there, in everything they propose!

Marquis de Fontenay-Mareuil, *Mémoires*

I

A LEGACY

In early September 1669 a group of men arrived at the Château de Colombes, seven miles north-west of Paris, on a mission of recovery. They had been sent by Ralph Montagu, the English ambassador to the court of Louis XIV, in search of paintings. Nothing remains today of the large building which was the country house of the Queen Mother of England, but many of the paintings that hung in her home survive, for instance Hans Holbein's *Noli me tangere*, Orazio Gentileschi's *Joseph and Potiphar's Wife*, and two pictures of her children by Anthony van Dyck: *Charles II when Prince of Wales*, and *The Three Eldest Children of Charles I*. Thanks to the diligence of Montagu these amazing pictures, with many others, were recovered from Colombes, returned to England, and are preserved within the royal collection.[1] There is no record of the fate of the little Indian box found in the queen's cabinet adjoining her bedroom, which contained a 'miniature of the King when he was Prince of Wales' and two rings, thought to be her wedding rings. These were her intimate keepsakes, totems of the queen's love for her dead husband, Charles I. They are among the open questions raised by the life of Henrietta Maria, famous as the unhappy queen – *'la reine malheureuse'* – but in reality a princess whose life combined stark tragedy with the greatest personal fulfilment and years of intense happiness.[2]

When Montagu's men arrived at Colombes, they did so because she died intestate and there was a quarrel about her possessions. To whom did they now belong? The same question can be asked about her legacy in history.

Henrietta Maria was a leader of the world that dissolved into civil war; in fact, she survived civil war in both England and France. Accounts of the queen – memories, descriptions, records of varying degrees of accuracy and wishful thinking – abound in the writings of her contemporaries and of historians, and we have many of her own letters. She can be seen bewitchingly in the canvasses of van Dyck, frozen forever in her early twenties, black eyes gazing into the modern day. To whom does Henrietta Maria now belong?

The best way of answering the question is to follow her story.

2

JUST ANOTHER GIRL

The bride entered Florence Cathedral in the company of three hundred young women, dressed in white. After a lengthy wedding service conducted by the Pope's nephew Cardinal Aldobrandini, scented by wafting clouds of incense and hymned by ethereal polyphony, Maria de' Medici, niece of the Grand Duke of Tuscany, emerged triumphant as the Queen of France. It was 5 October in the jubilee year 1600.[1]

That evening in the Salone dei Cinquecento of the Palazzo Vecchio, a feast was given by Grand Duke Ferdinando, followed by dancing. Above the guests a golden frieze showed the arms of the bride's relations: two popes, the Austrian Habsburgs, the Medici joined with those of Lorraine, the Este of Ferra and of Modena, the Sforza, the Spanish Alvarez de Toledo, the Orsini of Bracciano, as well as those of a previous Medici Queen of France, Catherine de Médicis. There were also the arms of Maria herself and her husband, Henri IV of France.[2]

A giant lily dominated the chamber, the emblem of France, decorated with gold- and silver-gilt vessels, silk tassels and other treasures. Many of the bowls and basins were filled with the worked semi-precious stones for which Florentine craftsmen were famous, with intaglios and clusters of jewels. The stem of the lily was surrounded by vases of crystal, lapis lazuli and amethyst.

Three silver-gilt knights on horseback stood guard. The base of the pedestal was engraved with the names of the married couple.

By the bride's table stood a large elephant and rhinoceros, beneath two spreading oak trees with white leaves and silver acorns. Doves and other birds nestled in the glittering branches, and the wintry leaves spread over bulls, wild boar and deer. There were meats, pies and other elaborate dishes that presented the labours of Hercules, heroes and gods, beautiful women, cupids, monsters and temples, and there was a figure of the groom made of sugar.[3]

*

For the time being, this sugar statue was all that Maria would see of her husband. The King of France had spent most of his adult life in the saddle, fighting in the apparently endless Wars of Religion which almost destroyed the French state in the last quarter of the sixteenth century. Now he was at war with the Duke of Savoy over the possession of the Marquisate of Saluzzo, a territory to the south of Turin.

Henri IV sent a group of gentlemen to represent him in Florence, headed by the Sieur de Bellegarde, who carried his proxy. Bellegarde was authorised to deliver it to Grand Duke Ferdinando, which meant that the Grand Duke stood in for Henri IV in the wedding ceremony as the proxy groom, so that Maria had actually married her uncle.

The party went on for days, with celebrations in the other main Medici palaces including a performance in the Boboli Gardens of the Pitti Palace of *Eurydice*, one of the first operas in European history, with music by Jacopo Peri; also performed was the *Abduction of Cephalus*, in the ultramodern theatre in the Uffizzi. After this the bride departed to Pisa, where there were fireworks, and then to Livorno, from where, accompanied by a fleet of galleys rowed by slaves, Maria embarked for France, chaperoned by her aunt Christina, Grand Duchess of Tuscany, who was responsible for the enormous cash dowry that travelled with them. To keep the Barbary pirates at bay, the seven Tuscan boats were accompanied by ten of the Knights of Malta and of the Holy See, and by one French galley.

*

Certainly the fleet was an attractive target. The cash dowry was 350,000 *écus,* and the Queen of France and the Grand Duchess of Tuscany would command incredible ransoms.

Then there was the jewellery – not just of the ladies but also of the main galley in which they travelled, which was a dazzling weapon of diplomacy. The crew was dressed in scarlet. A standard fluttered from the mast showing the Medici *palle* (balls) and the French lilies. Inside the galley, rooms were ornately painted. Outside, the prow was gilded and decorated with figures of men, masks, animals and mythical creatures such as harpies and winged horses; the stern was inlaid with sapphires, emeralds, topaz, pearls, amethysts; the deck was of sandalwood, ivory and ebony. When Maria stepped from the galley to the shore, it would be as if Cleopatra, or Juno herself, had arrived.[4]

Maria de' Medici landed safely at Marseille on 3 November. Unfortunately her arrival occurred in the absence, once more, of Henri IV, who was doomed never to see the miraculous Medici galley, which returned to Livorno with Grand Duchess Christina later in the month. Maria nonetheless appeared both royal and virginal in her dress of cloth of gold, her blonde hair dressed high and unpowdered, tied with simple ribbons, her face free of make-up and with pearls around her neck, which was ' left rather open'.[5]

It seemed the king would never appear. He was not waiting at Marseilles, but the French reception committee was stellar, boasting among its thousands the Constable of France, the Duc de Montmorency; the Chancellor, Pomponne de Bellièvre; three duchesses (Nemours, Guise, Ventadour); four cardinals (Gondi, Joyeuse, Givry, Sourdes); and ten bishops. Maria would now make a royal progress through Provence towards the waiting arms of Henri IV, who was attacking Savoyard fortresses north of Lyon. In this she was already a working queen, and from this time the Tuscan princess becomes the French Marie de Médicis.[6]

*

From Marseille the queen travelled to the capital of Provence, Aix, where, with reference to the terrible death toll of the religious wars, she was celebrated as

> the altogether perfect princess ...
> It will be you who make the beauty
> Of our towns blossom once more,
> You who will cause to die

The root of our civil hatreds and
By you peace will be assured[7]

Marie travelled to papal Avignon, and from there 125 chilly miles up the Rhone to Lyon, where she arrived at the beginning of December, made a stately entry to popular acclaim, through streets decorated with triumphal arches, platforms ornamented with Medici symbols and statuary, and settled in the Archbishop's Palace. The seven-year-old César de Vendôme, one of the king's illegitimate children, was now in her suite, so Marie was one of the family. Here Henri IV, who had concluded his war by taking the fort of Sainte Catherine, joined her. He arrived late on 9 December, at something like eleven o'clock in the evening. He was so keen to surprise his bride that he refused to let his men announce him as king, so the party had to wait an hour outside the city walls in the freezing rain before they were admitted. Marie was still eating her evening meal when Henri IV was granted entry. The queen was warned that the king was in the house, possibly by her childhood friend Leonora Galigai, possibly by the Italian Duchesse de Nemours. Marie blushed scarlet, refused any further food, and retired to her room. In fact Henri IV had been observing her as she ate, hidden on a gallery above. Having made his bargain, he wanted to check it out.

She was married in a cloud of virginal white, but the king's woman-loving nature was no secret to Marie. Of course they had not met, but they had corresponded, on his side in terms of rather un-courtly love. In one of his letters he said, 'If it is permissible to be in love with one's wife, I can tell you I am very much in love with you; but I would prefer to show what this means in a place where there is nobody except you and me.' Similarly, her uncle Ferdinando, the Grand Duke, was succinct: 'Whatever else, be pregnant.'[8]

The king came to his wife's room and covered her with kisses. He was taken with his voluptuous bride, but it is hard to believe that her first impressions were especially delicious. Henri IV was not a tall man, and was forty-nine years old to her twenty-five. He had a hooked nose, bad teeth and a white beard. He had come straight from the front line – and he hated washing.[9]

Probably the first conversation between the king and his new queen was gushing and incoherent, because Marie did not speak or understand much French. Henri IV retired for something to eat, and with blunt delicacy sent a message to Marie to say that, unfortunately, he had travelled so quickly from the camp to the palace that he had not brought any furniture with him, not even a bed. Would the queen object if he spent the night in hers? The queen replied that she was his humble servant.

*

The second nuptial ceremony took place on 17 December 1600 in Lyon Cathedral, once again celebrated by Cardinal Aldobrandini, but by then the wedding was consummated – repeatedly, we are told, and to the satisfaction of everyone concerned. It was not at all a private matter; people needed to know.

Marie was quickly pregnant. On 27 September 1601 the Queen of France was lucky enough to give birth to a healthy son, Louis, so at last there was a dauphin, an undisputed heir to the Bourbon throne.

For nine years after her marriage, Marie de Médicis proved what a good choice she was. On 22 November 1602, she had a daughter, Elizabeth. After a gap, on 10 February 1606 she had a second daughter, Christine. On 16 April 1607 another boy was born, Nicolas, who survived four and a half years, and the queen had a third son, Jean Baptiste Gaston (always known as Gaston), born on 25 April 1608.

Her last child was born on 26 November 1609. We have a clinician's account of the labour in the meticulous journal of Jean Héroard, doctor to the dauphin. From the onset of contractions it was two or three hours to birth. The labour was not especially difficult for the mother, although she took some time to recover. The baby's brother, the eight-year-old dauphin, was delighted and the courtiers flocked to see whether it was a boy, but once the baby was born people lost interest. The courtier Pierre d'Estoile recorded in his journal that there was no special celebration for the birth of the most recent daughter of France – just another girl. They named her Henriette Marie.[10]

3

A DELAYED CORONATION

During the winter the king and queen lived in Paris, so the baby was born in the Louvre, but the royal children were brought up outside Paris. In the sixteenth century the royal hunting lodge at St Germain-en-Laye was expanded into a magnificent palace-stronghold called the Château Vieux, sited on a wooded crest sweeping down to the Seine. Here the royal nursery was housed. At St Germain Henriette Marie and her siblings enjoyed an idyll, playing inside and out, in the terraced gardens, on the stairways leading to a quay, inside the grotto.[1]

There was no question of Henriette Marie being raised by her mother. Mme de Montglat, a tall, very thin woman, and her daughter Mme de St George, supervised the nursery, a full-time job because of the number of staff – every child had their own complement of attendants, wet nurses, regular nurses and rockers, and there was also a team of cooks, laundresses, cleaners – but also because of the number of children.

Together with her own six, the queen had to put up with five of her husband's other children at St Germain-en-Laye: three Vendômes and two Verneuils, the children of Gabrielle d'Estrées and Henriette d'Entragues respectively. Gabrielle had died in the course of her fourth pregnancy by Henri IV in 1598, but the catlike d'Entragues was still alive; in fact, she continued her affair with the king for several years after the marriage. These royal bastards were legitimised. César de Vendôme, the oldest, tried to make Marie de Médicis call him her son, but Henri IV thought this was going too far. It was arranged that the queen would address her husband's other children as her nephews and nieces.[2]

In emotional terms the haughty queen was rather distant from her children, especially from her eldest son, the dauphin, but she took a close interest, asking to know 'everything about them even to their private pastimes'. In 1607 she commiserated with Mme de Montglat when her husband died, but instructed her not to cry in front of the children and to be sure always to keep them in a state of effervescent jolliness. The journal of the dauphin's doctor, Jean Héroard, is peppered with references to the queen being in the company of the princesses, whether at St Germain, Fontainebleau or St Cloud.

We know how anxious Marie was when the toddler Henriette Marie had a fever in 1611, instructing Mme de Montglat to 'take care then that my said daughter lacks nothing that might afford any remedy or solace to her complaint' and sending one of her own physicians to check everything possible was done. Henriette Marie was small and suffered from scoliosis (curvature of the spine), and possibly needed extra vigilance.[3]

Henri IV was relaxed with the children. When he had the time, the king was a hands-on father. There is a famous story about the Spanish ambassador arriving for a formal audience – as the King of Spain's representative his contacts with the King of France were governed by the most refined rules of etiquette – and finding Henri IV on all fours with two of the children on his back. Henri IV was a warm, demonstrative man, happy to break the rules.[4]

Henriette Marie also knew a kind of aunt, who was really her father's first wife. Marguerite de Valois, now heading for sixty, heavily overweight, drenched in perfume, gorgeously dressed and bewigged, was famous in her youth for an exquisite glamour: 'You will take her for a Goddess from paradise rather than a Princess of the earth.' 'Queen Margot' lived in a brand-new palace on the other side of the Seine from the Louvre. She was especially fond of the dauphin, who adored her and called her '*Maman, ma fille*' ('Mama, my daughter' – all the French being the children of the king and his heir).

Queen Margot was the last daughter of the Valois line of the royal family. She had a past studded with adventure, including the annulment of her marriage to Henri IV, exile in the provinces, poems, an autobiography and countless lovers, but now she was a loyal friend to her ex-husband and his second wife, her blood relative.[5]

*

From Héroard's meticulous account of the dauphin's young life we can read across to the other children to learn that, once they stopped breastfeeding, they would be fed with bread and soups. Quite early the children started to drink heavily diluted wine. Chicken and duck were fed to the dauphin when he was two, and it is safe to assume the same was true of the others. Within seasonal constraints, royal children enjoyed a steady supply of fruit – strawberries, cherries, melon. The rule in the Catholic world was fish on Fridays, and from the age of five this seems to have been applied in the nursery. Children do not always take to fish, but the Friday diet of perch, trout and sole sounds reasonably appealing. From the age of five or six the children would start to tackle the richer food prepared by royal cooks, which included the full range of early seventeenth-century ingredients – pork, beef, spices, sugar, suet – and they also started to eat game, a staple in a family that loved hunting.[6]

This was luxury, but the children of Henri IV were not spoiled. A note has survived from the young Henriette Marie writing to her governess to ask forgiveness for her bad temper, and the letters of her mother imply that Henriette Marie was a strong-minded child who had to be curbed. Brattish behaviour was not allowed.[7]

Héroard records a conversation between the dauphin and his governess on 10 October 1605, when the four-year-old was trying to get a toy from Mme de Montglat:

> Mme de Montglat: Say 'please'.
> Dauphin: Don't want to say please.
> Mme de Montglat: Then you won't have it.
> Dauphin: I'll say it to Papa.
> Mme de Montglat: Say it now.
> Dauphin: When I have it [the toy], I'll say it.
> Mme de Montglat: Then you won't have it.

Dauphin: I'll hit you.
Mme de Montglat: I'll whip you.
Dauphin: I'll kill you.[8]

Mamangat, as Mme de Montglat was known, had authority to whip the children – 'whip' really does seem the right translation – and she did so, untroubled by fears of revenge. We do not know if the girls had the same physical treatment as the boys, but there is no reason to doubt the emphasis on discipline.

*

Five months after the birth of Madame Henriette, her mother was crowned Queen of France in the abbey church of St Denis, a few miles outside the walls of Paris. It was a day of brilliant sunshine. The thick, dark-blonde hair of Marie de Médicis was piled on her head, probably by Leonora Galigai, who had come with her from Florence in 1600 as her hairdresser. Marie's ample figure was enveloped in 'a velvet coat covered with golden *fleurs-de-lis* and lined with ermine, with a long train ... in her hair she wore jewels, and her jacket was covered with huge diamonds, rubies and emeralds'.[9]

Marie de Médicis walked slowly into the church under a canopy held by two cardinals. Her escort comprised Swiss guards in violet and sky blue, the king's gentlemen in white and violet, and the knights of the Order of the Holy Spirit in black velvet embroidered with silver. The ceremony at St Denis was a long, musical display of royal authority under God, attended by brocaded princes of the Church and court, and by Henri IV, who watched from a specially constructed box in the gallery. All the royal children were there, including the infant Henriette Marie, carried by Mme de Montglat and presumably wide awake throughout since the ceremony was filled with distractions – 'cardinals and bishops honoured the assembly, various concerts of music filled and delighted the ear'.[10]

The queen was annoyed that her husband had for ten years denied her the coronation. Marie de Médicis became desperate to be crowned so that everyone could see how God accepted her as queen, not least as a defence against her husband's girlfriends. Henri IV did not order the ceremony to please his wife, however; he did it because he needed her to act as his regent, with unassailable authority, when he left France on campaign. He was not entirely pleased about his decision, since he felt that crowning his wife was a bad omen for the rest of his reign, a loss of authority, or luck. The king had assembled an army of 22,000 in Champagne, which he intended to lead into the Holy Roman Empire to make war on the Habsburg family.[11]

4

THE HAND OF GOD

Henriette Marie was born into a world which was largely ruled by the Habsburgs, who were traditional enemies of France. In many ways the year 1610 was a good time to strike a blow for French prestige against the House of Austria, being a time of weakness in the two leading Habsburg states.

As well as colonial possessions in America and the East Indies, Habsburg Spain had a European empire which included all the Iberian Peninsula, all of south Italy, the Duchy of Milan and the Netherlands. Since 1558 the northern, Protestant part of the Netherlands – Holland and other provinces – had been in rebellion, which drained Spanish resources. A truce had therefore been signed in 1609 between Spain and the rebels, to last for twelve years while the exhausted combatants recuperated.

Another branch of the Habsburgs lived in Vienna and wielded an uncertain control over the German-speaking territories of the Holy Roman Empire. Although the Holy Roman Empire was big, its fractured nature and the emperor's fluctuating authority meant that it was a weak force in the greater world. The empire was not cohesive. It was part Catholic and part Protestant. Large numbers of German princes ruled as hereditary sovereigns over their different plots of land, owing obedience to the emperor provided he obeyed the complicated imperial constitution, and depending on their inclination to be compliant. The Austrian Habsburgs also had to look to their south-eastern flank on the borders of Europe, where the militarised Ottoman Turks pressed for conquests. In 1610 the imperial Habsburgs were also wracked by a family quarrel for power, known as the Brothers' Quarrel.

France was by comparison unitary, very large and, thanks to Henri IV, once more formidable. The brilliant medieval civilisation of France had given the country a claim to cultural leadership, which was then eclipsed by the Renaissance patronage of the much smaller Italian states and by the French Wars of Religion. The achievement of Henri IV was to unite his country and prepare it to assert its primacy in culture and politics. When Marie de Médicis was crowned, the personal authority of Henri IV was at its peak.

Other European powers were far from negligible, including the Duchy of Savoy, the Duchy of Lorraine, the papacy (with its crushing religious authority), the Kingdom of Denmark and the Stuart kingdoms of England, Scotland and Ireland, but these were all secondary powers. The British Isles were both protected and to some extent isolated from Europe by the sea. Although Britain consisted of three very different realms, all of them ruled by one man – King James I of England and Ireland, and VI of Scotland – they were all internally peaceful at this time.

*

Despite the supremacy of Henri IV, France was tested by internal tensions. By refusing to attend the queen's coronation, two powerful men challenged the queen's position and defied the king. Both were Princes of the Blood, the king's cousins. One was the Comte de Soissons, who kept away because his wife was not allowed to wear a dress decorated with royal lilies. The other was Soissons' nephew, the Prince de Condé, twenty-one at the time. Condé's reasons for avoiding the coronation were more interesting and easier to understand.[1]

Henri II de Condé was the senior Prince of the Blood. He was a child of scandal, born six months after his father's death in 1588 to a mother who was then imprisoned for poisoning her husband. This gloomy family history was due to a love affair of the Princesse de Condé with one of her grooms, which also cast doubt on the paternity of the young Henri, although his cousin the king later accepted Henri II de Condé as his heir – after any sons – and made sure the princess was exonerated of the charge of murder. Unsurprisingly, the young prince was damaged goods. He was considered surly, difficult and insignificant.

Thanks to the intervention of Henri IV, on 17 May 1609 Henri II de Condé married a daughter of one of the great families, the exquisite fifteen-year-old Charlotte de Montmorency, 'whom everyone found perfect in beauty'. The wedding was a low-key service at her father's Château de Chantilly. The king awarded his cousin an annual pension of 100,000 *livres tournois*, so in all respects he was lavishing favours on him, but nothing was what it seemed. Condé liked hunting better than women, and there was every sign that he liked men better than women too. That suited Henri IV, since, as the entire French court knew, the white-bearded king, old enough to be her grandfather, was desperately in love with Charlotte.[2]

When the king first saw the teenager in January 1609, she was rehearsing her part as a nymph for one of the entertainments that Marie de Médicis liked to present to the court, the 'Grand Ballet de la Reine'. At once he was smitten and succumbed to an attack of gout that lasted a fortnight. By marrying Charlotte to Condé, Henri IV interfered in her father's plans, since originally she was engaged to the king's friend, the ardent womaniser François de Bassompierre. Marriage to Bassompierre would not leave Charlotte free for an affair, while marriage to Condé almost guaranteed one. Bassompierre gave way to his master (with regret), but Condé was determined that the king would not touch his wife, although the marriage was not consummated.[3]

Rather than attend court, Condé retreated to Burgundy, taking Charlotte with him. The king and Charlotte exchanged letters in which he called her Dulcinée, the name of the heroine of Cervantes' *Don Quixote*, while she called him her star and told him to burn her letters, which he did not do.[4]

The Condés came to Fontainebleau in June 1609 in order to pay their respects to Marie de Médicis when it was clear that she was pregnant, but left again to take up residence in the Château de Muret, near Soissons, north of Paris. Henri IV pursued his quarry. At one point he disguised himself as a royal huntsman in his own livery, put on a false beard and an eye-patch, and posted himself at the side of the road to gaze longingly at Charlotte's carriage as it rumbled past, and as she gazed briefly back.

Condé became desperate. Three days after Marie de Médicis gave birth, he drove into the shadowy forest of Landrecies with Charlotte at his side and the two of them disappeared from view. 'Bassompierre, my friend,' said Henri IV when he heard the news, 'I am lost. This man has taken his wife into a wood. I do not know if it is to kill her, or to take her out of France.'

Charlotte survived her forest ride. The Condé cavalcade drove on through, and crossed the border with Spanish Flanders. The prince deposited his reluctant wife in the house of relations in Brussels, the Hôtel de Nassau, and put more distance between his own royal person and that of his cousin Henri IV by travelling down to Milan, where he could have discussions with the King of Spain's viceroy. He also talked about annulling his dangerous marriage. It was no surprise that Condé failed to turn up for Marie de Médicis' coronation on 13 May, since his actions made him vulnerable to a charge of treason.[5]

*

If love dramas played around the cradle of the newborn princess, so did dramas of war and religion. By early 1610 a stand-off had developed around the city of Jülich in the north-western part of the Holy Roman Empire, where Henri IV was planning to lead his army. This was the king's planned destination, his reason for leaving France, his reason for needing a regent.

The Jülich confrontation was caused by the claims of different German princes to the Duchy of Jülich Cleves, whose possession was in dispute following the death of Duke Johann Wilhelm on 25 March 1609. The childless duke's mental problems – he was known as Johann Wilhelm the Simple – contributed to the lack of preparation for his legacy, which was widely contested because he had a lot of relatives.

Jülich Cleves consisted of different hereditary territories under the personal union of the duke. Together they comprised a large and strategic area which bordered on the Dutch Republic and Flanders. The location alone made the duchy important, because Flanders was an economic jewel in the Spanish crown, and a military base against the Dutch.

By 1610 two leading parties had emerged in the Jülich Cleves dispute. The first party was that of the Habsburgs who intervened by imperial authority. The twenty-three-year-old Archduke Leopold was in occupation of Jülich with a fairly modest body of troops to support his position of imperial commissioner, which he himself had persuaded his cousin, the dithering Emperor Rudolf II, to grant him in July 1609. In theory this appointment was intended to guarantee fair play – Rudolf was supporting the claim of the Elector of Saxony – but in practice there was a fear that the Habsburgs would attempt to gain control of all or part of the duchy.

However, the Catholic Leopold was badly outnumbered by the combined troops of two Protestant princes, the Duke of Pfalz-Neuburg and the Elector of Brandenburg, jointly called the Possessors. As nephews of Johann Wilhelm (the latter by marriage) they had the best blood claim, and they occupied the duchy as a whole, with the intention of partitioning it between them. Their troops surrounded Jülich, penning in Leopold, who did not have enough soldiers to break out. Henri IV mobilised in support of the Possessors, in support, in fact, of 'German liberties' – this meant the rights of the princely rulers against the claims of the emperor – so as to face down Rudolf and Leopold, and build political capital. Clearly the risk was that a large French army invading the empire would trigger a general war, but Henri IV had won every war he had fought, so he was ready for that.[6]

To cement international friendships, Henri IV offered one of his daughters to the Duke of Savoy as a wife for his son. The support of Savoy was essential because of the Spanish Habsburg presence in northern Italy. Either Elizabeth or Christine was offered (both were still children). King James I of England was similarly caressed by the offer of Henriette Marie (not yet one year old) as wife for his eldest son, that is to say Henry Stuart, Duke of Cornwall. Here was the princess's first shot at an English marriage.

Among other blandishments Henri IV also sent his riding master, the Sieur de St Antoine, to teach Henry Stuart horsemanship – a great compliment since French equestrian skills were considered the most advanced in Europe. The offer of his youngest daughter, however, showed that Henri IV regarded the British king as his least important ally.[7]

The lovely Princesse de Condé was a common factor in the intrigues of early 1610. With 22,000 men at his disposal it was open to Henri IV to march to Jülich, but it was open to him to stop in Flanders too, to rescue Charlotte from the Hôtel de Nassau. He went so far as to draft a letter telling the Archduke Albert of Flanders that he would be marching through his territory, and asking whether he would be regarded as a friend or enemy.[8] Rescuing Charlotte would insult her husband, but it could also be a pre-emptive strike against Spanish interference in France.

The situation was therefore hard to predict, but the one evident message was imminent war.

*

In the afternoon of Friday 14 May, Henri IV took a ride in his carriage to see the arches, the rich tapestries hung from windows, allegorical figures, artificial rocks and trees, platforms from which poems and speeches could be declaimed, all the decorations that prepared the streets of Paris for the forthcoming triumphal entry of the newly crowned Queen of France. Henri's carriage was little more than an ornate four-wheeled covered cart, not sprung for comfort but containing cushioned seating and enclosed by flapping curtains of leather, not by glass panes. It trundled along at a pace which a running man could match. At his instructions, the main bodyguards did not accompany Henri IV on this pleasure trip, but some precautionary attendants ran behind and alongside.

The king was moody and indecisive. He needed distraction. He contemplated a visit to his chief minister, the Duc de Sully, at the Arsenal, but changed his mind and ordered the driver to head for the Rue St Denis, where the most splendid show was planned. In the Rue de la Ferronnerie, near the market of Les Halles, the road was narrow, crowded by a row of shops, which made it impossible for the king's escort to surround the carriage. They individually peeled off to go around the back, and catch up later, while two or three ran on ahead to clear a blockage caused by two carts, one carrying hay and the other vats of wine. When the carriage entered the Rue de la Ferronnerie, the king was sitting on the side of the carriage away from the row of shops, in other words where there was open space on the street side. He had his right arm around the Duc d'Épernon's shoulders, and was reading a letter.

The leather curtains had been rolled up, so the king was visible to all. It was easy for a brawny, red-haired man called François Ravaillac to jump up on to the wheels, draw a knife and stab Henri IV through the open windows. He did so three times, although only two blows struck home. The occupants of the carriage, Épernon and six other gentlemen, as well as the king himself, reacted in slow motion. 'It's nothing,' said Henri IV.

Ravaillac too was frozen. He made no attempt to escape. Once they absorbed what had happened, Henri IV's companions flew at the assassin. The Sieur de Saint Michel tried to kill him but was held back. Ravaillac was taken alive.

The Sieur de Liancourt was sent to the town hall to warn the mayor and his sheriffs of the attempt on the king's life, and the Baron de Courtomer was sent to the Arsenal to warn the chief minister, the Duc de Sully. Everything had happened in full sight of passers-by, so stories tore through the Parisian crowd. Courtomer ran into a group of eight or ten men on foot accompanied by two on horseback, all heading for the royal carriage, shouting, 'Kill, kill, he must die!' It was the second time that Ravaillac was threatened with immediate despatch, but he was again saved, the men breaking up and disappearing into the crowd. He was instead taken to the house of the Duc de Retz.

As word of the attack spread, the people were reassured that the king was only wounded. Henri IV was carried back to the Louvre and doctors were summoned, but they could hardly make a proper diagnosis because the worst injury was internal. The second blow had severed the inferior *vena cava*, the large vein carrying blood to the heart from the lower limbs. Henri IV was suffering massive internal bleeding, which was beyond treatment. Soon after he arrived back in the Louvre, the greatest king in Europe was dead.[9]

5

THE LOSS OF ELIZABETH DE BOURBON

Marie de Médicis had a migraine. She was lying on a 'summer bed', chatting with her friend Mme de Montpensier, when Henri IV was brought back to the Louvre. The ladies heard people moving and talking in the king's room, so Mme de Montpensier went to enquire, opened the communicating double doors, saw Henri IV lying on his back, white-faced, bloodstains on his chest, surrounded by attendants gripped by terror, and so she closed them again.

The queen shouted out, 'My son!' and ran to the doors, which her friend blocked. Marie de Médicis has not been given much credit by historians for her protective instinct towards the dauphin, the son whom she struggled to love, nor for her pathetic inability to think the victim was her husband. The dauphin Louis – or rather the child who was now King Louis XIII – was in fact out for a drive with his governor, M de Souvré, when Ravaillac struck and had since returned to the Louvre. The queen pushed Mme de Montpensier to one side and ran into her husband's room.

Hysteria seized the Queen of France. She repeatedly cried, 'The King is dead!' until the chancellor, Brûlart de Sillery, said to her, 'In France the king does not die – here is the king, madam,' indicating her son.

Marie arranged for the nine-year-old Louis to sleep in her room that night, together with the slightly younger Gaston de Verneuil, Henri's son by Henriette d'Entragues. The other children were assigned a special guard, while Sully and his colleagues on the council prepared for the next attack. However, there was no second attempt, no assault on any other royal person or official, and at last it became clear that Ravaillac had acted alone, as he had always insisted – or else that his mysterious puppeteers retreated into the dark. Marie de Médicis herself could not sleep for nine days, and it took years for her son Louis to overcome the trauma.[1]

In different circumstances from those she had expected, the queen, heavily veiled and dressed in mourning, was proclaimed regent the next day, 15 May 1610. Her regency – for her son – had been confirmed by the Parlement de Paris on the same day as the murder, but, more properly, was now announced in a *lit de justice* at which the boy king Louis XIII presented his mother to the Parlement.[2]

On 27 May 1610, Ravaillac was taken to the Place de Grève where he was burned with molten lead, sulphur and wax, then torn by four horses, shackled to each limb and driven off in opposing directions. People in the crowd helped the horses pull him apart. The assassin died two hours later, when one of his legs broke, perhaps torn off altogether. What remained of his body was attacked by the crowd, who hacked it to bits and burned the final remnants. In this way there was, after all, a cathartic bloodbath and the regicide was denied Christian burial – there was no body left for the resurrection that pious Christians expected on judgement day.[3]

*

Aged seven months, Henriette Marie attended her father's funeral, her second major royal ceremony, on 25 June 1610. Someone – Mamangat? – helped her sprinkle holy water on her father's corpse. On 17 October she was at the coronation of Louis XIII, where she was carried by none other than the exquisite Charlotte de Montmorency, Princesse de Condé. After the service she and the other children were removed from Paris to St Germain-en-Laye, because of 'factions and disturbance'. The baby's marriage to Henry Stuart was not pursued. Although talks continued, an alliance with the weak regency government of Marie de Médicis was not very attractive to James I.[4]

The queen regent had her strengths, however, and she had her policies – one of them a triumph. On 29 January 1612 Marie de Médicis announced a double engagement, that of her two elder children, Louis XIII and Madame Elizabeth, to the children of Philip III of Spain. Elizabeth was engaged to the Prince of the Asturias, later King Philip IV of Spain. Louis was engaged to the infanta Ana Maria, who as a Habsburg infanta – a princess of the House of Austria – was always known as Anne of Austria.

Marie turned around the policies of Henri IV, who wanted a coalition against the Habsburgs. She was related to both the Holy Roman Emperor and the King of Spain – she was the granddaughter of Emperor Ferdinand I – so it was natural to her to build on the Habsburg connection.

On Thursday 5 April 1612, three days of celebration began with a mock battle in the Place Royale, where the Castle of Happiness was protected by the Knights of Glory, led by the Duc de Guise and the Duc de Nevers, against their attackers, led by the more senior Prince de Conti and César de Vendôme. By nightfall, as drums sounded, the Castle of Happiness was taken by the Princes of the Blood. 'Their horses were all embroidery, cloth of gold and silver, silk.' The performance was repeated on the next two days. The same evening a torchlit display of dressage took place in the courtyard of the Louvre, also repeated the following evening. The young king and his mother were joyfully applauded by the Parisians, as they went to the Place Royale from the Louvre and back again. On 25 August 1612, the feast of St Louis – the ancestor of the Bourbon kings – the marriage contracts were signed in a private ceremony in the Louvre.[5]

Like all royal children, Henriette Marie was learning early about the stately world of seventeenth-century royalty. On 15 June 1614 she and her brother Gaston were christened in a double ceremony. Her godmother was her sister Elizabeth, and her godfather was the Cardinal de la Rochefoucauld, the most senior member of the royal council; while Gaston was also given an ecclesiastical godfather, the Cardinal de Joyeuse, and was probably delighted to have the generous Queen Margot as godmother. Although Marie de Médicis showed her Habsburg leanings in the marriage treaty of 1612, the choice of godparents for the younger children showed a conservative, France-only policy.[6]

In 1615, three years after they were announced, the Spanish weddings took place. The French court travelled from Paris to Bordeaux under the protection of three thousand infantrymen and one thousand cavalry, taking with them 1.2 million *livres tournois* in forty carts, the money being needed to pay the troops. On a day of sweltering heat, 17 August 1615, the army and its royal masters set off from Paris and tramped south, arriving unmolested in Bordeaux on 7 October.

Heavy security was needed because of a rebellion against the court by the Princes of the Blood opposed to the alliance with Spain. Whether it was the armed guards or a residual sense of dignity that kept them away, her husband's cousins did not assault the wedding procession. Marie de Médicis delivered Louis and Elizabeth to their weddings. In fact all the royal children came, including Henriette Marie, who was not quite six.

*

Once the court was settled, there were proxy weddings for the two brides, Madame Elizabeth's in France (Bordeaux) and Anne of Austria's in Spain (Burgos), both on St Luke's Day, 18 October 1615. In floods of tears, the two young princesses were sent to their new husbands, Elizabeth to the south, Anne to the north. Crossing paths, the girls briefly met on a floating platform in the middle of the River Bidassoa, the border between France and Spain.

After a truly miserable journey towards domestic bliss, Anne of Austria arrived in Bordeaux on 21 November. Louis XIII spent some time with her on 22 November when, having at last had a good night's sleep, the infanta was getting dressed. The two were barely teenagers, both fourteen years old. They got on. Anne wanted a crimson feather to go with a white one, so Louis offered her his hat, which had two, and said she must take what she needed. In return he asked for one of her ribbons. Laughing, she handed him one, which he tied around the remaining feather on his hat as a pledge.

A second nuptial Mass was celebrated on 25 November 1615, when Louis XIII married his Habsburg bride in person. She was close to perfect, with her blonde hair, lily-white complexion, blue-green eyes and vermillion lips.

After Mass the young Queen of France was presented to the people outside the church, dressed in violet embroidered with lilies and trimmed with ermine, wearing a closed imperial crown, while the king was in a white satin costume embroidered with gold, finished with a huge ruff. With them stood Marie de Médicis in mourning black, with a cross of diamonds fixed to her chest and three rows of pearls around her neck. The young people were expected to consummate the marriage, and the official version was that they did.[7]

Henriette Marie was too young to fully grasp the endless church services, but must have been fascinated by the processions and the crowds. Equally she cannot have failed to understand that she had lost Elizabeth. The sisters never saw each other again, although eight years later, in Madrid, Elizabeth would have a short conversation that settled her sister's future life.

6

BRIDGE OF SIGHS

That close childhood friend of Marie de Médicis, Leonora Galigai was thought to be the daughter of a carpenter. Her social obscurity supports the explanation that she was a servant's child provided as a companion to the Medici princess at the court of Florence. In 1601 Leonora married Concino Concini, a Florentine gentleman in Marie's train, whose status made it easier for her to receive the position of lady-in-waiting and therefore stay in France with her mistress when most other Florentines returned home. Around Leonora's unappealing figure – 'the hair of Medusa ... an elephant's nose, a harpy's hands, feet like a lobster's claws, thin as a buffalo' – a caucus of power developed.[1]

Until the death of Henri IV the Concinis had used their position close to the queen to make money through royal patronage and the traffic of influence, but the regency of Marie de Médicis sent their hopes soaring. 'A woman of shadows' who kept away from the court, Leonora was adept at managing the queen, although we hear that she was not very nice about her. The servant was 'so imperious and outrageous, that when she spoke of the king [Louis XIII] and the queen, his mother, she only used insults and threats, calling one an idiot and the other a clumsy oaf'. The power and wealth of the Concinis increased. In 1610 Concini became Marquis d'Ancre, and, on 19 November 1613, he was made a Marshal of

France, as part of a deal with Chief Minister Villeroy. Concini was now known as the Maréchal d'Ancre and was addressed by the king as *'mon cousin'*.[2]

A bad political dynamic took hold. The noblest subjects of Louis XIII resented the power of the queen regent, and detested her intimate friends, of whom *'les Maréchaux'*, as the Concinis were known – the Marshals – were the most intimate. The grandees started to protest against foreign influence, which meant both *les Maréchaux* and the Spanish royal marriages. It was ambition posing as patriotism.

Henri de Condé was welcomed back to court after the death of Henri IV, but, true to form, he led the discontents. On 13 January 1614 he left court, followed by the ducs de Nevers and Mayenne. Another Prince of the Blood, the Duc de Longueville, disobeyed the queen's command to stay in Paris and followed suit, as, after a spell of house arrest, did César de Vendôme. The princes demanded the summoning of the States-General, the body representative of the nation, to discuss the Spanish marriages. The States-General were called but the only result of their meeting was the rise to prominence of the future Cardinal de Richelieu, Armand-Jean du Plessis, Bishop of Luçon, whose eloquence swayed the delegates to the cause of Marie de Médicis.[3]

The grandee revolt of 1615 was a second attempt by the princes to stop the Spanish marriages. In 1616, the flight of the princes from Paris was a reaction to the arrest of the Prince de Condé on 1 September of that year, his twenty-eighth birthday, a move prompted by the fear that he was preparing a *coup d'état*.

The protests were not gestures. In 1615, while the royal marriage party was returning from Bordeaux to Paris, rebel troops were altogether out of control in Poitou, on the left flank of the royal convoy. 'They rape the girls right up to and inside the churches and then tie them to trees as fodder for crows. They fill the men's ears and noses with gunpowder and then apply flame. Others they throw into hot oil or half bury in the earth.'[4]

With cash and other concessions, Marie de Médicis bought off the rebels of 1614 and 1615. She made formal treaties with them as if they were foreign invaders: the treaty of St Menehould of 15 May 1614, and the treaty of Loudun of 3 May 1616. After the latter the queen regent made a triumphal entry into Paris, accompanied by Henriette Marie among others.[5] However, the royal council – or the royal insiders on the council under Concini – realised that the royal government could not give in to blackmail forever. That was why Condé was arrested in September.

*

There was also the question of the king. In order to upstage the Princes of the Blood, Marie de Médicis organised a tour around the west of France in 1614 for her son, where Louis XIII appealed directly to his people as their sovereign. Dressed as a knight of chivalry, the boy king rode in state to Orléans, Chambord, Blois, Tours and Poitiers, with five thousand gentlemen in his train.

At Amboise the Duc de Rohan, leader of the Huguenots, declared his allegiance to the king and invited him to the Protestant stronghold La Rochelle. Instead Louis XIII went to Nantes, where he touched six hundred sick people for scrofula, and presided over the session of the local States, which secured further declarations of loyalty, including the (reluctant) compliance of César de Vendôme on 26 August 1614. The tour pacified Brittany, but the more lasting result was that Louis XIII started to understand what it was to personify the royal authority of France.

On 2 October 1614, clad in cloth of gold, covered with diamonds, Louis XIII attended Mass in the Sainte-Chappelle, glittering in the light from its multi-coloured stained-glass windows, then addressed the Parlement de Paris in a *lit de justice* during which he sat enthroned on a dais covered with lilies. He declared his majority, then addressed his mother directly to confirm her as head of the royal council, second to him and in his absence. 'I desire and understand that you will be obeyed everywhere and in everything.' At this time Marie de Médicis stopped being regent, but maintained the title of queen, pending her son's marriage, when she would become queen mother.[6]

When he made this speech Louis XIII was only thirteen, since kings of France assumed their majority at the start of their fourteenth year. His mother therefore continued to treat him as a child, and kept him away from political power.

On one occasion the king turned up at a council meeting and his mother humiliatingly escorted him out. Louis XIII was allowed to marry, was allowed to play with his dogs, to fly his falcons, to hunt to his heart's content, to dance in court ballets, to rearrange the flowerbeds in the Tuileries gardens; he was not allowed anything more. 'The king ... saw himself reduced ... entirely distanced and excluded,' noted a courtier, who also referred to the 'tyranny of the Maréchal d'Ancre, and of Barbin, Mangot, Richelieu/Luçon' – the inner circle who dominated the council.[7]

Most unpleasantly, Concino Concini, the Maréchal d'Ancre, regarded Louis XIII as a stupid boy unsuited to rule. After the arrest of Condé, in October 1616, Louis XIII suffered from a gastrointestinal complaint that led to an acute depression, and on 31 October he had epileptic fits which took him close to death. D'Ancre made singularly little effort to show support to the young king at this difficult time. The boy continued to suffer from cramps and bouts of diarrhoea for some time, and suffered from low self-esteem in spades. On 11 November d'Ancre, surrounded by courtiers, walked into a room where Louis XIII was standing, in the company of two gentlemen, looking out of the window at the river. D'Ancre pretended not to see the king, and, his hat in his hand, just went on chatting with his friends (in the presence of the king the rule was to cover the head). He was bullying Louis XIII in public.[8]

By the end of 1616 Louis XIII was fifteen and boiling with rage. The teenager found a protective father figure in the handsome Provençal Charles d'Albert de Luynes, who managed some of his birds of prey. Luynes was made Captain of the Louvre, so that he could have a room within easy reach of the king's. With Luynes, and others of a modest standing at court, Louis XIII reviewed his options.

*

On 24 April 1617, at ten o'clock in the morning, the Maréchal d'Ancre arrived at the Bourbon gate to the Louvre, followed by a retinue of fifty to eighty men. He was walking slowly reading a letter. The Maréchal was wearing mourning clothes for his recently deceased daughter. His hat was decorated with black feathers, his doublet was black edged with gold, his high-heeled shoes were velvet grey and his cloak was grey. He was all show.

The gate crashed shut behind him. At the head of a troop of Swiss guards, the Baron de Vitry approached, but, nervous and distracted, walked straight past d'Ancre. The Maréchal had to be pointed out to Vitry, on the other side of the drawbridge. Vitry then challenged d'Ancre, saying, 'In the king's name I arrest you.' D'Ancre exclaimed loudly. Was it a call to his armed supporters? It was later said that he put his hand on the hilt of his sword. Vitry grabbed at the Maréchal, and five of his men shot d'Ancre in the head since they thought he was wearing chainmail beneath his doublet. He died at once.[9]

There had been no direct order to kill the Maréchal d'Ancre, but Louis XIII could not have done anything more popular. Parisians hated *les Maréchaux* – rich foreigners at the heart of power – and were delirious with joy. After d'Ancre was buried they found the body, removed it from the tomb, and cut it to pieces. At the same time, the destruction of d'Ancre pulled the rug from beneath the feet of the rebel princes, whose manifestos complained of evil advisers. They now protested their loyalty to Louis XIII, but Condé was for the time being left in prison.

D'Ancre's wife Leonora would soon be found guilty of witchcraft. The origin of the charge lay in the folk remedies with which she treated the nervous attacks which plagued her. She met her fate, execution, with dignity. The intelligent Leonora had wanted to go back to Italy; she was the only person in the queen's inner circle who had already seen that things had gone too far.

Marie de Médicis, who was used to running the royal council, was now on the receiving end of orders to stay in her room, so she soon understood the scale of the catastrophe, although she does not seem to have felt any great personal loss. She repeatedly tried to see her son and was repeatedly rebuffed. Mother and son communicated through third parties. Marie de Médicis asked to retire from Paris to one of her dower properties, in full enjoyment of her revenues as queen mother, to which the king agreed. They settled on Blois, a hundred miles south-west of Paris.[10]

Louis XIII refused his mother her request for Christine and Henriette Marie to live with her; the princesses must stay within his sphere of influence, they were his sisters, they were his 'children'. It was pouring with rain when, on 3 May 1617, Marie de Médicis was granted a brief audience in the Louvre. Louis XIII briefly thanked her for her help in governing France, and said that now he would rule as king, as it suited him. Rather coldly he told her that he would be a good son to her if she loved him. She made a humble reply and asked a favour for Claude Barbin (now in the

Bastille), which was ignored. She was then permitted to depart for her new provincial life, queen in name alone.

In this way the seven-year-old Henriette Marie, who never knew her father, and who lost her sister Elizabeth to the Spanish court, now saw there was a family quarrel which drove her mother far away. It would not last forever, but what was a child to think? The princess became careful with what she said, afraid of her brother's anger. We do not know what she thought about the Concinis, but it seems that she must have realised they were both dead. Her cossetted world was just a few steps away from violent death, and family ties seemed very easily broken.[11]

7

THE KING OF SCOTLAND

The wedding of Henriette's sister Christine to the Prince of Piedmont, the Duke of Savoy's son, took place at the beginning of 1619. During the ceremony the Bishop of Geneva, François de Sales, was struck by Madame Henriette, now a girl of nine. He saw in her face how 'God intended her to be a great support of the glory of the Church'.[1]

Henriette Marie was, anyway, the remaining French offer in Europe's marriage market. For reasons of honour and power, the royal game insisted on matches between ruling dynasties, even though royal marriages had unpredictable political results. It was the Habsburgs alone who achieved lasting alliances that way, by the intermarriage of the Spanish and Austrian members of the family. The courts of Madrid and Vienna supported each other consistently.

It was the Habsburgs, however, who were now hit by war. And, because of another marriage, it was James I's England – typically kept from expensive Continental entanglements – that became involved. These developments were critical for the French princess.

*

In 1612 the tall, beautiful Elizabeth Stuart, daughter of James I, had married the doe-eyed Frederick V of the Palatinate – the Elector Palatine. The Protestant Frederick V was a hereditary sovereign ruling the Upper and Lower Palatinates within the constitution of the Holy Roman Empire. It was the first time since 1554 that an English princess had married into Europe.[2]

Elizabeth and Frederick fell deeply in love. They had many children. The marriage had surprising consequences nonetheless, one being the determination of James I to find a Catholic bride for his son Charles. That policy arose from the King of England's wish to show the Stuart family bridging the Reformation divide – one of his children married a Protestant, so the other would marry a Catholic. The position of Elizabeth became difficult from 1619 onwards, and soon got worse, something that would become an English obsession. For James I, his daughter's problems reinforced his Catholic policy for Charles, because a Catholic power would be best placed to help Elizabeth.[3]

The avalanche began in 1618 with the rebellion of Bohemia, under Protestant leadership, against the Catholic Emperor Ferdinand II (who was King of Bohemia by election). In 1619, against the advice of almost everyone he asked, including his mother, Frederick V accepted the crown of Bohemia from the Bohemian states, and moved with his family to Prague. He and Elizabeth were crowned, and were known for the rest of their lives as King and Queen of Bohemia. Frederick was then defeated by imperial forces at the Battle of the White Mountain on 8 November 1620, a battle that took place in his absence, while he was having lunch in Prague with his wife and two English ambassadors.[4]

The Palatine family fled to The Hague, having lost not only Bohemia but both palatinates. Emperor Ferdinand II by contrast was on a roll. He eradicated Bohemian Protestantism, and started a drive to impose Habsburg Catholicism elsewhere in the empire, supported by the cash-rich Duke of Bavaria, who wanted his palatine cousin's electoral title and at least some of his lands. The Bohemian revolt led to general war in the empire and destabilised Europe. At the same time, another theatre of war was ready to open as the twelve-year truce between Spain and the Dutch rebels neared its end. Because of Elizabeth's exile, Stuart family honour was now on the line. A long, muddled campaign started to regain the palatinate for her.

*

At the same time the King of France was starting to look for Henriette Marie's husband. Louis XIII did not want a match for his sister that drew him into foreign war. He needed to solve two main problems, the first being the Huguenots, the Protestant French who lived in fear of losing their religious rights and therefore fortified their positions, in different parts of France, against his authority. The first years of Louis XIII's reign were dedicated to repeated Huguenot campaigns.[5]

England was considered the leader of Protestantism, a nation likely to help the Huguenots against Louis XIII. Perhaps this threat could be deflected by a marriage treaty.

If Henriette Marie married Charles, now Prince of Wales (his brother had died in 1612), her father-in-law James I would be friendly to the Louvre, and therefore unfriendly to the Huguenots. An approach was made by Louis XIII to James I in 1621, but unfortunately James I wanted his son to marry the infanta Maria Ana of Spain (largely because he thought she held the key to the Palatinate).

Louis XIII's second challenge lay in court intrigues, including his mother's, which pulled the Bourbon family apart. The marriage of Louis XIII and Anne of Austria had not produced children, or happiness for the married couple. Henriette Marie – who very unhelpfully took her brother's side against his wife – was well placed to shore up the Bourbons in these circumstances. Her cousin the Comte de Soissons, son of the man who refused to attend the coronation of Marie de Médicis, was delighted with the emerging plan that Henriette Marie would marry him. Together they would produce heirs to France.[6]

*

The wheel of fortune turned when, on 18 February 1623, two English gentlemen, attended by a Scottish servant, arrived in Dover. It had been a long day in the saddle, starting that morning outside Chelmsford. Two others waited for them in Dover. The night was stormy, but they embarked early next day, at sunrise in fact, and after a choppy crossing landed safe in Boulogne in the afternoon.

The travellers were heading for Paris, where they arrived on Friday 21 February. Here they lodged at a post house in the Rue St Jacques. The next day the young men went to the Louvre to watch the king and queen dine in public, as many did.[7] In the evening they returned to watch a ballet in which court ladies danced by candlelight, led by the queen, Anne of Austria, and her sister-in-law Madame Henriette. As foreigners they were lucky to catch the eye of the queen's chamberlain, who assigned them excellent seats.

They did not stay in Paris. On Sunday 23 February, the English party rode away from the Louvre, heading south. Carrying a fortune in cash and bills of exchange, they were lucky not to be attacked on the way. On the Spanish border south of Bayonne, on the Atlantic coast, an area known for banditry, the gentlemen rode ahead of the group, as if they were the servants spying out the land. If bandits appeared they would attack the three who followed. Fortunately the cunning plan was not tested by any bandits, and the group entered Spanish territory without trouble. Their destination was Madrid, which the impatient gentlemen, who left their companions behind, reached on Friday 7 March.

Not far from Madrid, at San Agostino, they picked a quarrel with some Spanish soldiers about a Spanish girl and her husband. It was later discovered that the furious Spaniards were on the verge of drawing their swords and putting an end to English presumption. Tempers cooled, the foreigners rode on.[8]

A Spanish postilion accompanied the Englishmen on the final stage, and took them to the house of the English ambassador, the Earl of Bristol. The taller of the two knocked on the door while his much shorter companion waited in the shade on the other side of the street. Harry Jermyn admitted the visitor, and went to find the ambassador. Bristol's nephew, Simon Digby, came to the door and recognised beneath the dust and grime the most powerful man in England outside the royal family, George Villiers, Marquess of Buckingham, favourite of James I. Buckingham had been hurt by a fall, so he was left inside while Simon went to find the other young man, waiting in the street, who was Charles, Prince of Wales.[9]

*

When Bristol met his visitors he was appalled. As Lady Bristol told a friend, her husband was 'altogether ignorant of any intention that the prince had of coming hither'. Their companions, who arrived the next day, were two courtiers deeply involved in the relationship of Spain and England, namely Sir Francis Cottington and Endymion Porter. Only the Scottish groom, Richard Grahame, was really a manual servant. It was a sensation that men so close to the King of Great Britain arrived in Madrid entirely unannounced.[10]

On 8 March 1623 Buckingham met his Spanish equivalent, the Conde-Duque de Olivares. Their conversation paved the way for the meeting, the next day, of Philip IV of Spain and the Prince of Wales. Because Charles had arrived incognito, which meant that officially he had not arrived at all, Philip IV was obliged to arrange an incognito meeting with him in the Prado gardens, where the king was found by Olivares and Buckingham 'walking in the streets, with his cloak thrown over his face, and a sword and buckler at his side'. Philip IV jumped into a coach and was taken to the prince. It was a friendly encounter, the king being seventeen and the prince twenty-five, and because everyone loves a lover.

By now it was known that Charles had come to Madrid to seal his marriage with the infanta Maria Ana. On 17 March the Prince of Wales made a formal entry into Madrid – in short, he arrived officially – and was lodged, with Buckingham, at the royal palace, for the brief period needed to settle a match that had been negotiated for seven years. The stalling (but never stalled) negotiation had prompted the prince to risk everything by coming in person since he had become obsessed with Maria Ana. Charles was in love with a girl he had never met.

*

The title used by Charles in Madrid was King of Scotland, so that he could have the critical royal precedence. Since the kingdom of Scotland predated that of Spain – 'the Spains' – this made it possible for him to take precedence over his host Philip IV. It did nothing to speed things up. Far from sealing the deal, the prince and Buckingham stayed in Madrid until the end of August.[11]

They were not isolated. Lord Bristol was there to help. Courtiers from England came in support, the first group following the prince a month after he left. Buckingham was made a duke by James I, to show confidence. The king was in constant touch with his son by letter. The Prince of Wales for the first time saw Europe's greatest collection of recent and contemporary art, which enchanted him. He loved the elegant formality of the Spanish court, so different from the messy seediness of his father's. However, things went from bad to worse.[12]

The infanta was alarmed by the arrival of the heretic prince, and was not permitted (and did not want) to see him for a private conversation. Charles was a coiled spring. He could not take his eyes off Maria Ana, and perhaps it was not that flattering: 'I have seen the Prince have his Eyes unmoveably fixed upon the Infanta, he watcheth her as a cat doth a mouse,' wrote a courtier. One day Charles managed to surprise her by jumping over a wall into a garden where she was walking, but she screamed and ran away.[13]

Olivares and Buckingham quarrelled. Buckingham and Bristol quarrelled. Philip IV thought Charles had come to Madrid to announce his conversion to Catholicism, which was not the case. Charles then felt he was being held hostage. A council of Spanish divines insisted on full toleration of Catholicism in England as the price of the marriage, which James I could not deliver, since he had to work with his anti-Catholic Parliament. The King of Spain made no promises about the future of the Palatinate, even though his troops occupied swathes of it (for his cousin the emperor).

Yet the astonishing result of six months in Madrid, of every possible misunderstanding, was that the marriage was agreed. When on 28 August 1623 Charles ceremonially bade Philip IV farewell at El Escorial outside Madrid – where the king's bedroom looked onto the high altar of the chapel, and where a whole community of monks lived and worshipped – he was committed to accept the infanta Maria Ana as his wife.

In the marriage articles James I and Charles consented to the repeal of penal laws against the English Catholics, the laws which had been in place since Elizabeth I's day. The Palatinate was unmentioned. In short, the Spaniards won every point except the conversion of the prince; but then, with the prince in their midst, the Spaniards held all the cards. Just one thing worked in favour of the English: the death of Pope Gregory XV in July meant that the essential papal dispensation – for a Catholic to marry a Protestant – had to be requested a second time, from the new Pope, Urban VIII. There could be no wedding before that arrived. If Gregory XV had lived longer, there was no reason to prevent the Prince of Wales from marrying Maria Ana then and there.

Charles signed the proxy document to validate a wedding in his absence, with one small victory – that his royal proxy was valid until Christmas. The King of Scotland and his companions then rode north to the Galician coast, where they were to meet the English fleet at Santander.

They were free.

On the way north, Charles sent Edward Clerke, a servant of Buckingham's, back to Madrid with a letter for the Earl of Bristol, to be produced when the papal dispensation arrived. The letter instructed Bristol not to proceed with the marriage until he had a guarantee that the infanta would not, after the betrothal, retire into a nunnery. It was a delaying tactic, although one that seemed more than justified by Maria Ana's own behaviour. Nonetheless the Prince of Wales was committed to marrying the Spanish princess.

Or was he? During the earlier stages in the visit, the prince found himself in conversation with Elizabeth de Bourbon, wife of Philip IV and sister of Henriette Marie. The Queen of Spain, correct in all things, asked for permission to speak with her guest in her native language, French. It was given. She made it clear that the conversation had to be brief, and warned him that the Spaniards killed men who flirted with their wives; but she had time to make her point. She said she wished he would marry her sister. After all, the Madrid trip pointed to Paris.[14]

8

THE FEMININE TOUCH

On 5 October 1623, the Prince of Wales and Duke of Buckingham landed at Plymouth harbour and set off for London. They spent the night with Viscount Annandale near Guildford and arrived early in London on 6 October, where they breakfasted at York House. After receiving the acclamations of the London crowd, ecstatic that their prince was neither dead nor Catholic – nor married to a Catholic – they travelled on to the king, who was staying at his hunting lodge at Royston.[1]

The weather was cold and wet. On 7 October, tears flowed with cups of wine as James I hugged his young men – known to him as Baby Charles and Steenie, the latter after St Stephen, famed for his beauty – while the people of London had alcoholic picnics in the middle of the street and 'were so mad with joy that if they met with any cart loaden with wood they would take out the horses and set cart and all on fire'. It was good news for a group of prisoners on their way to Tyburn to be hanged. They were reprieved by the king in celebration.[2]

The letter which Charles had sent to Bristol was re-spun. The prince wrote to Bristol and to Sir Walter Aston to say that the restoration of the Palatinate was the key; only if that were agreed would he marry the infanta. James I wrote to Bristol soon afterwards making the same point. There was no progress on the

Palatinate – in fact there was no time for progress, since any deal had to be agreed with the imperial court at Vienna, and that would take three months at least. At Christmas, the prince's proxy ran out.

On 28 December 1623, James I instructed writs to be prepared for the summoning of Parliament. This implied that the king was thinking of war, since raising troops required new finance that Parliament had to approve by vote. The king was in fact under pressure from his young men. Charles and Buckingham had indeed come to the view that war with Spain was better than marriage with Spain; the Palatinate had to be released and the debt of honour redeemed. Their Madrid experience killed their hopes of friendship with the young Catholic king, and Charles's love for the blonde infanta Maria Ana evaporated in the Atlantic breeze.

The feeling of change was suddenly electric. James I fell ill in November. Would he die? In January 1624 the Spanish ambassador produced new proposals which offered to return the Palatinate to the Elector Palatine by August – was this within the power of Philip IV? – and to work on military cooperation with England. But Charles decided at exactly this time that he would in no circumstances marry Maria Ana. Nor could the feint prevent the opening of Parliament, on 19 February 1624, in the middle of an exceptionally cold winter, by the now recovered James I.[3]

*

This was the Prince's Parliament, so called because the Members and Charles had – for the only time in his life – one shared preoccupation, that Spain was the enemy of England. The politics were tortuous, but the drift was clear.

The prince sat in the House of Lords as Duke of Cornwall and took part in the debates, including the attack on the Treasurer Lionel Cranfield, Earl of Middlesex, who was impeached on grounds of corruption and misusing the stamp of the Court of Wards. Cranfield headed the Spanish party on the Privy Council, and was manoeuvring against Buckingham, trying to replace the duke as the favourite of James I by drawing to the king's attention his own handsome brother-in-law Arthur Brett. In short, the attack on Spain, the attack on Cranfield and the defence of Buckingham were one and the same.

In early spring 1624, the House of Lords focussed on war

preparations while the Commons had to vote supply. This meant that every Member had to impose additional taxation on his constituency, and therefore each tended to dither. The Commons preferred to focus unhelpfully on the danger within, that is to say the spectre of a Catholic uprising in England.

The king was directly at odds with Parliament. He wanted peace in Europe, he wanted to avoid spending money on troops and he thought that the English Catholics were no threat. James I did not, however, try to defend Cranfield.[4]

The pace and focus of the debates and backstairs negotiations, punctuated by Buckingham's 'lightning dashes' to court – held variously at Theobalds, Royston, Greenwich and Whitehall – to counter the influence that the Spanish ambassador had on the king, were haphazard and unsettling. James I appeared to turn against his favourite, at one point accusing Buckingham of using 'cruel, Catonic words'.[5] The downfall of the favourite was predicted. Terrified of conspiracy all his life, James, torn between love and fear, really was worried about his own security. He ordered his Privy Councillors to take an oath on the Bible that they were not involved in a plot against him.

In May, the thirty-two-year-old Buckingham fell ill. He retired to Wallingford House. On 10 May 1624, the king's physician Sir Theodore Mayerne reported that Buckingham was vomiting saffron-coloured bile, and was close to death. The king panicked. He could not lose Steenie. James I stopped worrying about his own life and sent, among other things, the eyes, tongue and testicles of a recently killed deer to speed the duke's recovery.

Buckingham turned the corner, and by the end of May was convalescent. Desperate to accelerate the preparations for war, he went back to work early and suffered a relapse, so he retired again, this time to New Hall in Essex, with his wife and daughter. Here the king sent melons, pears, sugared beans, strawberries, raspberries and loving letters.[6]

It was almost a revolutionary atmosphere – plans for war, a restless Parliament, an overwrought king, the favourite close to death, the emergence of the Prince of Wales – in which Henriette Marie became a serious candidate for England.

*

In France, Marie de Médicis was back in favour. After an undignified escape from Blois in February 1619 – she slid down a crumbling wall in the middle of the night – the queen mother gathered her supporters and waged war on her son. Marie de Médicis was the patron of the French political faction called the *dévots*, those who subscribed to ultramontane Catholicism – close relations with the Pope – and who opposed toleration of any form of Protestantism. Unfortunately, the 'Wars of the Mother and the Son' led to repeated defeats of Marie's troops.

All was forgiven in the interests of the Bourbon family. Marie's reconciliation with Louis XIII was easier after the death of Luynes, whom Marie considered responsible for her disgrace. The ex-falconer had been given a dukedom, massive wealth, a beautiful, much younger bride from the ancient nobility; he became the most senior military official, the Connetâble de France; and he earned Louis XIII's hatred.

One day when Luynes came into the room with an escort of Swiss guards, the king said to an astonished François de Bassompierre, 'Look at the king come in! You don't know him. He thinks I owe him much more than he already has, and he wants to play king, but I'll fight him for as long as I live.' Luynes was saved from disgrace by death, after catching scarlet fever on campaign against the Huguenots in 1621.[7]

It was to Marie de Médicis, therefore, that Buckingham reached when he realised that the Spanish match would be abandoned. In autumn 1623 the duke sent Fr Gray, an English or Scottish friar, from Santander to Paris for a confidential conversation with the queen mother about her daughter Henriette Marie. Would she be prepared to think of an English marriage treaty?[8]

In October 1623 Fr Gray told the duke that Marie de Médicis was in favour of the English proposal. Well before the final rejection of the infanta, another bride was being lined up for the Prince of Wales. Buckingham followed up by sending Henry Rich, Viscount Kensington, to Paris in February 1624 to investigate further. The etiquette required the English prince to chase the girl, but Marie de Médicis was not taking any chances. She persuaded her son to indulge in some sporting diplomacy to encourage James I to make enquiries by sending a man to Whitehall 'with a present of fifteen or sixteen cast of hawkes, some ten or twelve horses and as many dogges'.⁹

*

As well as being Catholic, as James I wanted, Madame Henriette was young, came from the oldest royal dynasty in Europe, could bring a large dowry, and France was a military power – and the traditional enemy of Spain.

Suddenly there was momentum. Kensington's mission was, in the usual way, a delicate mix of the personal – was the girl attractive enough? – and the political – was she available? She was, it turned out, a pretty fourteen-year-old, 'a lovely sweet young creature', and it was soon obvious that she was indeed available.¹⁰

By contrast with this innocent doll, Lord Kensington was 'one of the most beautiful men in the world, but with an effeminate beauty'. The sensuous envoy, on the most sensitive mission in Europe, was soon involved in a passionate affair with the Duchesse de Chevreuse, who was none other than the widow of Luynes, remarried even more grandly. Marie de Chevreuse helped her lover; indeed, the early stages of the wooing of Henriette Marie are a textbook case of feminine power.¹¹

When Lord Kensington arrived in Paris in February 1624 it was, again, to Marie de Médicis that he addressed himself. She was now installed in her magnificent, modern Palais de Luxembourg, south of the Seine. Kensington's letters make it clear that Marie was a driving force. 'I find the Queen Mother hath the only power of governing in this State,' he wrote to Buckingham, 'and the Queen Mother told me, she had not lost those inclinations ... to desire her daughter may be given to the prince.'

Another advocate of the marriage was Anne of Austria. The Spanish queen was 'so truly French' she wanted the Prince of Wales to marry her sister-in-law rather than her sister. Kensington wrote to the Prince of Wales, 'She [Anne] was sorry when you saw them practise their masques, that Madam her sister [Henriette Marie] ... was seen at so much disadvantage by you, to be seen afar off, and in a dark room, whose person and face hath most loveliness to be considered nereby.' This was a reference to the sight observed by Charles and Buckingham on their way to Spain of the French royal ladies dancing by candlelight. After all, their Paris incognito had fooled nobody.[12]

Nor was Madame Henriette slow to show interest. She was incapable of the required passivity. Knowing the mistress of the house where Kensington was staying, she ordered this lady to borrow from him the portrait he had brought of Charles, so that she could take a look. The miniature was duly taken to Henriette. 'She opened the picture in such a haste as showed a true picture of her passion, blushing in the instant of her own guiltiness. She kept it an hour in her hand.'[13]

At the end of March, Kensington was joined by the Earl of Carlisle, a man of charm but no looker – Elizabeth of Bohemia called him 'camel-face' – who had worked on a previous and unsuccessful embassy to France in 1616. His arrival as ambassador extraordinary showed the marriage was being negotiated formally. When Buckingham was sick in May, things were looking good in France. In June, Kensington paid a visit to London to report in person. He announced that modest commitments had to be made in the marriage treaty, in support of the English Catholics, but nothing much.

The Prince of Wales could be married before Christmas.

*

The Prince of Wales was not married before Christmas. The least of the obstacles was the fury of the rejected Comte de Soissons. He 'stormed and received the Lord Kensington's salute scornfully'. The Spaniards, too, were enraged. In Madrid, Olivares told Aston that he would authorise the sack of Rome if the Pope delivered a dispensation for the French marriage.[14]

More important, the Bishop of Luçon, now Cardinal de Richelieu, joined the royal council. His arrival caused the departure of the previous Chief Minister of France, La Vieuville. When he returned to Paris in July, Kensington found Richelieu in place and a new set of conditions, most alarmingly the demand that English penal laws against Catholics be suspended. It looked almost malicious, but Richelieu only demanded tighter conditions because he knew the Pope would not supply a dispensation otherwise.

The Stuarts failed to anticipate this sort of thing, but then the nature of English politics made it hard to cater for everyone. The Prince of Wales had already publicly said there would be 'no advantage for the recusants at home' if he married a Catholic. It was not a throwaway remark. Charles made this commitment to the House of Lords, to persuade the House of Commons to tone down a petition against recusants that it wanted to present to the king. The Commons cooperated, and the king did his part, when the watered-down petition was presented on 23 April 1624, by saying that 'no such condition (concessions to English Catholics) be hereafter foisted in upon any other treaty whatsoever'.[15] In short, the Pope was bound by his leadership of the Catholic Church to require concessions, and James I was bound by his leadership of Protestant England to rule them out.

James I was more than up to the challenge. He found a solution. In a side letter, called an *écrit particulier*, he promised to free his Catholic subjects of persecution (a revolutionary commitment). This document, signed by the king and his son, was acceptable to Richelieu and Louis XIII, and was not quite acceptable to Urban VIII, who asked for a commitment to abolition of the penal laws in Latin, which James I refused. The momentum was back.

This year it was a warm winter, but it was very rainy when, on 12 December 1624, James I, then in Cambridge, accepted the marriage articles with France. Only the king, his son, Buckingham and Secretary of State Conway reviewed and signed the articles – the king wanted the details kept secret. Even then things were not settled, because the papal dispensation was still pending. By now the Pope, under pressure from France, could not back out, and with great reluctance – he thought Henriette Marie would be unhappy as a Catholic bride in England – he sent the dispensation in February 1625.[16]

*

The future of Madame Henriette was now decided. She would leave France. She would be a princess in the ancient islands off the European coast, and rule, as consort, over a people who were almost all Protestant. At the same time she was expected to remain thoroughly French, to speak for French interests and to support Catholicism. The marriage treaty confronted these difficulties with the following main articles:

The wedding would take place in France and it would be a Catholic service.

Henriette Marie with her household was guaranteed freedom to practice the Catholic religion. In each of her residences in England, she would have a Catholic chapel. She would have twenty-eight Catholic priests with her in England, including a bishop as her grand almoner.

All her household would be both Catholic and French (but all would take an oath of loyalty to the king).

Until their thirteenth year, all children of the marriage would be brought up as the queen directed.

She would bring a dowry of 800,000 crowns (£267,000), half to be paid before the wedding and half a year after.[17]

In March 1625, the Duke of Buckingham had sent his carriages to Dover to prepare for his entry to Paris with the prince's proxy for the wedding when James I again fell ill. The sovereign was staying at his favourite residence, Theobalds in Hertfordshire. Charles and Buckingham were also at Theobalds, and here they remained as the king's condition worsened.

Buckingham and his mother, the Countess of Buckingham, tried different remedies to supplement the doctors' efforts. The countess tied a plaster on the king's wrist, which was meant to dissolve into the patient and cure him, while Buckingham administered a 'julep' which the king sipped. Nothing helped. On 27 March 1625, James I died.

The satisfying story spread that the Buckingham family poisoned the king to speed the accession of Charles. It was widely credited, but murder does not otherwise figure in the careers of Buckingham and his pious mother, and it can be ignored. At once, the Prince of Wales succeeded as Charles I.[18]

The king is dead, long live the king!

9

THE WEDDING

Louis XIII announced his sister's engagement to King Charles I on 8 May 1625, in a gorgeous ceremony held in the Louvre. Madame Henriette had to forgo the ballet that had been planned as the court was in mourning for the King of Great Britain, but mourning was forgotten when it came to her clothes. For the betrothal Henriette Marie wore a gown of cloth of silver embroidered with gold *fleurs-de-lis*, covered with diamonds and pearls.[1]

The death of James I had made necessary a whole new set of papers, with the new king's agreement to the marriage treaty, but nothing would now stop the wedding, which took place three days later at Notre Dame Cathedral, based on the precedent of the 1572 marriage of Henri de Navarre and Marguerite de Valois. Instead of Buckingham, the (Protestant) Duc de Chevreuse held the proxy of his relation Charles I.[2] It was splendid.

First came a hundred Swiss guards of the king, drums beating, fifes whistling, then twelve hautboys (playing oboe-like woodwind instruments), then eight drummers. The king's French guard was next, followed by twelve trumpeters. Then came the master of ceremonies and the Chevaliers de l'Ordre du St Esprit, followed by two marshals of France, Vitry and Bassompierre. The Duc d'Elboeuf came next, a man with a royal wife, Catherine Henriette de Vendôme, the daughter of Henri IV and Gabrielle d'Estrées. With Elboeuf came Chevreuse, whose wife was having an affair with Lord Kensington, who came next in the procession with Lord Carlisle. Both ambassadors were dressed in shimmering silver.

The ambassadors of England preceded Henriette Marie, who was escorted by her two brothers. The great ladies followed: first the Queen Mother of France; then Anne of Austria; then the Princesses of the Blood; then the senior duchesses, Guise, Chevreuse and Elboeuf, with other ladies. After these people, who were all royal or quasi-royal, or symbols of the French state through their office, came the noblemen of France, and they were followed by the king's principal guard. The procession took place eight feet above ground level, on a purpose-built platform extending from the Archbishop's Palace into the nave of Notre Dame, held up by pillars covered in violet satin embroidered with Bourbon lilies.[3]

The bride was in gold, wearing a crown chased with diamonds and a gown so encrusted with golden lilies that eyewitness accounts failed to note the cloth of which it was made, presumably invisible beneath the field of *fleurs-de-lis*. Chevreuse was in perfumed black cloth cut upon cloth of gold and richly lined. He wore a jewelled cap of cloth of gold, a short cloak embroidered with gold and set with diamonds, and, to finish the whole understated effect, a scarf embroidered with roses and powdered with diamonds and pearls. Henriette Marie stood beneath a golden canopy on a raised dais which extended into the church, and was covered in violet satin embroidered with *fleurs-de-lis*.

The Cardinal de la Rochefoucauld, the senior member of the royal council, performed the ceremony, which took place outside so that the Protestants were not compromised.

While all this splendour broadcast royal power, spectators were treated to a harsh reminder of physical reality. The painter Rubens was present, having just put the finishing touches to his cycle of paintings about Marie de Médicis, hung in the Palais de Luxembourg. He watched the ceremony from the platform reserved for the English ambassadors' suite. Under the weight of the spectators, it buckled and collapsed. Standing at the end, Rubens was fortunately unhurt.[4]

*

Within the church waited the presidents of the parlements of France, clad in scarlet, with gold mortarboards on their heads. Below them sat the councillors of the parlements. Opposite the lawyers were the provost of the merchants of Paris (business) and the sheriffs (law enforcers) of Paris and of other cities. A Mass was celebrated, not attended by the English ambassadors, nor by the Duc de Chevreuse.

The people were not excluded. Coins were flung to the crowds featuring Cupid, holding flowers, on one side with the words 'Love pours out lilies mixed with roses' ('*Fundit amor lilia mixta rosis*'), and on the other Charles I and Henriette Marie, with the words 'The Great Charles and Henrietta Maria, King and Queen of Great Britain' ('*Carolus mag. et Henrietta Maria, rex et regina magnae britanniae*').[5]

After Mass, Cardinal Richelieu gave a feast in the Archbishop's Palace 'worthy of the magnificence of France', accompanied by volleys of cannon and the lighting of bonfires in the streets, with fireworks and more music. The houses of Paris had candles in the windows 'to make day out of night'. Within the palace, Henriette Marie sat on the left hand side of Louis XIII with the place of honour on his right reserved for their mother, whose status as the queen of queens was broadcast throughout the wedding celebrations. The ravishing Anne of Austria was next to her mother-in-law.[6]

The perfumed Duc de Chevreuse was next to the new Queen of England. On the other side of the *mari complaisant* sat Camel-Face and the seductive Lord Kensington. The whole deafening business continued with 'music, dancing and revel' in the Louvre. There was a symbolic ceremony of consummation when Chevreuse briefly got into Henriette Marie's bed. The next day she retired to a convent outside Paris in Senlis to compose her thoughts in prayer. Similarly, she had spent the night before the wedding in a convent, that of the Carmelites on the Faubourg St Jacques.[7]

When news of the wedding reached London, people lit bonfires in the streets and all the churches rang their bells. To help Anglo-French friendship, the new royal government loaned eight ships to Louis XIII to help him attack Genoa, the bankers of Spain.[8]

*

With the arrival in Paris of the Duke of Buckingham on 24 May 1625, the frenzy returned. As Master of the Horse, he had attended the funeral of James I, and was then consulted by Charles I about the countless official appointments that must be confirmed or changed. He himself continued to be favourite and chief minister.

Buckingham's glamour amazed even the French. He had a retinue of at least four hundred followers, including 120 musicians and 45 kitchen staff, and brought three coaches for his personal use, each pulled by eight horses. He had thirty suits in his luggage, variously embroidered, laced and covered with diamonds and pearls. The most costly was valued at £4,000.

The duke stayed at the Hôtel de Chevreuse, and topped the bill at a succession of parties. The story went round that he wore necklaces of pearls which were deliberately tied loosely so that they broke and scattered jewels in his wake for anyone to pick up. He caused 'admiration in the people, joy and something in addition to joy among the ladies, jealousy among the young bloods, and more than jealousy among the husbands'.[9]

The duke's mystique resulted from his looks – long-limbed, lean-bodied, with strong cheekbones, soft features and large, dark eyes, 'everything in him full of delicacy and handsome features' – combined with fizzing energy and great charm of manner. Having spent some years in France before he started his career at the court of Whitehall, Buckingham spoke French well. Nor can the aphrodisiac of power be forgotten. Buckingham was 'well made, with a beautiful face, he was magnificent, liberal and the favourite of a great king'.[10]

The braggadocio was politics, to persuade Louis XIII and Richelieu that Charles I was a great king, a power of the first rank. Buckingham's job was to obtain more than the person of the royal bride. He was instructed to explore the formal military alliance with France that would help the new king restore the Palatinate to his sister's family. Cardinal Richelieu could not, however, be persuaded. While the Huguenots presented a challenge to royal authority within France, there was no question of Louis XIII signing a full alliance with the King of England, who wanted to make war in Germany.

*

Henriette Marie spent the day before her departure at the convent of the Grandes Carmelites, where she served the nuns at table with her own hands. On 2 June the French court accompanied her on her progress to the coast. She left the Bourbon capital in a litter of crimson velvet embroidered with gold, carried by mules who were themselves wearing crimson velvet topped with white plumes, under the control of the royal mule driver, 'no less magnificently dressed'. Before her went three companies of mounted archers, five hundred mounted burghers, the aldermen and other officials, and thirty archers of the Grand Prévôt. On the way to St Denis, outside the city walls, she exchanged her litter for a carriage.[11]

Louis XIII took his farewell at Compiègne. He was recovering from an infection, and did not want to go further. The king made sure his sister was accompanied to the coast with the magnificence that her birth and her new status required. At Amiens, the three queens – the queen mother, the Queen of France, the Queen of England – and their still vast entourage found the words '*en amis*' ('as friends' or 'in friendship') spelled out in flowers over the city gate, an anagram of the city name. However, Marie de Médicis fell ill before they reached Amiens, and decided they must rest when they got there. Seven pageants entertained the visitors celebrating the princess's marriage, the last of which showed all five French princesses who had become Queen of England so far, starting with the sixth-century Bertha.[12]

While the queen mother convalesced, the courtiers amused themselves. Thanks to the management of Marie de Chevreuse, Anne of Austria one day found herself walking in a riverside garden in the shade of trees, accompanied by the Duke of Buckingham. Marie de Chevreuse and Kensington followed at some distance. Behind the public celebrations, the lovers were having fun trying to convince Anne that Buckingham was in love with her, and vice versa. The surprise riverside idyll resulted. Rounding a corner, leaving their dawdling companions well behind, the queen and Buckingham were alone for a time beneath the trees. The duke seized the moment.

Sources give different accounts of what happened next – more than a kiss? – but we know that Anne screamed and her servants came running. The news spread like ripples in a pond, reached the ears of Henriette Marie, also more to the point those of Louix

XIII. He sacked those of his wife's servants who should have kept her in their sight, and his distrust of his wife multiplied, despite her flight to virtue.[13]

*

Since there was plague in Calais, Henriette Marie travelled to Boulogne. Her train now included the two Chevreuses; two French ambassadors, d'Effiat and de la Ville-aux-Clercs; the Bishop of Mende as her grand almoner; Père de Bérulle as her confessor; the daughter of Mamangat, Mme 'Mamie' de St George, as lady-in-waiting; and a vast retinue of servants. One historian puts her total retinue at a thousand people. Of her family, only Gaston was at her side.[14]

At Boulogne, Buckingham pretended to receive news from England which required his return to Amiens, to Anne of Austria, who was forewarned, and lay in bed to receive him in the company of a lady-in-waiting, the elderly Comtesse de Lannoy. Buckingham sank to his knees and burst into tears but the queen was unmoved, and the Comtesse de Lannoy told him this was not normal behaviour in France.[15]

The English fleet was waiting, but the weather was bad. There was a delay of several days. Henriette Marie, quite plainly dressed, made a good, in fact a strong, impression on one of the waiting courtiers, Toby Matthew, who thought her 'a most sweet lovely creature … full of wit … she is not afraid of her own shadow'. With Gaston she took to a small boat to experience a ride on the sea for the first time. On 22 June she set sail in the flagship, the *Prince*. She was lucky with the crossing, which took seven hours, although she was seasick.[16]

PART TWO

THE ENGLISH MATCH

If men could be contented to be what they are, there were no fear
in marriage.

William Shakespeare, *All's Well That Ends Well*, Act 1, Scene 3

10

QUEEN MARY

Some kind of fatality, too, the English imagined to be in the name
of Marie which ... the king rather chose to have her called by,
than the other, Henrietta ...

Lucy Hutchinson, *Memoirs of Colonel Hutchinson*, c. 1665

With her arrival at Dover the French princess, on the king's orders, assumed an English identity as Queen Mary, at once recalling the previous Queen Mary Tudor, known for burning Protestants. Anyway, it was better than 'Queen Henry', which was first used in prayers in the king's chapel, in a wild attempt to make her English. The princess herself continued to use her French name, signing letters – almost always written in French – 'Henriette Marie'. Historians have followed her lead, only anglicising her to Henrietta Maria.[1]

Henrietta Maria, then, was met at Dover by a brilliant group headed by the Earl of Arundel, the Earl Marshal. Although James I had died so recently, the English courtiers did not wear mourning. She was taken to Dover Castle to spend the night, where nine rooms had been prepared for her on Buckingham's orders. Her French servants had to find lodgings in the town, which was a cause of complaint, although their arrival was a bonanza for Dover. It was a low-key arrival.[2]

Throughout her bridal journey, the king ordered ceremonial to be kept to the minimum because of the difficulties arising from the outbreak of plague in London. He wanted to make a splendid show when he and his wife were crowned. It looked as though their joint coronation would take place in October.[3]

Henrietta Maria woke in the gloom of Dover Castle on 13 June 1625.[4] With the assistance of Mamie de St George and her maids, she dressed for her first meeting with her husband. At about eleven in the morning Charles I and his, by French standards, modest entourage clattered over the drawbridge to find the queen having breakfast. Unlike her mother in similar circumstances, she did not retire to her room but came to meet her husband.[5]

Both king and queen were small. Charles had been a sickly child who never developed an impressive physique, despite his passion for hunting and his later life as a soldier. He was at most five feet and five inches tall. Henrietta Maria was shorter, coming up to his shoulder. People had been worried about her height. Was the king marrying a midget? Would she ever have children? Lord Kensington had written from Paris the previous year, 'Her growth is very little, short of her age.'

But Charles found his wife rather taller than feared. They spoke together (in French) for an hour by themselves, then joined the court. We hear that at the first meeting the king looked down at the hem of her skirt to see if she was wearing high heels, and she said to him, 'Sire, I stand upon my own feet; I have no help from art, thus high am I, neither higher nor lower.' The princess wore shoes that had heels, of course, as women's court shoes did, and they were concealed beneath long skirts to the ground. In short, the story makes little sense except that it shows perhaps she was taller and generally better than expected. It also shows what a number of observers quickly saw: she did not hold back.[6]

What were her other attributes? The princess had a thorough practical education. The nuances of court life – the nuances of power – were instilled at St Germain-en-Laye, as was a love of music and spectacle. Henrietta Maria had a beautiful singing voice and liked dancing. She knew how to ride. She knew how to follow Catholic Mass and the other services (in Latin). She knew nothing about the history of England, and could not speak English and did not read much anyway. On the other hand, French politics was a school in itself. The young queen came from a family torn by violence, from a country accustomed to civil conflict. In this she was more sophisticated than her husband, whose first political outing, his trip to Madrid, was recent.[7]

Henrietta Maria had softly curling, dark-brown hair, not yet seen to its best advantage. At this time rich women wore their hair pulled back from the forehead and brows, held neatly in place by wires, often padded for volume. It was a formal coiffure, easy to decorate with jewels. The languorous van Dyck look, which she would make famous, had not come into fashion. Although small, Henrietta Maria had a 'perfect shape' and had large, black eyes and an oval face – 'a countenance that opens a window into her heart'.[8]

She burst into nervous tears at the first meeting, but Charles I was thrilled with his childish bride and 'rapt her up in his arms and kissed her with many kisses'. The large, soulful eyes of the king, his slim waist, his delicate hands and above all his wonderful manners did not compensate for the disappointment that she felt. He was smaller, thinner and duller than she had hoped, and was not magnificently dressed, since he was in mourning for his father. In fact, Charles I, always insecure in his heart, was not entirely sure how to deal with Henrietta Maria. She was well brought up, though, and found her poise. She told her husband she was young, and knew nothing of his country, and was likely to make mistakes. She begged him to be the first to point them out to her.[9]

*

At dinner the king himself served his wife with pheasant and venison. One of the Catholic priests reminded the queen that it was a Catholic fast day, and told her she must refuse the food. She ignored him and ate her fill. Watching like so many vultures, the courtiers concluded her Catholicism was skin-deep. When they set off for Canterbury, the king wanted only English ladies to accompany the queen in her carriage, while Mme de St George thought it her right to stay with the queen – it probably was – but she was excluded. The royal party stopped on the way on Barham Downs, where the queen met more English ladies and gentlemen, and saw some of the beauties of the English landscape. She had arrived in England late, delayed by her mother's illness and bad weather. People were impatient to assess their queen, who herself was just starting to get to grips with the English.[10]

Was there a second wedding at Canterbury? A tradition survives that Charles and Henrietta were married in the great hall of St Augustine's (not in the cathedral), which was part of the grand residence added the previous century to the ruins of St Augustine's Abbey, outside the city walls.

It would have been a good place for the second wedding because of associations with Queen Bertha who figured in the Amiens pageants, and also in the endless lecture given to the French royal council by Richelieu when he recommended the marriage.[11] But the marriage treaty prevented a Protestant service, and Charles could not have taken part in a Catholic one. There was no religious ceremony.

The wedding night was spent in Canterbury, in the royal bedchamber above the Fyndon Gate of St Augustine's. Charles I made sure of his privacy by keeping curious attendants at bay. He allowed in two servants only to undress him then 'bolted all the doors round about', shutting everyone out. It was a characteristic contrast with the almost public bedding of other royal brides of the seventeenth century. The next day Charles was all smiles, but his young wife was withdrawn. In fact, Henrietta Maria was not well. She had asked – or on her behalf, her mother had asked – if she could rest at Dover before meeting Charles I, and she missed several important ceremonies in the next few days.[12]

*

There was an outbreak of plague in London. Before it ran its course, this plague would kill a fifth to an eighth of the capital's population, one of the worst casualty rates of the century. In order to avoid infection, the king had decided that his wife would not make the usual triumphal entry through the streets, but would arrive like a sea nymph on the River Thames. The coronation of king and queen was delayed for the same reason. Attended by the knights and gentlemen of Kent, and by the local militia, Charles and Henrietta Maria drove from Canterbury to Gravesend. Here they embarked on the royal barge for the last part of the journey.[13]

On 16 June 1625, the welcome of the English fleet at Gravesend, a deafening cannonade – 'fifteen hundred great shot' – was a message about the brute force which Charles I commanded. Before arriving at the Channel coast Henrietta Maria had never seen the sea, so this display was something new. The royal barge was accompanied by a milling fleet of barges of the nobility and merchants, oared vessels with elegant curved prows, carrying ornate cabins at the back, multi-coloured on the water. It took several hours to reach London.

The numbers increased. There were 'many other barges of honour ... and thousands of boats ... infinite numbers, besides these in wherries, standing in houses, ships, lighters, western barges, and on each side of the shore.' As they neared the Tower of London, fifty ships saluted Henrietta Maria with their guns, only to be topped by the cannon of the Tower itself.

It was pouring with rain. Despite 'the vehement shower', all the windows of the royal barge were open so that the king and queen, both dressed in conspicuous spring green, were visible to their subjects. People did not stop and think; there was almost a calamity when two hundred people rushed to the side of one ship which was not securely moored. It turned over in the water, but everyone found their way back to dry land safely.[14]

The English were decidedly pleased with their young queen, although some thought she was rather small, and pallid – but then she was not well, and the cold weather did not help. Henrietta Maria arrived in style. In the words of a prominent historian of the period, 'the princess came with a virtual auxiliary court and its furnishings, down to the curling irons and the chamber pots'. She bought half the dowry in cash, which probably also came by water for safe delivery, and a 'staggering number of horses and carriages'. A copy of the inventory of her trousseau runs to more than thirty folios. With her goods came her men of religion, her grand almoner, her confessor and the others, people who had not been seen in royal palaces since the days of Mary Tudor. It was, in short, an arrival of great splendour and state and to some extent surprise.[15]

She too found herself surprised. The Queen's Side, the set of rooms dedicated to Henrietta Maria's use, was located on the east side of Whitehall Palace, overlooking the river. When she inspected her bedroom, Henrietta Maria saw that the bed of state had come from an Elizabethan storeroom. She complained that it was the oldest bed she had ever seen. She had brought with her, as part of the trousseau, a luxury modern bedroom set of crimson velvet, drapery for the bed, a matching dais, carpets, a dressing table, chairs and stools. Not surprisingly, she was taken aback.[16]

Whitehall Palace, her new home, was huge, but it was old-fashioned, not stately. The rambling complex was little changed from the days of Henry VIII, who took it away from Cardinal Wolsey and built it out. There was just one modern building, the splendid classical Banqueting Hall designed by Inigo Jones. Compared with St Germain-en-Laye, compared with Fontainebleau, Whitehall disappointed.

The next day a feast was held for the Chevreuses. There was a ceremony at which the marriage was 'confirmed, declared to be lawfully consummated, and the queene proclaimed queene', but Henrietta Maria was recuperating and did not attend. The marriage articles were signed by the king and the French ambassador. The next day Buckingham gave another banquet for the Chevreuses, who were lodged luxuriously at Somerset House. When Charles I opened Parliament on 18 June, Henrietta Maria again was absent. Nonetheless, she was welcomed, applauded, accepted as the sovereign's consort. However, Members of Parliament were uneasy. Even before the queen's arrival, they had complained of 'being here in danger of the plague'.[17]

11

PIOUS HOPES

A visitor saw the queen's anger at first hand on 2 July 1625. 'Divers of us being at Whitehall to see her (being at dinner and the room somewhat overheated with the fire and companie) she drave us all out of the chamber. I suppose none but a queen could have cast such a scowl.' The cold weather continued, and Henrietta Maria's nerves were on edge. Whether it was health or nerves, the new queen did not at once take up the English court, but stayed in her rooms with her French attendants – and did not receive English ladies. Perhaps she was aware of English prejudice. One Englishman told another, 'The queen hath bought such a poor, pitiful sort of women, that there is not one worth the looking after, saving herself and the Duchess de Chevreuse, who, though she be fair, paints most foully.'[1]

On 11 July Parliament was prorogued, to the relief of the Members. It would meet again the next month in Oxford, thought to be safer. At the end of July Secretary Conway wrote to his son to say, 'I ... in earnest do marvel that anyone who may be called reasonable would be now in London.' Plague deaths were climbing, the Trinity term of the law courts was cut short, Londoners were forbidden to attend fairs, anyone who could afford to leave the capital did so.[2]

The Venetian ambassador, Zuane Pesaro, sent a despatch to Venice describing plague infection in Whitehall Palace 'although among low officials'. Business came to a standstill: 'A new proclamation has forbidden commerce with the court on pain of death.' The king and queen at once left, first for Hampton Court, followed by short stays at Windsor, Oatlands, Nonsuch and Woodstock.[3]

They moved further. Henrietta Maria settled at Titchfield in Hampshire, while Charles stayed on the other side of Southampton Water at Beaulieu – the size of the two courts made it hard to find a building large enough to house both at the same time. None of this helped marital relations. There were more arguments about seating. At Hampton Court the king asked for a smaller carriage, so that there was literally no room for Mamie St George. Charles I was amazed at Mamie's confidence – she even contradicted him directly – so the less he saw of her the better.[4]

*

Religion kicked in. Before she was married, Madame Henriette wrote to Pope Urban VIII, saying, 'I will not choose any but Catholics to nurse and educate the children who shall be born, or do any other service for them', and wrote to her brother Louis XIII, 'I will make no selection of persons to bring up and serve the children who may be born except from Catholics.' The Pope urged her to be 'the Esther of her oppressed people, the Clothilde who subdued to Christ her victorious husband, the Adilberga [Bertha] whose nuptials brought religion into Britain'. The marriage treaty gave her control of the education of her children until they reached their thirteenth year, so naturally she intended to teach them Catholicism.[5]

Before she left France, Marie de Médicis gave her daughter a letter of guidance (partly written by Bérulle) which was equally clear. 'Remember my daughter that you are a daughter of the Church, it is the first and greatest quality that you possess ... It is for the Church to speak for you, and for you to preserve the simplicity of the faith.' The insistence of the French court on Catholic orthodoxy was not crude. The queen mother and Bérulle also instructed her that 'after God and your religion, your first duty is to the king ... Always show a respectful familiarity towards him, considering him as your leader ... your quality of queen ties you to England, and separates you from France.' However, it was easier to write the words than to follow their sense in real life, as Henrietta Maria found.[6]

At first everything went like clockwork. In April, Charles I ordered his Lord Keeper, the Bishop of Lincoln, to send out circular letters suspending proceedings against all but the most dangerous recusants. It was done before the Notre Dame wedding, let alone the arrival of Henrietta Maria in England, let alone the meeting of Parliament. The king wanted to show Louis XIII that he was abiding by the side letter on the penal laws. He wanted to receive the dowry money. Once Parliament met, it was likely to send petitions about recusants to him, and he could hardly forget his personal commitment to the Lords in 1624 that a Catholic marriage would never bring advantages to English Catholics as a whole.[7]

Most Members of Parliament naturally regarded the French marriage as a lesser evil rather than a positive good. Nonetheless, once it assembled, the 1625 parliament was not provoked by the Catholic marriage to mount an assault on Catholicism at once. It was accepted that royal marriages were for the king to decide. Still, Parliament could not leave religion alone.

There was a *cause célèbre* very close to an attack on Catholicism. This was the Mountague case. For his religious tracts, Parliament committed Richard Mountague, rector of Stanford Rivers in Essex, to the custody of the Serjeant-at-Arms. Mountague had taken up the pen in 1622 in order to attack Catholic proselytisers in his parish, but his difficulties arose because people considered him a crypto-Catholic. He was arrested during the first session of Parliament after the death of James I.

Mountague's publications included the catchily titled *A Gagg for the new gospel? No, a new gagg for an old goose* and *Apello Caesarem: a just appeale from two unjust informers*. His style made him hard to ignore. The difficulty for the House of Commons was that he balanced his dislike of Rome with an equal dislike of strict Calvinism. He wanted a middle way in religion 'to stand in the gapp against Puritanisme and Popery, the Scilla and Charybdis of antient piety'. To Puritan eyes, he was a Trojan Horse.[8]

The attitude of the Puritans to Mountague and to others who thought like him was neatly expressed by a Catholic historian: 'They deemed it the first of their duties to eradicate popery, which like a phantom haunted their imagination day and night; wherever they turned, they saw it stalking before them.'[9]

Mountague was rescued by Charles I, who appointed him a royal chaplain-in-ordinary, so that he was answerable to the king, not the Commons, and the matter was dropped. Later Mountague received further royal favour when he was made Bishop of Chichester, then of Norwich. The Mountague affair was important because it marked the start of a visible split in the Church of England, as the Arminian (religiously moderate) leanings of centrist churchmen found support from the Crown. The most prominent of these ministers in the coming years would be William Laud, who was at this time Bishop of St Davids. Their opponents were as trenchant as Mountague. Francis Rous, a Cornish Member of the Commons, said 'an Arminian is the spawn of a papist'.

For Henrietta Maria, these arguments within the Protestant fold seemed irrelevant. What did differences between heretical sects matter to her? Much later on, they would matter a great deal.[10]

*

With the battle for religion, the battle for the queen was heating up. She abandoned the docility she showed at the first meeting with her husband. Household appointments became a battleground. It was not personal but political. If Henrietta Maria, as advised by the French ambassador, could take control of the senior appointments in her household, she would establish herself as a patron. In addition, the marriage treaty did appear to confirm that the members of her household should be both French and Catholic.

When the king and queen were in Hampton Court, moving out of plague-ridden London, Charles I sent some of his councillors to her to ask if her household could be run on the same basis as that of his mother, Anna of Denmark. He told Buckingham about her response. 'She hoped I [Charles] would give her leave to order her house as she list herself.' The king was appalled at this public retort, but could not convince his wife she had done anything wrong.

Later, when the jointure was settled, and it needed only the final decision of the king to set the household up formally, Henrietta Maria took the initiative. One night she handed her husband a list of the people she wished to appoint, both English and French names. Charles I told her that he would read the paper the next day, but in any case the English names, if he agreed, would go forward, but none of the French. 'Then she fell into a passionate discourse, how miserable she was, having no power to place servants.'[11]

At Titchfield there were tricky moments that showed how household appointments and the faith divide connected. At dinner one day Bérulle said grace and made the sign of the cross, whereupon the king strode out of the room, taking the queen with him. The Countess of Denbigh, Buckingham's sister, arranged, another day, for Protestant preaching to take place in the queen's guardroom, but the queen and her ladies deliberately walked through the service chattering and laughing, accompanied by barking dogs.[12]

With the women of her household the queen mocked the lack of structure in Protestantism, pointing out that Catholics had a panoply of prayers, and times to say them, spelled out in their prayer books, while the English courtiers, 'who have much spare time', neither prayed in the same way, nor had any encouragement to do so. The Protestant ladies asked Charles I whether something could be done, so he commissioned a collection of prayers from Dr Cosin to supply the gap, 'so the court ladies and others (who spent much time in trifling) might at least appear as devout, and be so too, as the newly-come-over French ladies'. The teenage Henrietta Maria was far from incapable of winning her arguments.[13]

There would be complaints in London, when the court returned, about the Oratorian fathers who said Mass every day and strolled around the palaces of Whitehall and Somerset House in their long clerical robes. It was the shock of visible Catholicism. The reality of English Catholicism was in fact complicated, the community fractured and antagonistic. However, just as the quarrels within Protestantism were of no interest to the queen, so the internal Catholic struggles meant nothing to spectators.[14]

Financially, Henrietta Maria did exactly what was expected, exactly what was required, but this also led to discomfort. Despite her vast trousseau, Henrietta Maria was pleased to find that as queen she could spend any sums of money that she liked, and proceeded to do so, even though in the early days her revenues had not been formally settled. She made it up by borrowing from her French courtiers.

Later her patronage would turn to the monuments of the reign which we see today, such as the pictures of van Dyck and Orazio

Gentilleschi, the buildings of Inigo Jones, but most of the money went on clothing (including the clothes of her pages, music boys and dwarves), jewels, furnishings and gifts. Her rooms were frequented by 'dressmakers, organ tuners, strewers of herbs'. The power of her patronage was felt by many suppliers, including for instance the pin maker Thomas Ardington, who sent in quarterly bills of £10 for '13,500 middle vardingale pins, 100 fine needles, 1,500 velvet pins, 21,000 round head pins, 17,000 middle round head pins and 17,000 short round head pins'. The court masques which she at once started to commission and act in were costly. While she brought a large cash dowry, the immediate financial impact of the delightful young queen was worrying.[15]

As for the critical question of her relations with Charles I, Henrietta Maria was not well served by the Oratorian priests who counselled her to abstain from sex on certain days, and for longer periods, as though she were a partial nun, which is undoubtedly how they saw her. Charles I was literally frustrated.[16]

The queen's most senior religious servant, her Great Almoner the Bishop of Mende, had been appointed because he was the nephew of Cardinal Richelieu, but he was a young man and perhaps lacked judgement. The queen's confessor Bérulle was a priest of great personal piety, but he was at sea when surrounded by heretics – he considered Henrietta Maria as a 'flower surrounded by thorns' – and anyway he returned to France in the late summer of 1625 to report back to Louis XIII. These were the wrong men to head the queen's religious establishment in England.

Stories spread about the penances the queen was required to undergo, including, it was said at one time, walking to Tyburn barefoot and praying for the Catholic martyrs who had died there. Charles I certainly believed that his wife had walked to Tyburn, possibly as part of an extended walk in the royal parks, and had said some prayers there. What seemed a private act to Henrietta Maria was to others public.

Everything ran together. If she were privately devout, was she publicly subversive? If she were a patron of industry, was she profligate? If she commanded her household, did she defy her husband?[17]

*

Much later, Henrietta Maria told her friend Mme de Motteville that there had been distance between herself and Charles I in the early days of her marriage thanks to the interference of Buckingham. The duke tried to bully the queen. 'He [Buckingham] took great pains to lessen the king's affection towards his young wife, being exceedingly jealous'; 'he ... had brought himself to a habit of neglect, and even of rudeness to the Queen'. Buckingham seems to have told her, accurately enough, that 'there had been queens of England who had lost their heads'.[18]

Buckingham's attitude to the queen was due not to jealousy but politics. He had to show Parliament that he was not the poodle of the French. Nor were confusions in French policy the fault of Henrietta Maria. The Bishop of Mende identified Buckingham as the enemy of France, while Louis XIII's inclination was to 'oblige the duke'. In fact, Buckingham in private conversation advised the king to be considerate and kind with his wife. Nor is there any sign that the queen was intimidated by Buckingham; quite the reverse. Henrietta Maria made a habit of using her French identity as a barrier against her husband. She refused to learn English and insisted on the king making any requests of her through a servant. She kept away from him, 'eschewing to be in [his] company'.[19]

This was more than a spoiled teenager making life difficult for everyone else. At the age of fifteen, Henrietta Maria had to confront a deliberate policy against her French retinue – against the marriage treaty. At the end of July 1625 she was asked to accept three new ladies into her household: Buckingham's wife, sister and niece. The French – that is to say the queen as advised by the French ambassador – were prepared to accept Buckingham's mother, the Countess of Buckingham, because she was a Catholic, and the others were permitted to visit her quarters, but non-Catholics could not be part of the household. When these scuffles were reported to Paris, Richelieu decided that not even the Countess of Buckingham was acceptable.[20]

In October 1625 the king told Buckingham that 'my wife begins to mend her manners' and also that her French servants, the 'Monsieurs', would soon be sent home. Forty Frenchmen were then returned to France, although the great majority remained. None of this was abnormal. Foreign queens needed to become English and to work and live, therefore, in an English environment.

The difference for Henrietta Maria was her marriage treaty, which was very specific because she was a Catholic.

To complicate the situation, Charles I's own credibility with the French had been hit when on 8 August 1625 he went back on his word, and on his earlier decision, when he promised Parliament full enforcement of the recusancy laws. He did this as a response to the inevitable petition on recusancy.[21]

The king's decision to show his Protestant face was certainly influenced by his wife's behaviour. Action led to reaction. Buckingham told the House of Lords that the king was happy to support the penal laws because he wanted to carry out his father's instruction – when was this given? – to show 'as soon as he was married that he did not marry her religion but her person'. On 12 August, Charles I dissolved Parliament for the reasons that were becoming usual – the reluctance of the Commons to vote adequate supply for the attack on Spain that was now being organised. Even so, by now he had for a second time told Parliament that he would support their view of legislation against Catholicism.[22]

*

Two expeditions were organised against Spain, aiming to recover the Palatinate for Elizabeth of Bohemia, the first in January 1625, while James I was still alive. The plan was to march into the empire and repossess the Palatinate by force. The English troops raised to fight under the mercenary general Mansfeld never came close to the Palatinate itself. They mostly died of cold, malnutrition and disease in winter quarters in the Dutch Republic or on board their vessels before they could disembark – 'we die like dogs'.[23]

Buckingham was held responsible, although it would have been fairer to point the finger at James I. It was the king who was intent on avoiding a direct confrontation with Spain, and therefore refused to divert the English troops to Breda, which was besieged by Spanish forces. As a result, Louis XIII decided that England was not serious about taking the fight to the Spaniards and withdrew his support for the expedition, which he had promised informally.

A second attempt to harass Philip IV took place in October 1625. Sir Edward Cecil, created Viscount Wimbledon in anticipation of his success, led a sea expedition to the south of Spain to attack the Spanish silver fleet, or, failing that, a major port such as Cadiz, the fleet's home port. The fleet sailed under the flag of the Elector Palatine to make the point.

The English ships reached the Bay of Cadiz, and the troops landed, not, at first, to attack the city directly, but to take the bridge which linked the city to the mainland, and therefore cut the garrison off. When they went ashore, on 24 October 1625, the men were lucky enough to find a wine store which they plundered and drained. They became hopelessly drunk. The defenders of Cadiz were not, therefore, taken by surprise.[24]

The season was late – autumn storms in the Bay of Biscay had already damaged the fleet – so Cecil decided to give up and come home. Popular feeling was expressed by Sir John Eliot when he said to the House of Commons, 'Our honour is ruined, our ships are sunk, our men perished, not by the sword, not by the enemy, not by chance, but ... by those we trust.' The last remark referred to Buckingham, who was Lord Admiral.[25]

These failures did not stop the duke. In October 1625 he was in The Hague, where he secured an alliance with the Dutch and the Danes against Spain. Louis XIII and Richelieu still refused French involvement, since their struggle against Huguenot power continued at home. The loan of the eight ships to Louis XIII, however, was held against Buckingham, since they were not after all used against Genoa but against the Huguenots. The English crews refused to serve, but this only made it harder to regain the ships later.

12

FRISKING AND DANCING

The reign of Charles I began badly because of his decision to attack Spain. At the same time, he found his wife overspending, refusing to sleep with him and parading herself as a Catholic proto-martyr. At least the dowry money could be (partly) used to finance the Cadiz expedition, and at least the king had their long-delayed coronations to look forward to.

The plague infection rate dropped with winter weather. On 29 January 1626, there was a general thanksgiving in London for the reduction in plague deaths, making it possible for the coronation to take place on Candlemas Day, 2 February 1626.[1] This was the feast of the Presentation of Christ in the Temple, commonly known as the Purification of St Mary the Virgin, so the date was a compliment to Queen Mary, Henrietta Maria, but, to add to her reputation, she now refused to be crowned, even to attend. A special screened area was offered within Westminster Abbey to no avail. Henrietta Maria would not lend her support to a Protestant service.

It was not brattishness. The queen tried to secure a coronation by her own Catholic Bishop of Mende, but the Archbishop of Canterbury, George Abbott, blocked her. Henrietta Maria sent Mende to consult with Paris. Naturally, she was 'quite happy that France took responsibility for the refusal [to be crowned]' but it was true that, however it may have seemed to the English nation, the decision was not really hers. She was cast in the role of a Catholic envoy by the marriage treaty and all other decisions stemmed from this. The coronation of Charles I therefore went ahead without Henrietta Maria and she herself was never crowned.[2]

*

Having travelled from the Tower of London, by boat, on the evening of 1 February 1626, Charles I arrived at the Palace of Westminster, which stood on the site of Edward the Confessor's eleventh-century royal palace. The eve of the ceremony took the king to the two ancient seats of royal government in England. At Westminster, the king was presented with a red silk shirt, 'open and looped at the places of anointing'. This was to be worn the next day over his own shirt, to show where he would be anointed with holy oil. The king returned to Whitehall by boat, and spent the night there in prayer.

The next morning, 2 February 1626, Charles I returned to Westminster, again by boat from Whitehall. The boat journeys were an innovation. Traditionally the sovereign rode in a procession through London, from the Tower to Westminster, but the risk of plague infection was still there, and water travel was much cheaper.[3]

Here he was dressed in virginal white, not the traditional purple, and without using the scarlet tunic after all. Archbishop Abbott of Canterbury, lame with gout, plus the Archbishop of York accompanied by the other bishops and the officials and choir of the abbey, met Charles I in Westminster Hall in a solemn procession. The king was already attended by his secular peers and other dignitaries.

At about ten in the morning, the procession to the abbey started. The marshals were first through, to clear the crowds, followed by the aldermen of London, the judges, the Knights of the Bath, officers of the Crown, and the choir. The peers came next, including the bishops, in ascending rank. Immediately before the king walked the favoured peers, who carried the coronation regalia: the crown imperial, the chalice, the paten,[4] two sceptres, the ivy rod ornamented with a dove, and 'St George's spurs', emblems of knighthood.

The religious regalia were carried by bishops, the secular regalia, including the crown imperial, by secular peers. Three peers, the earls of Dorset, Essex and Kent, carried three ceremonial swords, standing for mercy and justice temporal and spiritual. The king walked under a canopy of purple silk carried by the barons of the Cinque Ports. His train was six yards long.[5] He was supported by the bishops of Durham and Bath. His train was carried by the Earl of Warwick and Lord Maltravers. The feet of the great people never touched the ground, because they walked on a cloth spread over newly laid gravel from Westminster Palace to the abbey.

Inside the church, a stage had been built near the altar with a throne placed on it, raising the king, when he sat there, above the level of the altar. The stage and the altar rails were covered with cloth of scarlet. At the level of the altar, where the king would be crowned, another chair was placed, covered with cloth of gold. There was seating for the religious and secular peers.

As the king entered the abbey, the choir sung an anthem to the text of Psalm 122, starting, 'I was glad when they said unto me, we will go into the house of the Lord', followed by Psalm 84, starting, 'Oh how amiable are they dwellings, thou Lord of hosts!' The king then sat on the raised chair of state and the Archbishop of Canterbury proclaimed him from each side of the stage, accompanied by the Earl Marshal (Arundel), the Lord Constable (Buckingham) and the Lord Keeper (the Bishop of Lincoln), and asked the assembled dignitaries whether they were willing to do homage. The archbishop was asking the people of England to accept Charles I as their king.

The king descended from his chair of state on the dais to the level of the altar for prayers and a sermon. The archbishop then administered the coronation oath:

> Will you grant and keep, and so by your oath confirm to the people of England the laws and customs to them granted by the Kings of England, your lawful and religious predecessors; and namely the laws, customs and franchises granted to the clergy by the glorious King St Edward [the Confessor] your predecessor, according to the laws of God, the true profession of the gospel established in this kingdom, and agreeing to the prerogative of the kings thereof, and the ancient customs of this realm?

Charles replied, 'I grant and promise to keep them.'

After elaboration of the coronation oath, the king swore on the bible to 'perform and keep' the things he had promised. There were prayers and hymns, then the archbishop anointed the king in the palms of his hands, on his chest, on his back between the shoulders, on each shoulder, in the crook of each elbow and on the crown of the head. Although the scarlet shirt had been rejected, the clothes worn by Charles I were of course made with gaps and loops to make this possible. Bishop Laud, as deputy Dean of Westminster, then arrayed the king in the coronation robes over the pure white costume he had arrived in.

The spurs of St George and the king's sword were presented to Charles by the archbishop, The spurs were tied on by Buckingham. As the sword was buckled around the king by a peer, the archbishop charged Charles with his sacred duty as protector of the holy and the weak:

> Protect the holy church of God and his faithful people, and pursue heretics no less than infidels, defend and help widows and orphans, restore the things that are gone to decay, and maintain those things that are restored, be revenged of injustice...

The king was then lifted up on the chair of state on the stage, and the peers religious and secular, led by the Archbishop of Canterbury, paid homage to him, kissing him on the cheek. Communion followed, then the procession out of the abbey and back to Westminster, from where Charles I returned to Whitehall by boat. It was now four o'clock in the afternoon.

The mind of Charles I was indelibly impressed by the promises he made to protect English religion and to act justly at all times. Henrietta Maria did not stand back entirely from this seminal event in her husband's life. She watched the procession from a window in Sir Abraham Williams' house. Her French ladies could be glimpsed 'frisking and dancing' behind her. They were bored.[6]

*

Hard politics returned with the meeting of the 1626 parliament, which Charles I opened on 6 February, after progressing the short distance from Whitehall to Westminster. It was arranged that the queen would watch this other procession from the rooms of the Countess of Buckingham. The queen and Buckingham's mother, seen together, would provide a statement about solidarity at the top of government.

Unfortunately, on 6 February it was raining heavily. To reach Lady Buckingham's rooms, the queen needed to go outside, walking along a muddy path. She asked if she could stay inside and watch from the Great Hall. Charles said yes, understanding the inconvenience of the rain and the importance of an immaculate appearance. His wife, having listened to the advice of the French ambassador, the unpopular Blainville, then changed her mind. Mud or no mud, she went after all to the countess, and now the exasperated Charles – she listened to Blainville but did not listen to her husband – ordered her back to her own rooms, and went on to threaten the expulsion of her French household, especially of the controversial Mme de St George.[7]

13

DEPARTURE OF THE FRENCH

While the king and queen sparred, pressure was building in the country. Buckingham was drawn into the emerging religious confrontation.

In the early seventeenth century religion and politics locked together. The war in Germany continued, with the intervention of Christian IV of Denmark on the Protestant side and the King and Queen of Bohemia still based in The Hague, still trying to work out how to repossess the Palatinate. It was a war of religion and politics at the same time. The same was true of Louis XIII's campaigns in France against the Huguenots, and of the Dutch rebellion against Spain.

With the arrival of Henrietta Maria, England faced a unique situation. A Catholic queen – as quickly became clear, a woman (a girl!) of outstanding vivacity and determination – raised fears about Catholic influence at court, while the real disagreements lay in the Church of England. The confusion between Protestant quarrels and Catholic invasion would later be important; for the time being, the developing Protestant split headed the agenda.

Taking up the suggestion of another rich peer, the Earl of Warwick, Buckingham sponsored two days of religious debates, on 11 and 17 February 1626 at York House. The Bishop of Lichfield opened the case against Mountague – the case against

Arminian moderation – with support from the clergyman John Preston. During the second session, Mountague argued back. The arguments were put before an audience which included the earls of Pembroke, Warwick and Carlisle, Lord Saye and the Secretary of State Sir John Coke.

All this led to no conclusion. The Earl of Pembroke said, 'None returned Arminians thence, save such who repaired thither with the same opinions.' The York House Conference was a double failure, first a failure of Buckingham as a Protestant champion and second as a failure of Warwick and his supporters to achieve government endorsement of Puritanism.[1]

*

Foreign affairs, too, became tied up in dizzying complexity. Buckingham tried to help Louis XIII settle with his Huguenot subjects by sending the Earl of Holland (Viscount Kensington) and Dudley Carleton to mediate in Paris. Their mission bore fruit in the Treaty of Fontainebleau, an agreement between Louis XIII and the Huguenots (26 January 1626).[2] In this way France became free to join the attack on Spain, which was of course Buckingham's objective.

Preparations were therefore made for a French invasion of northern Italy, where Milan was a Spanish possession. The Duke of Savoy would assist the French. This would force Philip IV of Spain to move troops from the Palatinate (and/or the Dutch war) to defend his strategic Italian interests, with the long-desired – by Charles I, by Buckingham, by the English nation – result that the Palatinate could be saved.

Unfortunately the war plans were Richelieu's smokescreen to cover his more important and secret negotiations with – not against – Spain, which came to a head in the Treaty of Monçon, concluded on 23 February 1626. This permitted both France and Spain to travel through the key area of northern Italy, the Valtellina, which would be controlled by the Grisons, or Swiss Grey Leagues, who were French clients. Richelieu achieved a low-cost result for France, security on the Italian border, by stabbing his English and Savoyard friends in the back. No French attack on Milan, therefore no Spanish panic, no easy way to the Palatinate.

The Duke of Savoy deplored 'the perfidiousness of this treason, which is the greatest of all that were ever seen in like cases amongst Turks'. Sir John Coke described the promises of the French as 'the dreams of sick men'. Having attempted a war with Spain, with no result except lost money and dead Englishmen, Buckingham was coming to think that a war with France would be needed to remove Richelieu from the leadership of Louis XIII's government.[3]

The queen, already struggling with her marriage, was now exposed politically. Henrietta Maria's country was cooperating with the Spanish enemy, apparently seeking a Catholic domination of Europe. Richelieu began a shipbuilding programme, so that France would have her own strong navy, and founded a trading company based in Morbihan, south Brittany. The company had the right to build ships and guns, and to develop trade with North America, the East and West Indies and the Levant, in competition with the maritime English.

Worse, Richelieu detected and unravelled every conspiracy against him, the most recent of which involved Gaston, the favourite brother of Henrietta Maria, and the Comte de Chalais. Richelieu struck against his enemies in April 1626. Chalais was executed in August 1626, two weeks after Gaston – forgiven, in the traditional way, by his royal brother and, in the traditional way, bought off – had married the rich Mlle de Montpensier, and been made Duc d'Orléans.

Kensington's lover Marie de Chevreuse was involved. She was now the lover of Chalais and was not an innocent bystander. She was banished from the French court for her involvement and did not take her punishment lightly. The duchesse was 'transported by rage, and went so far as to say that people did not know her, they thought she was only suited to flirtation, that she would make it clear in time that she was good for other things, there was nothing she would not do to avenge herself, and rather than fail to win satisfaction from her enemies she would give herself to a peasant guardsman'.[4]

Henrietta Maria watched her friends and family at each other's throats. Buckingham, too, was fighting with his back to the wall. On 8 May he paid the price for the two failed Spanish expeditions, and for his York House failure, when he was impeached (indicted) by Parliament on thirteen charges, the last of which was the administering of medicine to James I without the permission of the king's physicians. It amounted to a scandalous charge of murdering the king.[5]

*

Henrietta Maria was more than a witness of these fascinating events; her fingers were already burned. A month after the row about the rain, the king ordered the arrest of the Earl of Arundel, the Earl Marshal. Henrietta Maria twice pleaded for the earl and was twice refused. The reason given for the arrest was the marriage, or elopement, of Arundel's son Lord Maltravers with Lady Elizabeth Stuart, who was a royal ward, and whose marriage required the king's consent for that reason. The challenge to royal authority was an affront to a king who was insecure personally and who especially liked ceremonial respect. It was more than this, however. Arundel, who was probably not aware of his son's romantic plans in advance, was involved in manoeuvres against Buckingham. By supporting Arundel, the queen therefore added to the pressures on Buckingham, and had to be denied.[6]

Possibly Henrietta Maria's retreat soon after to Somerset House was linked to this argument. It was a retreat in the religious sense. She ordered a gallery in her palace to be partitioned into cells, a refectory and an oratory, and here for a time she lived with her ladies as if they were all nuns, singing the 'Hours of the Virgin'. Charles I must have recalled his fears of the infanta Maria Ana retiring into a convent to avoid marriage.[7]

Two Members of the Commons, Sir Dudley Digges and Sir John Eliot, were also arrested because of the words they had used, or were reported to use, about the medicine given to King James. All three arrests were defences of Buckingham by the king. All three arrests turned up the temperature. Because the House of Lords was appalled that one of their Members was arrested while the house was sitting, Arundel was out and back in the Lords by 8 June.

The parliament did not last. Again Charles I saw how the Commons wanted to make supply conditional on the satisfaction of grievances. While this was traditional – Parliament was the forum for expressing national complaints – the personal attack on Buckingham broke the deal. Buckingham himself was much less concerned. He and other senior members of the council begged Charles I to allow Parliament to continue. The duke was confident he would survive the impeachment charges, but on 15 June the king ordered the dissolution, having decided to raise money by other means, namely a compulsory loan from his subjects.

Not long after the dissolution, the duke, as Lord Admiral, had to provide for coastal defence, since the government had intelligence of invasion plans from Spain: two hundred ships and forty thousand men were being gathered in Flanders. In addition, the king needed to raise money to pay the subsidies promised, under the Hague agreement, to his uncle Christian IV of Denmark. The future of the Palatinate depended on the success of Christian.

*

It was a year when many demands were made on the attention of a young and inexperienced king.[8] Unsurprisingly, it was now that Charles I's suspicion of the French men and women at the heart of the royal establishment boiled over.

At the beginning of July Charles I paid a visit to the Queen's Side in Whitehall. Instead of the decorous court that he favoured, he found 'some French, her servants, unreverently curvetting and dancing in her presence'. The king snapped. He took his wife by the hand, dragged her into the Privy Gallery, and led her into his own apartments, locking the door behind them. Lord Conway was sent to tell the French that they must go to Somerset House until the king had decided what to do with them.

'The women howled and lamented as if they were going to execution.' Henrietta Maria was beside herself. She drummed her fists on a window in her attempt to get through to her servants, now in the courtyard below, and broke the glass. She clutched the iron bars of the window but the king dragged her away, tearing her gown and grazing her hands. She threatened a hunger strike, and this at last made her husband relent a little, by ordering that Mlle du Vantelet could attend her. Even by the combined standards of the Bourbon and the Stuart families, it was an amazing scene.

On 1 July 1626 Charles I went to Somerset House to tell the French they would have to go back to France because he wished to 'possess his wife absolutely'. Her loyal followers kept their hands on the queen's expensive wardrobe, arguing that possession of the clothes was a right if they lost their employment. They were paid their wages, and demanded more money. They did not make arrangements to leave. On 26 August 1626 Charles I wrote to Buckingham to make things clear: 'I command you to send all the French away tomorrow out of the town – if you can by fair means, but stick not long in disputing – otherwise force them away like so many wild beasts.'

Henrietta maybe glimpsed her husband's side of the story when she was left with barely any clothes to wear. Her senior courtiers, Mende, the Comte de Cipière and the Comte and Comtesse de Tillières cannot altogether be blamed for their behaviour, because they thought they would not be repaid the loans they had made to their mistress. This was the 'only reason' they accepted the valuable jewels offered as gifts by the king to show his appreciation of their service.[9]

The legend arose that Whitehall was cleared of the French; in fact, about twenty were permitted to stay. Nor was the dismissal as theatrically spontaneous as it seemed, since, just before – in preparation? – the king had sworn in four English women as ladies of the queen's bedchamber: the Countess of Denbigh, the Duchess of Buckingham, the Marchioness of Hamilton and the Countess of Carlisle.[10]

14

BASSOMPIERRE

Henrietta Maria's rage exposed Cardinal Richelieu. She had not been crowned and she had no children. Her marriage was not consecrated in a Protestant church. The princess could be sent back. It was his fault. He had insisted on the tough marriage treaty and he had ordered a policy of no compromise. If so, that would be the end of Cardinal Richelieu, since Henrietta Maria's mother and brother would hardly accept the scandal without demanding a pound of flesh.

The cardinal reacted very quickly by sending a knight in shining armour. Barely a month later, an ambassador extraordinary from Paris arrived at Dover, instructed to negotiate a new deal for the Queen of England. The dark-haired, woman-loving forty-seven-year-old Maréchal de Bassompierre – the man once engaged to Charlotte de Montmorency – was an experienced soldier and diplomat, trusted by Louis XIII and Marie de Médicis.[1]

On arrival in England in October 1626, Bassompierre retraced Henrietta Maria's steps. He stayed a night in Dover Castle, then moved on to Canterbury. The queen sent her barge to Gravesend to ferry him to Greenwich, where he was met by the Earl of Dorset, her newly appointed Lord Chamberlain. The king's barge took him to the Tower, and from there he went to his lodgings, which he had to pay for himself. The same night, the Maréchal received a private visit from Buckingham and Wat Montagu. Complaints on both sides were discussed amicably.[2]

The first meeting with Charles I was planned for Hampton Court, on 11 October 1626. While Bassompierre waited in an antechamber, in the company of a 'handsome collation' and Lord Carlisle, Buckingham came with unexpected instructions. Charles I had decided that he did not want Bassompierre to raise the subject of his visit.

Henrietta Maria would be present. She 'might commit some extravagance, and cry, in the sight of everybody'. Anyway, the king himself was prone to fly into a rage when his marriage was discussed, and this 'would not be fitting in the chair of state, in sight of the chief persons of his kingdom, both men and women'. So the audience was cancelled. Instead, there would be a private meeting another day.

The maréchal had *savoir faire*. He explained to Buckingham and Carlisle that he was obliged to present his credentials, but the king, he said, could give and the king could take away. After the initial courtesies, he went on, the king could cut short the audience, saying that it was late in the day, and that he, Bassompierre, had to return to London; but His Majesty could at the same time say that he, Bassompierre, must return for a private audience later on, when there was more time. In this way the king would avoid the embarrassment of another scene, but the embassy would be preserved.

Buckingham embraced the ambassador, exclaiming that he was delighted to help him, but he clearly needed no help. After Buckingham had relayed this solution to the king, Carlisle and he led Bassompierre into the audience chamber. Charles I was seated on a chair of state with the queen at his side, also seated. They stood as the ambassador bowed. He presented his letters and made his compliments. The king interrupted the opening speech, invited his distinguished guest back for a private conversation another day, and the business remained unmentioned. Bassompierre exchanged a few words with Henrietta Maria. 'The company was magnificent, and the order exquisite.'

Blows were traded meanwhile. In his train, Bassompierre brought Père Sancy, an Oratorian priest originally in Henrietta Maria's English household. The priest was more than a simple Oratorian, having been sent before as French envoy to Constantinople. The example which Charles I tried to make of him is a tribute to the calibre of the men who came with the queen in 1625.[3]

Sancy's presence was a show of support for the queen, so the king sent at least three messages before the visit to Hampton Court asking Bassompierre to send him back to France. The messages were ignored. Surrounded by English lords, the maréchal was about to step back into his coach outside Hampton Court while Buckingham chatted with him 'expressly to give the secretary time to catch me'. The secretary – Secretary of State Conway – came running to say, once more, that Sancy must return to France, or there would be no second audience. The ambassador did not blink. Sancy was his confessor, would stay within his lodgings, was not permitted to leave the house, could not stray among the English. If Sancy went back to France, Bassompierre would go with him.

The knight in shining armour won his point. He met the queen at Somerset House on 13 October, then the king and, separately, the queen once more at Hampton Court on 15 October. At about the same time Henrietta Maria was reported to be happy and cheerful, spending much of her time at Somerset House with her English ladies, who now included the Catholic Countess of Rutland, the Catholic Countess of Buckingham and the Catholic Lady Savage. With Charles, Bassompierre had a discussion so heated that at one point Buckingham intervened. The interruption – not the emotion – shocked Bassompierre, who at once took off his hat to show the character of the conversation had changed (what was private became public). When Buckingham stood back, he put his hat back on again.[4]

Further meetings took place, reports were penned to Louis XIII, replies received. On 24 October the royal husband and wife had a row, followed by Charles speaking privately to Bassompierre, 'making me complaints of the queen, his wife'. On Sunday 25 October there was a general reconciliation, the king with the queen, the queen with Buckingham.

Charles I was now so pleased with Bassompierre that he showed him his collection of jewels. The next day the queen quarrelled with the ambassador, but they made it up two days later. On 1 November (French date) the Privy Council met to discuss the embassy, to see whether a solution could be agreed as to the management of the queen's household. Henrietta Maria was still uneasy, but Buckingham and Bassompierre had found common ground. The duke brought his adored four-year-old daughter Mall (Mary) to see the French ambassador. Mall was the one straightforward person involved in the entire episode.

On 6 November (French date) a blanket of fog covered London, and the Privy Council gave Bassompierre a written response to his embassy, blocking the French position. He responded by speaking to the councillors for an hour 'with great vehemence, and better, to my own liking, than I had ever spoken in my life'. He then saw the queen, who was delighted with his performance. Stalemate.

Bassompierre was tired out. He lost his voice when he was required, on 7 November, to resume talks with the council. Now things went well. He agreed to some English presence in the household, and the English agreed to the reinstatement of French Catholic priests. The Oratorians were gone for good, but Capuchins would replace them, and the queen was allowed a bishop too.

On 9 December, Bassompierre enjoyed the splendid ceremony of investiture of the Lord Mayor of London at Cheapside, 'the greatest that is made of any office in the world'. The queen went out of her way to pay him compliments, seating him with her in her coach. Then 12 December, a day filled with visits, ended badly. Bassompierre paid a call on Henrietta Maria, during which the king arrived. The couple had a row. The king swept out. The queen turned her black eyes, filled with tears, to her French friend for support, but from his eyes the scales were dropping. Bassompierre said that he would now leave England, return to Paris and tell Marie de Médicis and Louis XIII that the problems in the Stuart marriage were the fault of the queen, not the king. On that satisfactory note he went home, only to find that Père Sancy, having received a letter from Henrietta Maria, was urging the queen's case 'with such impertinencies that I got very angry with him'.

The queen commanded Bassompierre's presence the next day, but he refused to obey. François de Bassompierre had called Her Majesty's bluff. It was the turning point.

Henrietta Maria now accepted the Privy Council's decision. The remainder of the embassy was passed in feasting and music. A banquet of great theatricality – 'the most magnificent entertainment I ever saw in my life' – was given by Buckingham at York House in honour of the ambassador, on 15 November 1626. The performers served the meal 'with sundry representations – changes of scenery, tables and music'. The king was served by Buckingham, the queen by Carlisle and Bassompierre by Holland, all three, the royal couple and the ambassador extraordinary, sitting at the same table, to show concord.

After they had eaten, there was a second entertainment in another room, at which Buckingham himself danced. The central imagery of the entertainment was that of Marie de Médicis presiding over Europe as a peacemaker, through the agency of her children, the Duchess of Savoy, the Queen of Spain and the Queen of Great Britain. Finally everyone joined in country dances. The party went on until four o'clock in the morning. The next day the king threw another party at Whitehall. Symbolically the guests listened first to a performance by the Queen's Music, followed by general dancing, followed by a play. Eleven days later Henrietta Maria organised yet another masque in which both French and English performed.[5]

It is worth reflecting that the queen, who showed extremes of petulance and refined diplomatic skill, were celebrating her seventeenth birthday.

*

When the maréchal left the queen's household was settled, with her agreement, but after all that the relationship between France and England was not. Both Buckingham and Bassompierre were criticised for giving too much away. There were compensations. The king gave Bassompierre a valuable jewel – 'four diamonds set in a lozenge, and a great pearl at the end' – and the queen gave him a large diamond. The Earl of Suffolk gave him a horse, and the Earl of Holland three horses.

However, the maréchal lost money. He arrived at Dover with a train of four hundred including some sixteen English Catholic priests released from gaol, to take them back with him to France. He had promised to pay the expenses of everyone coming with him, not realising they would be delayed fourteen days at Dover, a cost of 14,000 *écus*. In addition he lost twenty-nine horses to thirst at sea because their transports could not land in the stormy weather and did not have enough fresh water, also losing two carriages which were thrown overboard to steady the boat in rough weather. With these went 40,000 francs worth of clothes, which the maréchal had bought to use as gifts.[6]

Once he left London, Bassompierre heard that Louis XIII was not satisfied with the settlement; in fact, he repudiated it. To repair the damage, Buckingham decided to travel to France to convince the king personally. Bassompierre, having set sail, had to return to Dover because of the winds. He went to meet Buckingham, Carlisle and Holland in Canterbury, where there were further lavish entertainments. Here he did his best to dissuade the duke from pursuing the return embassy. How could Buckingham be acceptable to Louis XIII? He had flirted with his wife and insulted his sister.

Meanwhile, Henrietta Maria arranged to spend Christmas Day 1626 at Somerset House, where she could celebrate the religious festival according to Catholic rites. After this she returned to her husband and Whitehall to prepare a court ballet. The queen had found a way to compromise.[7]

15

THE DUKE'S DESTINY

There was still a quarrel between France and England. Before Bassompierre arrived in England, Charles I had nearly sent six thousand troops to help the Huguenot Duc de Soubise defend La Rochelle, on the Breton coast, against the government of Louis XIII. In addition, as part of the war with Spain, English vessels had been instructed to seize and inspect (and sometimes confiscate) any vessels that might be harbouring Spanish goods. French ships were caught in the trawl.[1]

The most controversial was the *St Peter*, captured in 1625, then released after petition by its owners, but held again on Buckingham's orders in early 1626. His personal intervention was the true reason for the prominence of this single vessel. The Commons argued that his action provoked French reprisals.

Reprisals, anyway, there were. At the end of 1626, after the departure of Bassompierre, the entire English wine fleet, two hundred fully laden ships valued at 'more than three millions', was seized by France while they lay in dock at Bordeaux, at a time when there were just fifteen French ships under legal review in English hands.[2]

The hostile acts of the French royal government in the second half of 1626 convinced Buckingham that he was right about Richelieu, whom he thought to be the enemy of England. If Buckingham could not himself visit Paris and charismatically subdue Louis XIII, nor give comfort to the cardinal's French enemies, there remained military action.

In short, two years after her marriage – when she was the living emblem of Anglo-French friendship – Henrietta Maria found England and France at war.

*

La Rochelle, a walled town built around a superb natural harbour on the Breton coast, lay at the centre of the English strategy. The plan was to encourage a general Huguenot uprising by occupying this virtually impregnable port and threatening an English invasion in support. The conclusion would be the dropping of Cardinal Richelieu by Louis XIII from a great height.

In early July 1627, six months after Bassompierre had gone home, Buckingham was in personal command of nearly a hundred ships moored off La Rochelle. Despite the presence of the Duc de Soubise, and the assistance of his mother the old Duchesse de Rohan, who lived in the town, the mayor of La Rochelle could not be persuaded to allow the English soldiers to occupy it. Buckingham decided instead to occupy the neighbouring Isle de Rhé, an eight-mile-long island that stretched out into the Atlantic from the town, held by French royalist troops. It would be a good alternative base. To secure it he had to capture the Fort St Martin on the Isle de Rhé. Once the fort was taken, and reinforcements arrived from England, the mayor of La Rochelle would surely change his mind.

Buckingham almost did it. Unfortunately, Richelieu took personal charge of the French response, and managed to deliver supplies to the starving garrison of Fort St Martin by sending a flotilla of small boats at night, the tide pushing them direct to the fort, steered where they were least expected, through the middle of the besieging English squadron.

This seemed decisive against the attacking English, but Buckingham threw everything into an assault on the fort. It was repulsed. When he arrived back in England on 12 October he had lost four thousand of his men. Had reinforcements arrived, Buckingham's expedition could have been a game-changer. It was lack of money and bad organisation that delayed the reinforcements, which were just setting off from Plymouth the same time that Buckingham arrived back.[3]

*

In summer 1628, the duke was busy organising another expedition against France in support of the Huguenots. On 23 August Buckingham was talking to Thomas Fryer, one of his colonels, in the crowded parlour of the Greyhound Inn in Portsmouth. The colonel bowed to him, in the manner of the time. Buckingham courteously bowed in return, and was straightening up when John Felton pushed forward and stabbed him in the chest. The single blow was fatal.

The murderer ran away into the kitchen, then gave himself up. Before his own death, on 29 November 1628 (he was hanged at Tyburn after being found guilty of murder), Felton repented what he had done, saying, 'It was abhorrent, I have much dishonoured God in it.'[4]

Felton fought under Buckingham's command on the Ile de Ré, and was angry at not being promoted to the rank of captain, and bitter at the debts he had incurred because of arrears in his pay. When he read the 'remonstrance of the house of Parliament' – like its predecessors the 1628 parliament turned on Buckingham (and presented Charles I with a Petition of Right, an attempt to codify English liberties with royal approval) – he decided that killing Buckingham was a patriotic duty. Many agreed. Buckingham's failure at Ré was another blow to his reputation. For his glamour, his success, his failures, he had become a hate figure in the country, so Felton was regarded as a hero. Popular ditties circulated praising the murderer.

> Live ever Felton; thou hast turned to dust
> Treason, ambition, murder, pride and lust.[5]

*

Far from heralding an English collapse, the death of Buckingham came just before a relaxation in foreign affairs. From 1628 to 1631, Spain and France devoted their energies to a conflict with each other at last, the War of the Mantuan Succession, with the consequence that both wanted to make peace with England and did so, France in 1629, Spain in 1630. After the surrender of La Rochelle later in 1628 to French royal troops, Richelieu considered the Huguenots were under control and left them their religious rights after all. What had it all been about?

For Charles I, the loss of Buckingham was a deep wound. There would never be a second all-powerful favourite during his reign, never a second friend. The king's character is pathetically illuminated by a description of his reaction when he heard of the murder.

On 23 August 1628, Charles I was at divine service in Southwick House, outside Portsmouth, when a messenger arrived and whispered into his ear the devastating news.

> [Charles I] continued unmoved, and without the least change in his countenance, till prayers were ended; when he suddenly departed to his chamber, and threw himself upon his bed, lamenting with much passion and with abundance of tears ... and he continued in this melancholic ... discomposure of mind many days.[6]

Henrietta Maria was the one intimate companion the king now had. The marriage had always been based on strong attraction and sympathy, even though their terrible quarrels sometimes looked like the end. As is so often the case, the rows were caused by emotional bonds which were never to be broken.

In early 1627, before Buckingham died, the French envoy du Moulin noted the closeness of the royal couple, and recorded the queen's pleasure when Charles gave her a large diamond in April that year. When Buckingham was killed, Henrietta Maria was at Wellingborough in Northamptonshire, where the waters were meant to help women conceive. She was only eighteen, but after three years of marriage she understood quite well how her husband's shyness, lack of confidence and inflexibility were destructive companions to his adamantine sense of royal entitlement and his driving energy. Nor should her own feelings be disregarded, when she had to absorb the news of yet another violent death so close to her family.[7]

By October 1628 the courtiers were noting the king's new habit of lying 'with the queen every night'. On 22 July 1629, the painter Rubens, who was in London as a diplomat, wrote to the

Conde-Duque de Olivares in Madrid that 'the king is very fond of his wife and she has great influence with him'. Marie de Médicis helped by writing a number of letters encouraging her daughter to obey her husband, 'matters of religion only excepted'.[8]

Henrietta Maria and Buckingham were reconciled by the time he died. Having opposed their appointments, she became close to the Villiers ladies, and especially to Lucy Carlisle, then Buckingham's girlfriend, who for a long time was her favourite. After surviving smallpox, Lucy was even permitted by Henrietta Maria to wear a mask at the queen's court, which was a very rare privilege (Charles I forbade masks as part of his new rules on orderly, respectful court procedure).[9] Buckingham's death did, however, mark a new stage in her marriage, allowing Charles I to turn to his wife.

When Charles I celebrated his twenty-ninth birthday, the year after the loss of Buckingham, Henrietta Maria had relaxed into her marriage and had become fond of the English court. She ordered a birthday feast for her husband at Somerset House, and was irritated when the Duke of Saxe Lauenburg, and a junior member of the ducal family of Württemberg, both visiting to look for support against the emperor in Germany, made it clear they wanted to attend.

'The queen withstood it, saying she should be less happy than any common country gentlewoman if she would not make one meal in a year without the presence of unknown faces.' Henrietta Maria did not want Charles's birthday to be a diplomatic occasion, she wanted a family party.[10]

PART THREE

YEARS OF PEACE

How charming is divine Philosophy!
Not harsh, and crabbed as dull fools suppose,
But musical as is Apollo's lute.

John Milton, *Comus*

16

HEIRS TO THE THRONE

In March 1630, a ship travelling from France to Dover was captured by pirates. The prisoners included the party of Monsieur Garnier, consisting of several women and a boy. The chief pirate was a Dunkirker, one of the entrepreneurs, based in the Flemish port, who made a living by stealing from travellers crossing the Channel and ransoming them.

The Garnier group was quickly released and back on their way to England, thanks to the intervention of the Archduchess Isabella, governor of Flanders. The pirates had already made a fortune from the swoop. The party handed over jewels and other presents they were bringing for the Queen of England from her mother, valued at £7,500, but these people were worth more than jewels to Henrietta Maria, who was reduced to tears when she heard. After news of the kidnap arrived at Whitehall, 'they were more upset at court than if they had lost a fleet'.[15]

With Monsieur Garnier, who was the husband of the queen's nurse, came Mme Peronne, a renowned midwife, to manage the birth of the queen's second child, with more French nurses. Henrietta Maria had lost one baby already. Her first child, a son, was born early, not quite in the seventh month of pregnancy, on 13 May 1629 at Greenwich. The infant was quickly baptised – given the name Charles – but died about an hour after a breech delivery, having been 'turned overthwart in her belly'.[2]

This labour came on so quickly that the only midwife present was a local woman from Greenwich who was terrified by the responsibility, so the dangerous delivery was performed by the surgeon Peter Chamberlen, summoned from London. Charles was buried in Westminster Abbey after a stately funeral in Westminster Abbey, held at night, which neither parent attended. The tiny coffin was carried by six sons of earls, and six sons of barons were also in attendance. There were fears that the queen was physically damaged, but she recovered after several weeks lying in a blacked-out bedchamber heated by a roaring fire. By early 1630 she was pregnant again.[3]

Nonetheless, the queen's tears were probably shed on behalf of the twelve-year-old Jeffrey Hudson rather than anyone else. Henrietta Maria loved Jeffrey. He had gone on the mission to France as an adventure. The boy's father was an Oakham man who 'kept and ordered the baiting bulls for George, Duke of Buckingham'. When he was nine, Jeffrey was presented as a gift by his parents to the Duchess of Buckingham, and briefly attended her at Burley-on-the-Hill, one of the Buckingham mansions. Duchess Kate then made a surprise present of Jeffrey to the queen in 1626 or 1627, by putting him inside a 'cold-baked pie' out of which he burst in the middle of a dinner given for the king and queen. The child was traded and exhibited because he was a dwarf, less than eighteen inches tall at this time, being delicate and 'wholly proportionate'.

While he was presented as if he were a puppy or a parrot, Jeffrey was the winner, since he became one of the queen's most beloved servants and therefore lived a life of luxury. Not long after he had arrived at Somerset House, Jeffrey fell out of a window, and on this occasion too the queen was reduced to tears; in fact, she was so worried about Jeffrey – who was not damaged – that she did not get dressed all day. He would stick to his mistress through thick and thin until, much later, she was forced to banish him from her court. He would then have another pirate experience.[4]

The queen's household accounts show how richly Jeffrey Hudson was dressed. In 1628 an order was given for 'an ash colour barracon suit and cloak with sleeves for Mr. Jeffery' and other receipts have survived for a green taffeta suit and blue stain suit for him. Another dwarf – 'little Sara' – was elegantly attired in petticoat waistcoats 'bound with gold and silver parchment' and an 'Italian gown of scarlet bays bound with gold and silver'.[5]

While it made Henrietta Maria miserable, Jeffrey's time in the hands of the Dunkirker provided others with creative ideas. On 24 April 1630, the Revd Joseph Meade told his regular correspondent Sir Martin Stuteville that 'there is a poem which I cannot yet get, called "Geffreidos", describing a combate between Geoffrey, the queen's dwarf, and a turkey-cock at Dunkirk.'[6]

*

Henrietta Maria was settling. Her religious household returned to strength with the arrival at the end of February 1630 of twelve Capuchin friars with the new French ambassador, the Marquis de Fontenay-Mareuil. Thanks to their piety and the clothes they wore – and the clothes they did not wear – the Capuchins became a sensation, attracting crowds in their 'hundreds and thousands' to the queen's chapel, as well as increasing interest in the chapels of the Catholic ambassadors, and giving rise to at least one conversion to Catholicism.[7]

The essence of Capuchin rule was the original Franciscan simplicity, a dedication to utter poverty. The friars lived in a house near Somerset House. They wore brown-hooded, belted habits, no shoes, and prayed with passionate, introspective spirituality. Obedience to these principles, an exotic and, in the circumstances, rather showy absence of self-love, challenged the godly Protestants, who preached a different type of pared-down Christianity. The hostile Puritan reaction to the Capuchin craze gave the king an opportunity to be a Protestant champion. Charles took a public stand against the crowds, ordering arrests of people who went to hear the Capuchins, who were, by treaty, dedicated to the service of the queen and her household alone. He also announced that in the nursery of the new baby there would 'neither be nurse, rocker, nor any other office ... save only Protestants'.[8]

While some of her mother's presents were lost to the Dunkirker, a sedan chair arrived by another ship. The queen could now enjoy fresh air during her pregnancy without risking the strenuous walks which had possibly caused the early birth or the terrible jolting of coaches, which her husband seems to have thought responsible. The chair was 'handsomer than I [Henrietta Maria] deserve'. Not all the French blandishments were accepted. Charles I allowed the renowned Mme Peronne but blocked a French doctor, who never saw Henrietta Maria.[9]

On 29 May 1630, the nervous young queen – 'I hope God may grant me the favour to go to the end of my term' – gave birth in St James's Palace, without complications, to the future Charles II. A brilliant star was seen shining in the daytime sky. Henrietta Maria was now established as mother of future English kings, and Mme Peronne received £1,000 for her work. After his Protestant strictures, Charles I announced that the governess in charge of the prince's household would be the Catholic Countess of Roxburghe.[10]

*

There followed a Protestant christening, in St James's Palace, on Sunday 27 June 1630. The aldermen of the City of London, dressed in scarlet, led the procession, followed by the judges and the lord mayor – representatives of business and law. Then came the peers, followed by the godfathers, who were the two brothers-in-law of Charles I, the King of France (represented by the Duke of Lennox) and the King of Bohemia (represented by the Marquess of Hamilton). The baby was carried by the Marchioness of Hamilton (Buckingham's niece), supported by the Earl Marshal (Arundel) and the Treasurer (Weston), who was followed by a nurse.[11]

When the procession went outside, a canopy was held over the tiny prince by several lords. The Duchess of Richmond followed, as the representative of the godmother Marie de Médicis, her train carried by Mall Villiers, now eight. Frances Richmond was collected from her house by the queen's Master of Horse, Lord Goring, and transported to St James's in the queen's carriage, and decided that she herself had been chosen as godmother, or anyway behaved as though she had been.

It was not a ludicrous idea, since her late husband was a Stuart cousin, and, apart from the king, the only double duke in Great Britain – Scottish Duke of Lennox and English Duke of Richmond. Nobody complained when Frances generously presented the baby with a large diamond ring, the queen with another jewel and

Mme Peronne, the nurses and others with gold plate and jewels, her entire outlay being about £10,000. Court ladies followed the duchess, led by the Countess of Kent and Lady Strange, a Frenchwoman. The crowds were so great that they had to be roped off for safety.

The King's Chapel was hung with cloth of gold and tapestries. Galleries had been built on each side for the musicians, and the pillars which supported these were covered in 'crimson satin flowered with gold silk and silver'. The Bishop of London (Laud) officiated, on a carpeted platform erected in the middle of the chapel, raised several feet above the floor and fenced in by railings covered by cloth of gold. The Earl of Bedford carried in a 'great gilded covered basin for the font'.[12]

Charles I watched from a window on an upper storey, but Henrietta Maria did not attend at all. The baby's mother did not have an official role at the christening, and she had unchangeable views on Protestant services.

After the ceremony the baby's titles were proclaimed by heralds, and the people 'gave their loud acclamations, seconded by the sound of drums and trumpets, and by the thundering of canons from the Tower and the shops on the Thames'. The procession returned the same way as it had come, taking the baby back to the Queen's Side, where Charles and Henrietta Maria waited in the queen's bedchamber. They gave their blessing to their son 'and thence back to the nursery'.

Of course, the queen was desperately proud of her son, who lived at St James's Palace under the supervision of the woman who was finally appointed his governess, the Protestant Countess of Dorset, wife of the queen's chamberlain.

Henrietta Maria regaled Mamie St George in Paris with stories of baby Charles: 'He is so fat and so tall that he is taken for a year old, and he is only four months; his teeth are already beginning to come: I will send you his portrait as soon as he is a little fairer, for at present he is so dark that I am ashamed of him.' 'He is so ugly that I am ashamed of him, but his size and fatness supply the want of beauty ... he is so serious in all that he does, that I cannot help fancying him far wiser than myself.' The boy would grow into a tall, ugly yet attractive man, unlike his exquisite parents but similar to his Medici forebears, and also, in height, to his great-grandparents Mary, Queen of Scots and her husband Lord Darnley.[13]

Mamie also heard about the Summer progresses from palace to palace – 'the progress, from which we have only just returned a week ago ... you know the place, it is at Titchfield; now we are at Hampton Court, where we will stay six weeks' – and about the health of other houschold members – 'you will have heard of the illness of Rantelet, she has been very near death, but now she is well again'. Clothes feature: 'I have ordered Pin to be written to, to know from him whether he would be so good as to return into England to serve me; but only to make my petticoat waists'; 'send me a dozen pairs of sweet chamois gloves, and also I beg you to send me one of doeskin'. Also mentioned is the garden, when for instance she wrote to her mother, 'I am sending this man into France to get some fruit-trees and some flowers.'[14]

*

The birth of the second Charles heralded a succession of pregnancies. On 4 November 1631 Henrietta Maria had a girl, Mary; on 14 October 1633 a second boy, James; on 28 December 1635 a second girl, Elizabeth; on 17 March 1637 a third daughter, Anne; on 8 July 1640 a third son, Henry. One other child she lost soon after birth, Katherine, born on 20 January 1639. A last child, Henrietta, would be born on 16 June 1644. Each birth – except the last, which was in new circumstances – was momentous. The queen would be showered with gifts. When Elizabeth was born the Dutch ambassador gave the queen a large piece of ambergris, two basins of Chinese porcelain, a beautiful cloak, and four paintings by Tintoretto and Titian.[15]

With the exception of the last two, the children were born at the oasis St James's, a less formal residence than Whitehall with large gardens, an orchard and a park. 1637 was a plague year but Henrietta Maria still insisted on St James's for her lying-in, when pregnant with Anne. Not all were easy pregnancies. Mary was a small, sickly baby, not expected to survive, but she lived to be a pivotal figure in British history. While she was pregnant with James, Henrietta Maria had a very difficult time, including a spell of paralysis in her right arm.[16]

By 1640 the king and queen were the most successful royal

breeders in England since the fifteenth-century Edward IV and Elizabeth Woodville. Each one of the children – three boys, three girls – was a potential king or queen of Great Britain.

*

After Buckingham died, Henrietta Maria worked with her husband to re-establish the royal court, which had lost its star. For instance, she helped with the Marquess of Hamilton, who had to be coaxed into the consummation of his marriage with Buckingham's niece, Mary Fielding, so that he could take up his new appointment of Master of the Horse without scandal.

Hamilton lived in Scotland, separately from his wife, because, as a Scottish grandee, he felt he had been forced into a *mésalliance* with the daughter of a Midlands squire; but also because Mary was ten when they married (in 1622). Also, when his father died in 1625, he was left with enormous debts. Now he was recalled to Whitehall as the most prominent Scottish noble, and a man trusted by Charles I, whom he had joined in Madrid in 1623. The king lent him a nightshirt, and the queen sent him a posset drink with stimulative ingredients. The result was a daughter named Henrietta Mary, followed by five other Hamilton children.[17]

Similarly, soon after Buckingham's death, the king and queen made a state visit to one of Buckingham's opponents, the Earl of Arundel, to view his art collection, as a compliment to the man who was premier earl, Earl Marshal, and one of the king's richest subjects. The earl had recently been reinstated on the Privy Council; in fact, he had been recalled to court from internal exile. He was a voice both in the royal government and in Parliament, as a peer. The visit was a political act.[18]

Because of the marriage treaty, Henrietta Maria was involved in international politics from the word go. She went further. When war with France loomed in 1626–7, the queen offered her personal mediation with her brother Louis XIII (Charles I refused it). Henrietta Maria met foreign ambassadors separately from the king, and less formally. She allowed the diplomatic representatives of France and Savoy the privileges of members of her household but she did not give the same favour to Spanish representatives. The queen went out of her way to favour France.[19]

Despite her sister Elizabeth in Madrid, Henrietta pursued an anti-Spanish policy. Peace with France was agreed in April 1629, something Henrietta Maria wholeheartedly supported; and with Spain in November 1630. The queen was so opposed to peace with Spain that she wore her plainest clothes when she attended the ceremonies that celebrated it, and ordered her servants to do the same.[20]

The key to understanding later events is that Henrietta Maria found her feet as Queen of England at a time when her husband decided to work without calling Parliament. His experience of the 1628–9 parliament convinced him that another way should be tried. The years of personal rule began, when the king kept away from war, and found the finance he needed without summoning Parliament. His wife therefore had no real experience of the force of Parliament until much later on. She has been regarded with condescension as at best a court politician, but that was the only sphere of English politics, as consort, that she was placed to exploit. In fact, neither Henrietta Maria nor Charles I understood the risks of his decision to govern without Parliament, the most important he ever took.

17

THE EXCITEMENTS OF MARIE DE MÉDICIS

At the end of August 1630, Henrietta Maria's brother Louis XIII fell ill while staying at the Abbaye d'Ainay near Lyon. On 27 September, he was anointed with holy oil on his eyes, ears, lips, hands and feet, and given the Holy Eucharist. This was Extreme Unction, the Catholic sacrament given those who are dying. Three days later he had a haemorrhage in his guts, and was again given the sacrament. Although he recovered, the King of France did not seem destined for old or even middle-aged bones – at the time he was twenty-nine – which meant that his heir, his brother Gaston, was put on notice that he would be king, perhaps soon.[1]

Cardinal Richelieu's power was crumbling. He had the support of Louis XIII, but for how long? Louis XIII was unreliable. The king first loved the Duc de Luynes but came to hate him. As for Gaston, he was not the cardinal's friend. Gaston was part of the Chalais conspiracy against Richelieu in 1626. Anne of Austria hated Richelieu too. In short, Richelieu had risen thanks to the patronage of Marie de Médicis, so all he needed was for the queen mother to turn against him and he would have no friends at all.

This was the background to the meeting of the French royal council held on 10 November 1630.

*

In the Palais de Luxembourg, Marie de Médicis lived as a great power. Here, every day, she could walk in the gallery which Rubens had embellished with his famous cycle of paintings about her life. In the painter's glowing canvasses – most of them were more than twenty feet wide and twelve feet high – the queen mother could gaze upon twenty-four heavenly visions of herself going from strength to strength. Why should such a queen need one particular servant when there were others waiting in the wings? For instance, her *dévot* friends the Marillac brothers – one, Louis, a general leading useful troops in the field in northern Italy, the other, Michel, the Keeper of the Seals.

Because of building works at the Louvre, Louis XIII was staying in the Hôtel des Ambassadeurs, the sumptuous home of the Concinis. Respectfully he came to his mother's (larger) palace to chair the council meeting. In the course of the 10 November meeting, the council granted supreme command of the French troops in northern Italy to the maréchal de Marillac.

After the meeting, and in the presence of Louis XIII, the stately fading blonde Marie confronted Richelieu, dismissing him from the posts he held in her household, those of 'Surintendant' (financial controller), head of her council and Great Almoner. It was the second time she had attacked him in this way, the man who ten years before had been her *protegé* and champion. Richelieu had indeed lost his last friend.

*

The next day Louis XIII visited his mother in the Luxembourg again. Mother and son had a long conversation. No servants and no Crown ministers were present. Marie made sure the doors to her apartments were closed and guarded. She wanted to be certain there would be no interruptions.

There was no record, but it is safe to conclude that she was bashing the final nails into Richelieu's coffin when interrupted, despite her precautions, by the sudden arrival of none other than Richelieu himself. Thanks to his forethought in placing a number of spies among her attendants, he knew about the meeting and bypassed her defences by finding a corridor at the west end of the Luxembourg, running past the chapel, leading to a hidden stairway.[2]

Marie de Médicis could not keep Richelieu out of her rooms,

let alone her life. The bile of the fifty-five-year-old queen mother overcame her famed royal dignity. 'She could not conceal the hatred which she felt for him.' In front of her son, she turned on the cardinal, berating him with his utter unworthiness, his failure to serve. His surprise appearance had failed and he was reduced to submission. Richelieu told her that 'he no longer wanted to live because he was so unfortunate to have lost her favour', kissed her robe and left. Louis XIII did not intervene.

The king said farewell to his mother and retreated to Versailles, at the time a modest hunting lodge. News of Marie's triumph instantly spread. The Luxembourg was soon thronging with courtiers who came to congratulate her on her victory. 'The crowd was so great that you couldn't even turn around in it.'³

*

The next day the Secretary of State of the navy, Henri-Auguste Loménie de Brienne, called on Marie de Médicis. He had been sent to 'let the queen mother know, on behalf of the king her son, of the changes that he made in his council, in removing the seals from M. de Marillac'.

Marie de Médicis' Master of the Wardrobe, Luca Fabbroni, had advised her to follow the king to Versailles to be sure of him, but she stayed at home to receive the acclamations that now sounded so desperately hollow. It was Richelieu who followed the king to the hunting lodge. At Versailles the cardinal was received with effusive warmth by Louis XIII. The same evening the queen mother's man, the Keeper of the Seals, was deprived of office; and, even more critically, a message was sent to the maréchal Schomberg in Italy to arrest Michel's brother Louis (he was later executed).

In a replay of the events of 1617, when the Concini regime imploded, the fall of Marie's favourites was the fall of Marie. Louis XIII wanted Richelieu as First Minister, so if his mother could not work with Richelieu, it was his mother who must go. By the end of July 1631 Marie de Médicis was living in the Spanish Netherlands as a guest of the archduchess infanta Isabella. She would never return to France.

The events of 10 and 11 November 1630, when Louis XIII seemed to support his mother as she berated Richelieu, are known as the Day of the Dupes. It is a key episode in French history, because it established Richelieu in power for the rest of his life. To the court of Whitehall, these events were not a quarrel in a faraway country. They were a violent eruption nearby, and they struck at Henrietta Maria.[4]

*

In 1631, the Queen of England was pregnant with Mary. Her half-brother César de Vendôme came to London in November 1631, and stayed until Christmas 'to wear out some time of his commanded absence from the court of France'. Vendôme was another enemy of Richelieu. On arrival in London he was taken by Charles I to see Henrietta Maria 'with a French liberty, not ten hours after she had been brought to bed of a princess'. This was a colossal breach of etiquette. Usually it was two or three weeks after giving birth that the queen saw anyone other than her husband and the nurses. The family discussion which followed was secret.[5]

The problems of Marie de Médicis were a catalyst for her daughter's independence from France. Henrietta Maria tackled the French ambassador on her mother's behalf, with no result. She also wanted to keep her old confessor in England, an Oratorian, rather than send him back, as the Louvre wanted, now that her religious household was re-established. This became another reason for Henrietta Maria to stand apart from Paris.[6]

Marie de Médicis proceeded to ruin herself financially by pawning her jewels to finance a three-part abortive attack in 1632 on the royal government of France, from Calais (to be led by its governor), Lorraine (to be led by Gaston) and Languedoc (to be led by the Duc de Montmorency). His lustre increasingly tarnished, Gaston survived the disaster while, to the horror of the French court, Montmorency was executed on 30 November 1632. At Whitehall Charles I could congratulate himself on his superior management of his own family and on the stability of England.[7]

His wife could not stand by, however. At once there followed another plot against Richelieu, involving the Marquis de Châteauneuf, who had been ambassador to England and therefore knew Henrietta Maria well. The beautiful Duchesse de Chevreuse, considering Richelieu the lowest of the low, was inevitably part of this conspiracy, having buttered up Châteauneuf with a lively flirtation. When Châteauneuf's papers were confiscated in February 1633 – the cardinal was always ahead of the game – they were found to contain twenty letters from Lord Holland, thirty-two from Walter Montagu and thirty-one from the Queen of England.[8]

Henrietta Maria became involved on her mother's behalf and went too far. As part of the conspiracy, a plan was formed to oust the English minister Weston from his office of Treasurer and First Minister, because he was tolerant of Richelieu. Weston was also (in contradiction) considered a friend of Spain, and certainly opposed to war with Spain to regain the Palatinate – there was no escape from the Palatinate – and therefore had other enemies in the Puritan camp (who backed the Calvinist Queen of Bohemia as an alternative Stuart line). Although he had sent his son Jerome to Paris to talk Louis XIII into diplomatic support on the Palatinate, Weston was therefore vulnerable. So far, so confusing.

*

The queen disliked Weston personally, disliked him because he was opposed to her mother's requests to come to England and because he was a cost-cutter who liked to starve her of funds. Henrietta Maria suffered from Weston's austerity measures. When she was resting after the birth of Charles, she was pleased to see the old Duchesse de la Tremouille, who had come to England to visit her daughter Lady Strange, but ordered all the windows of her room to be closed and curtained so that the duchesse, admitted in the gloom, would not see the shabby condition of the furnishings in her room. Accordingly, if the Earl of Holland became Lord Treasurer instead of Weston, there would be a united front against Richelieu and a friend in power at home, not to mention more fun.[9]

The Châteauneuf conspiracy came to nothing – every conspiracy against Richelieu came to nothing – and Jerome Weston returned to London in March 1633 with two letters that he had taken out of the diplomatic pouch of a royal courier, one from Holland and one from Henrietta Maria. He was afraid they contained proposals against Richelieu and his father, although, when they were opened, they were found to be harmless. Holland challenged Jerome to a duel for this dishonourable behaviour, but Charles I defended Jerome, understanding that he was trying to contain a potentially highly embarrassing situation, and suspended Holland from the Privy Council, briefly placing him under house arrest (where he was besieged by visitors).

To show repentance for her encouragement of Holland – perhaps for more – Henrietta Maria was obliged to offer to put her affairs in the hands of Jerome's father. In addition to being implicated by her correspondence, she also was known to be seeing the Sieur de St Croix, a man sent by Marie de Médicis to look for English military support against the French regime. None was given.[10]

18

A PERFECT WORLD

Bourbon misery contrasted with Stuart happiness. Charles and Henrietta Maria liked to spend time with their children, both at St James's, where they joined them for the evening meal when they could, and at Richmond, where the nursery decamped for country air. The family was relaxed and affectionate – natural, not cramped by royal etiquette.[1]

The queen watched carefully over the children's health. In September 1635 the Venetian Ambassador informed the doge and senate that the queen was staying at Richmond to keep an eye on the five-year-old Prince of Wales, who was sick, and later in the same year recorded the boy's recovery, so that the queen was now moving between other houses nearby, probably Hampton Court and Nonsuch. She was heavily pregnant with Elizabeth at this time. Henrietta Maria's first letter ever written to her eldest son urged him to take the medicine that his doctors prescribed and that he, probably aged eight, was refusing. In May 1636, the brother of the Landgrave of Hesse Darmstadt made a private visit to England and came at the end to say farewell to the king and queen, but his audience with Henrietta Maria was put off by a day, being 'hindered by the Princesse Elizabeth's sudden indisposition'. The queen wanted to look after her baby herself. She was 'the best wife and mother in the world.'[2]

Early the children were put to work. In March 1634, Henry Oxenstierna arrived in London as ambassador extraordinary of Sweden. Having had a public audience with the king, whom he addressed in Latin, and the queen, whom he addressed in French, Henry had a private audience with the king, and then visited the children. He met Charles (nearly four) and Mary (two and a half) together, and separately paid his respects to James (five months old) 'as he lay sleeping in his nurse's lap'.[3]

Audiences with ambassadors continued as the children grew. They joined their parents for dinners of state at times, so that the crowds could see the next royal generation. Charles was made a knight of the garter when he was eight, and joined his father every year for the annual garter ceremony, which Charles I had made the centrepiece of his policy to promote and renew the nobility.[4]

*

It was a life of constant movement. Winter was spent at Whitehall. In spring the king and queen went to Greenwich, where it was still possible for Charles I to transact business, and easier for him to combine it with hunting. In the summer – when it became harder to locate the king and secure his time – there was a progress to royal residences such as Theobalds (Hertfordshire), Oatlands (Surrey), Nonsuch (Surrey), Woodstock (Oxfordshire), Holdenby (Northamptonshire) and the houses of the nobility, among which Lord Pembroke's Wilton near Salisbury was the one most loved by Charles I. There were feasts and entertainments throughout. In 1634 the court travelled north via Lord Rutland's Belvoir to Welbeck, home of the Earl of Newcastle, who entertained the king and queen at another house, Bolsover, with a masque written by Ben Jonson, the whole entertainment costing the earl £14,000–15,000. The entourage would move on to Windsor Castle and Hampton Court before returning to Whitehall for the winter.[5]

The queen travelled with a huge household, including small birds, dogs, monkeys and priests, although some exotic attendants stayed behind in London. As well as Jeffrey and other dwarves, Henrietta Maria was served by a Welsh giant called William Evans, seven feet and six inches tall, who worked as porter at Somerset House for £25 a year. There was a great interest in human curiosities at the Caroline court, which also briefly housed 'Old Parr', a man from Shropshire said to be 151 years old in 1635. When asked by the king for the secret of his long life, Old Parr replied, 'Please your majesty, I did penance for a bastard when I was above a hundred years old.'[6]

*

Henrietta Maria loved theatrical court entertainments. She had known them, and acted in them, since childhood at St Germain-en-Laye. They were the reason for the reputation she gained, among those who thought that fun was a sin, for flighty immorality, although the evidence that we have suggests the exact opposite. Her confessor Fr Philip is on record as saying that 'as to faith, or sin of the flesh, she is never tempted'.[7]

Others were tempted and fell. Henrietta Maria's friend Harry Jermyn made Eleanor Villiers pregnant and refused to marry her, on the grounds that he had no fortune. The queen persuaded her husband to readmit Jermyn to favour even though both king and queen were trying to raise the moral tone of the court.[8]

The masques and plays were one way of doing this. They were expensive – austerity did not apply to them – and usually took place during the winter season, celebrating the two royal birthdays, both in November, and the feasts around the Christmas period. They were statements of principle, of philosophy, and could be alarmingly high-minded. The court theatricals were promoted by both king and queen but there is no escaping the conclusion that they were one of the ways that Henrietta Maria personally introduced French discernment into the English court. They were spectacles of ravishing beauty.

The shows started with a bad reception back in November 1625, when the newly arrived queen arranged a masque which combined speaking parts with music and dance. The locals were not amused. The first French masque was 'disliked of all the English, for it was neither masque nor play, but a French antique'. As time passed the queen supplemented the traditional masque entertainment with 'pastorals' in which mythical settings were used for a narrative about love and virtue.[9]

In February 1626, the first pastoral was performed to a select audience in Somerset House. This was *Artenice* by the French playwright Racan. It was given in French, and consisted of the play itself followed by a dance. The title role was taken by Henrietta Maria, who excited respect for her ability to remember '600 French verses by heart' but also concern. It was an all-female cast, which meant that some of the ladies performed trouser roles, wearing fake beards, something not seen before. The Catholic queen was avant-garde.[10]

The text of *Artenice* was almost subversive, promoting romantic love. The heroine Artenice is destined to marry a man chosen by her parents, but she is already in love with Alcidor. Artenice takes refuge in the temple of the 'Good Goddess', where she decides she must dedicate herself to a life of the spirit – become a nun – but she realises that her love for Alcidor is so powerful that his death would mean her death, and so Artenice ends up in a happy marriage with the right man.

The allegory was illuminated by ruminations on the nature of the world and the purpose of life, based on Neoplatonic traditions of thought, which combined Christian orthodoxy with classical philosophy. For the production Inigo Jones constructed a stage. His designs included a village street of thatched country cottages and a colonnaded building.[11]

Incidentally, *Artenice* is evidence for the success of the queen's marriage well before the expulsion of the French entourage and in the same month as the coronation. Henrietta Maria was lively and active but she would not have invoked the perfect love relationship to taunt her husband publicly.

At the end of 1626, Ambassador Bassompierre was entertained by a masque arranged by the queen, held at Somerset House, in which subtle diplomatic points were made about Anglo-French cooperation – too subtle, really – and on 14 February 1626 Henrietta Maria and her ladies performed in a Whitehall masque which required 1,000 yards of taffeta and satin. At Christmas 1627 there was another masque, featuring both Jeffrey Hudson and William Evans. This was probably the masque in which Evans reached into one of his pockets and pulled out a loaf of bread, and reached into the other and pulled out Jeffrey.[12]

Henrietta Maria used visual display outside the court. In July 1628 she went on royal progress to Wellingborough, in Northamptonshire, where there was a spring which helped women conceive. She brought with her a number of blue calico tents decorated with gold lilies, pyramids and stars. On this or another progress she also set up a mock castle made of canvas, a 'French military camp ... set up *inside* the bounds of England'.[13] This was the time, just before Buckingham's death, when her husband was preparing for another attack on the French mainland. The queen supported her husband, and was hoping of course to become pregnant with an heir to the throne of England, but she made a statement about her French origins with her beautiful tents, showing she could be French and English at the same time.

*

Charles I, too, arranged and performed in masques. On 9 January 1631 he performed in Ben Jonson's *Love's Triumph Through Callipolis* at Whitehall, and this masque was again given on 22 February 1631 together with the queen's masque *Chloridia*, also by Ben Jonson, among whose players was Jeffrey Hudson, 'richly apparrelled as a prince of hell'.

While Henrietta Maria did not perform in *Love's Triumph*, she was sitting at the heart of the watching court, and was heavily invoked by its plot, in which 'depraved lovers' who have invaded the 'beautiful city' are brought under control.[14] More Neoplatonism, but in the end the point is the ravishing vision of the fecund royal marriage.

> Who this King and Queene would well historify
> Need only speake their names. Those them will glorify.
> MARY and CHARLES, CHARLES with his MARY named are,
> And all the rest of Loves, or Princes, famed are.[15]

The plot of *Chloridia* combines the raising to heaven of the nymph Chloris (played by Henrietta Maria) as the goddess Flora, together with the discords inflicted by Cupid, whose mother has denied him a place in the council of the gods on grounds of age. Cupid, having descended to hell to find allies, namely Jealousy, Disdain, Fear and Dissimulation, is pacified by Juno (goddess of marriage), assisted by Chloris, and the masque ends with the nymph's apotheosis.

In the disturbances of Cupid are echoes of the rift between Louis XIII and Marie de Médicis, a quarrel whose outcome was not

clear at the time the masque was performed. In addition, Henrietta
Maria found herself complimented as semi-divine and as a creator
of harmony at home.[16]

On 8 January 1632, Charles I appeared in the masque *Albion's
Triumph* by Aurelian Townshend. This was followed on 14
February, also at Whitehall, in the Banqueting House, by the
queen's *Tempe Restored*, also by Townshend, who had succeeded
to Ben Jonson's position as writer of royal masques. Henrietta
Maria played Divine Beauty, whose job is to restore harmony to
the Vale of Tempe, after the sorceress Circe, a 'lovelorn woman',
consoles herself with chaotic antimasque dances of wild animals
and barbarians. Joining with Heroic Virtue (played by Charles
I), Divine Beauty exerts her influence with the result that Circe
surrenders her golden wand to Minerva (goddess of wisdom) and
calm is restored.[17]

*

The queen's second pastoral was something of a watershed. *The
Shepherd's Paradise*, written by the queen's friend Wat Montagu,
was performed at Somerset House twice over the Christmas period
in 1632/3. Once again there were trouser roles for the queen's
ladies; ten out of fourteen roles were male. The weird, indeed
testing, script – 'one of the worst [plays] in the language' – was
partly designed to help Henrietta Maria with her English, in which
she was making slow progress.[18]

Bellessa ('Beauty', played of course by Henrietta Maria) rules
the paradise of the title, which is the Elysian refuge of both men
and women dedicated to platonic – non-sexual – love. It is always
ruled by a queen, never a king. In the end Bellessa, revealed as the
disguised Sapphira, Princess of Navarre, abandons the paradise to
marry Prince Basilino, whose great friend, previously known as
Agenor, turns out to be her brother Palante.

For much of the baffling action the boys are love rivals but
Palante finally marries Basilino's sister. The moral heart of the
drama, if drama is the word, is Fidamira, who for much of the time
is disguised as the moor Gemella, and arouses great admiration,
but is yet another princess of Navarre (called Miranda), the sister
of Sapphira and Palante. Gemella/Fidamira/Miranda at last takes
over as the chaste queen of the paradise. As Mr Beaulieu wrote to

Sir Thomas Puckering on 10 January 1633, 'This night, our queen have acted her costly pastoral in Somerset House, which hath lasted seven or eight hours.'[19]

Shortly after *The Shepherd's Paradise* was shown, a 'pamphlet' was published by the godly William Prynne, a lawyer in his early thirties. *Histriomastix* covered 1,100 pages and raged against the indecency of stage plays and all other theatrical entertainments. It was not the first or only such attack but it became prominent because its publication led to the trial of the author by the Star Chamber for sedition. William Laud said that it would take sixty years of an ordinary man's life to read the sources cited by Prynne in *Histriomastix*, meaning those which were critical of the theatre. Of the theatre itself, for instance of the plays of Shakespeare, Prynne appears to have known almost nothing.[20]

Even though there was no direct attack on the king, Prynne was found guilty. The problem was that the index at the back included a description of women actors as 'notorious whores', a reference apparently added after Henrietta Maria's star turn as Bellessa. It was because of this almost sacrilegious attack on the queen, as it appeared, that Prynne was sentenced to have both ears cut off, to a fine of £5,000 and to life imprisonment.[21]

*

Henrietta Maria's Bellessa was her last performance in a speaking part. There were other reasons than Prynne for the queen's retreat from an active role on the stage. Declaiming a language over which she had imperfect control cannot have been much fun, especially when the script was so bad. Another reason could be the painful pregnancy she suffered when she was carrying James, who was born on 14 October 1633. After that, as mother of three small children, she may have felt it right to stop.

Another family reason could be concern for her husband, who fell ill in early December 1632, at just the time *The Shepherd's Paradise* was being finalised for performance. Maybe she felt guilty.

Henrietta Maria's care for her husband was selfless. Doctors explicitly diagnosed smallpox – it was a light attack which did not bother him much, but he was covered with spots – but Henrietta Maria continued to sleep with him and refused to stay away from him during the day. The mutual devotion of king and queen was now famous. When Sir Ralph Verney needed a reason to avoid a meeting with a friend, he said, 'According to the example of our gratious sovereign, I must obey my wife and she commands my presence on the 26th.'[22]

*

During the next winter season Henrietta Maria sat through a performance of Shakespeare's *Richard III* that Charles I offered for her twenty-fourth birthday in November 1633. Both this and her production for his birthday, *The Young Admiral* by James Shirley, were performed by companies of professional actors (*Tempe Restored* also used professionals) not by courtiers, and both were held in the relative intimacy of St James's Palace.

Charles I used the theatre to teach his wife something about English history and did this – on purpose – soon after she lent her support to conspiracies against the chief ministers of England and France. The story of *Richard III* features a French queen of great ferocity (Margaret of Anjou), a usurping brother (Richard himself), as well as vulnerable children – the tragic Princes in the Tower – and a number of political murders, and was probably chosen to help Henrietta Maria think such people, such situations, through. The queen's patronage of the theatre continued, as did the performance of court masques, but her personal involvement from then on was more thoughtfully judged.[23]

The philosophical approach, however, stayed. It was once more evident in *The Young Admiral*. While her husband offered her the bloody story of the last Yorkist King of England, she offered him a tale of split loyalties in which the virtuous Cassandra and Rosinda save the mutually destructive men of an imagined conflict in the south of Italy. Her choice was considered by the master of the revels, Henry Herbert, 'a pattern for other poets, not only for the bettering of manners and language, but for the improvements of the quality'.[24]

The elevated tone was characteristic of the court of Charles I and Henrietta Maria. At this period, young noblemen were sent on long tours of the Continent to broaden their horizons, an aim which could, if they were lucky, include a good deal of low life. When they came to take their leave of the king before setting off,

Charles therefore gave the young bloods a moral lecture, saying that 'if he heard they kept good company abroad, he should reasonably expect they would return qualified to serve him and their country well at home'. Husband and wife made high moral purpose a joint endeavour.[25]

19

HOLYROODHOUSE

Having ruled Scotland since 1371, the Stuart family abandoned their ancient home when Elizabeth I died in 1603, preferring the wealth of England. The historic succession – by the descendants of Henry VII's daughter Margaret Tudor – solved the English problem of legitimate power, but deprived the Scots of the patronage of a royal court. While James I (James VI of Scotland) understood the dynamics of Scottish politics, having presided over the Scots as their king for so long that he pulled off the difficult trick of long-distance government of Scotland from Whitehall Palace, this knowledge could not be inherited by his son. It required experience. The ignorance of Charles I lay at the heart of the coming storm,

In 1633 – the year when Londoners for the first time saw a bunch of bananas, exhibited in the shop window of the apothecary Thomas Johnson in Snow Hill[1] – Charles I travelled north for his coronation as King of Scotland. It was not a great compliment to go eight years after his father's death, but he went. Henrietta Maria was four months pregnant, carrying the future James II (James VII of Scotland). She stayed behind.

Organisation started early. In February 1633, fifty 'fair-carts with necessary provision' were costed (at £427 3s) to accompany the king. Charles was to be accompanied by his Lord Chamberlain (Pembroke) and Treasurer (Portland), the Earl Marshal (Arundel), one of the two Secretaries of State, six Lords of the Bedchamber, six more earls and four bishops, and his lesser servants, including two physicians, three surgeons, a barber (with three servants), sixty guards, twelve trumpeters and six drummers. The bishops had forty servants to look after them, as well as two deans and four chaplains, and fifty horses. A chapel choir was sent by boat: a subdean, twelve choirmen, three choristers, two organists and four deans of vestry. Adding everyone together, including all the 'servants' servants', nearly a thousand people went with the king. Almost all the foreign ambassadors also went. The queen's household stayed at Greenwich, looking after their mistress and the two royal children.[2]

On 8 May 1633, Charles I set off from London. He made slow progress. After delays caused by hunting, by an interview with an agent from Germany and by the hospitality of landowners and towns on the way, he arrived at Berwick on 4 June 1633. He entered the country of his birth in state, making a triumphal entry into Edinburgh on 15 June 1630.[3]

The king installed himself at the royal palace of Holyroodhouse, which was much smaller than the accommodation he was used to. It had been renovated in preparation, and brushed up: the mounds of sewage left by travellers on their way to and from Musselborough were cleaned from the walls of both the palace and the abbey church.[4]

On 17 June the king transferred to Edinburgh Castle, where 'the captain of the castle saluted His Majesty coming up to the gate with 52 shots of great ordinance'. A banquet was held that night. The next day he was crowned in the abbey church of Holyroodhouse. The ceremony started at about eight o'clock in the morning of 18 June 1630, when Charles I walked into the Great Hall of Edinburgh Castle to join eight bishops dressed in black, and fifty-seven Scottish peers in crimson velvet.

The king wore red. As in England, he had a shirt with slits, where he would be anointed; over that he wore a red silk coat, also with slits; then a 'princely robe' of crimson velvet with a train 'of prodigious length'. Accompanied by the peers of Scotland, Charles I rode from Edinburgh Castle to Holyroodhouse, his long train being carried behind him, where he dismounted and walked on a path covered with blue cloth, under a crimson canopy fringed with gold, carried by six eldest sons of peers. At the door of the abbey church, the king was met by Archbishop Spottiswood of

St Andrews and four other bishops.[5] These clerics were in violet silk cassocks, over which they had white rochets (narrow-sleeved surplices), and copes (cloaks) of cloth of gold.

There was a similar sequence of events to the English coronation, leading to the coronation oaths which included the following question, from Spottiswood:

> Sir, will you promise to serve Almighty God to the utmost of your power, as he hath required in His most holy Word, and, according to the same Word, maintain the true Religion of Christ, now preached and professed within this Realm, abolishing and gainstanding all false religion, contrary to the same?

The king replied, 'I promise faithfully so to do.'

The crown was placed on Charles's head about two o'clock in the afternoon, with prayers and music to follow. The newly crowned king returned in procession to Holyroodhouse, so that the ceremony in total lasted about six hours.

On 20 June the king opened the Scottish parliament, which passed 186 pieces of legislation, including a substantial grant of taxation. By the end of July the king was back in the south of England after a 'very hurried and almost flying journey', arranged because 'he wished to take the queen by surprise, so as to make his return more welcome to her when she was not expecting him'.[6]

Soon after his return the pregnant Henrietta Maria had a fall, so 'the king ordered her to go to bed at once', but fortunately it was not serious. The baby was safe. This absence of almost three months was the longest the king and queen had spent apart since they were married. Henrietta Maria missed her husband, but it was not a time of abject misery. Among other diversions, she organised a barge race with Lord Goring on the Thames.[7]

*

The calling of the Scottish parliament encouraged the idea that an English parliament might also be called, which did not happen, but this was not the worst of the damage. Thanks to the king's behaviour, the subtext in Scotland was resentment. 'From the outset, Charles upset his Scottish hosts with a notable lack of tact', preferring the company of his English nobles to the Scots whom he barely knew, but whose loyalty it was very much in his interest to cultivate. The coronation ceremony was itself offensive because the English prayer book was used and bishops officiated, elaborately dressed. The Communion table was railed off and positioned by the altar, rather than in the middle of the church as the Calvinist ministers preferred. It was 'popish'.[8]

While the royal program for the Scottish parliament was a success, it was clumsily managed. When, in the traditional manner, a petition of grievances was drawn up, Charles refused to read it. The worst mistake was to order the prosecution of Lord Balmerino the following year, when Charles was back in England, because Balmerino had kept a copy of the petition, made notes on it (which softened the complaints) and showed it to John Dunmure for his comments. Balmerino was tried and found guilty of 'divulging and dispersing' a 'scandalous libel' and sentenced to death. Although he was pardoned by the king in July 1635, the sentence was considered a scandal.[9]

Would Henrietta Maria have charmed the Scottish lords if she had gone with her husband? Could she have changed the future? The answer has to be no. Scotland was devotedly Calvinist. Scottish Protestantism was attuned to the hard and joyless values of William Prynne, not those of the tolerant and sophisticated Henrietta Maria.

20

THE SOUND OF SILENCE

Nonetheless, the next steps of Catholicism in England were down to Scots influence. When she had survived a difficult pregnancy and produced James, a second male heir, the queen's energy – belied by the graceful, poised portraits now being painted by the Flemish artist Anthony van Dyck – fixed her eyes and her heart on her faith. The Vatican considered the Queen of Great Britain a frivolous woman dedicated to dancing in public. The arrival in Rome in spring 1634 of Sir Robert Douglas, a Catholic Scot, therefore surprised the Cardinal Secretary of State Francesco Barberini, since Douglas came with a request from Henrietta Maria for the creation of a British cardinal.

It was this initiative of the queen that moved Catholicism up the English court agenda. She was always devout, but since the settlement of her household following the Bassompierre embassy her faith had not been a broader issue. This would now change.[1]

The queen wished to favour another Scot, George Conn from Aberdeenshire, whose achievements included a pious biography of her husband's Catholic grandmother, Mary, Queen of Scots, published in 1624, and a history of Scottish Christianity. Conn had lived most of his life on the Continent. He was a Franciscan, and part of Cardinal Barberini's household.[2]

Barberini advised his uncle Pope Urban VIII to find out more before committing to an appointment that would sound alarm bells across Protestant Europe. An envoy was sent to spy out the land, Gregorio Panzani, who arrived in England in December 1634. Panzani was instructed to settle disputes among the Catholic clergy, to obtain royal permission (if he could) for a Catholic bishop to be sent to England and to see whether Catholics could be officially exempted from all oaths sworn to the government.

Henrietta Maria obtained Charles I's permission for Panzani's presence in England, accredited to her court, provided he kept his work low-key. She also secured Panzani an audience with her husband. According to Panzani himself, the king vowed that he would have given his right hand if only England had not broken religious communion with Rome, a remarkable comment from the head of the Church of England.[3]

It was not even half true. The king liked old institutions, but he did not mean that he liked the authority of the Pope, or that he was thinking of conversion. Charles I accepted the legacy of the Tudors, and, having twice sworn coronation oaths (to God) which placed him at the head of English and Scottish religion, took his religious responsibilities seriously. But he had to be polite. He also hoped for diplomatic support from the Pope in a number of important matters, inevitably including the Palatinate.

*

Charles I had his own agenda of English religious reform, which was being executed by the devoted William Laud, Archbishop of Canterbury – devoted to Charles I and devoted to a seemly English Church. Laud was imposing a disciplined uniformity on the Church of England. Neither king nor archbishop intended these changes to make the English Roman Catholics, but the insistence on ceremonial – the beauty of holiness – had a Catholic appearance. These would be important confusions.

For both practical and political reasons, the Elizabethan settlement of the Church (1558–9) allowed, within a framework of theology, and with public constraints, a rather wide pattern of worship. This more or less successfully accommodated the Puritans on one side[4] and the Catholics on the other, to begin with. Elizabeth's settlement was Protestant, she was the governor of the Church of England, but there was in practice a measure of toleration. Elizabeth I did not want to 'make windows into men's souls'.

Under Archbishop Laud the emphasis changed. Rules still aimed at the outward rather than the inward, but the archbishop (and the king) wanted narrowly defined forms of worship, a universal commitment to order and ceremony in which aesthetic considerations were highly valued, and in this way Laud (and Charles I) challenged the Puritans, who disliked hierarchy and shrank from the apotheosis of appearance. The fact that Laud was diligent and competent – his programme was known as 'thorough' – made the challenge dangerous.

At the same time, while the presence of Henrietta Maria in England showed how the Catholic challenge had softened, Catholicism was still feared, and indeed the conversion of England was still a policy aim in Rome. There was also a continuous stream of news from Germany about the destructive war of religion which raged on through the 1630s.

Anyway, it was Pope Pius V who intensified English Protestantism with his 1570 Bull *Regnans in Excelsis*, which freed Catholics of their oath of allegiance to Elizabeth I, excommunicated her and deprived her of the right to be queen. From this came the Armada of 1588. It encouraged attempts such as the Gunpowder Plot of 1605 (which threatened not only the royal family but all the Members of Parliament). In short, it was Pius V who created the visceral anti-Catholicism that bedevilled seventeenth-century England.[5]

Henrietta Maria's ignorance of English history, her lack of sensitivity to it, was therefore a problem. She only saw the arrival of Panzani as an opportunity to pursue the mission she was given at the age of fifteen, to nurture English Catholicism.

In response to Panzani's request, Charles I did not allow a Catholic bishop to be sent officially to England, but he treated Panzani, and Conn, his successor as papal envoy (to the queen), with respect and friendliness. He was not just being polite. The king instructed Walter Brett, designated as the queen's envoy to Rome, to ask the Pope to help secure the return of the Palatinate to his nephew Charles Louis (Frederick V of the Palatinate died in 1632) and to permit English Catholics to take the Oath of Allegiance. He wanted something in return for his hospitality.[6]

*

On 13 March 1635, the Lord Treasurer of England, Richard Weston, Earl of Portland, died at the age of fifty-eight. The undercurrents of the Stuart court became visible in the widely believed story that, while he had been a practising Protestant during his tenure of office, Portland died a Catholic after a deathbed conversion secured by Tobie Matthew.[7] At almost exactly the same time, March 1635, a new ambassador extraordinary arrived from France, the Marquis de Senneterre, 'a perfect courtier of ladies' who knew how to handle Henrietta Maria, which helped Anglo-French relations. In short, there was new chemistry at court. In April 1635 Senneterre reported back to Paris that 'the queen apparently has more power than previously because the Archbishop of Canterbury ... wants to get along with her and the other ministers do too, since she is in fact very influential and loved by the king'.[8]

The queen's support commanded a premium now that senior posts were juggled. Laud wanted to become Lord Treasurer himself, but the office was awarded to William Juxon, Bishop of London, in March 1636. Henrietta Maria was involved in the decision, consulting in September 1635 with Lord Cottington, who held the junior financial post of Chancellor of the Exchequer, to see whether he was happy for Juxon to be promoted (Charles I wanted to retain Cottington's services).[9]

George Conn arrived in London in July 1636. He turned out to be a man who 'knew men and business well' and furthermore was 'graceful in his person ... affable in his conversation'. The Venetian ambassador Anzolo Correr thought Conn was too evidently clever. 'His ability, which may be read in his face, will certainly rouse the jealousy of that suspicious people [the English] who are always afraid of being deceived.' Charles I enjoyed his company, playing cards with him and discussing theology with him. Henrietta Maria took Conn to visit her children at Richmond. He even dined with Juxon, a senior Protestant bishop.[10]

*

The royal couple were wooed with gifts. In January 1636, Panzani reported to Rome that a number of oil paintings had arrived, sent by Cardinal Barberini as a present for the queen, with the intention that she would pass them on to the king. They were meant as a surprise but Fr Philip told Henrietta Maria, who told the king, who could not wait.

Shortly after the pictures arrived, Charles I, none the wiser, impatiently asked his wife when they were coming. She said they were not coming – because they had arrived. This was considered hilarious by Charles I. As etiquette required, the heavily pregnant Henrietta Maria reviewed the pictures first, especially liking those by Leonardo and Andrea del Sarto, but she told Panzani unfortunately she could not keep the pictures, since the king was going to steal them. Panzani also wrote that she regretted the absence of devotional pictures, which sounds like a rebuke to the Vatican.[11]

To see the pictures as soon as possible, Charles came over to the Queen's Side of Whitehall with the earls of Pembroke and Holland, and Inigo Jones. He was delighted. He took the labels off the pictures, then asked his friends to guess the painter of each one. Inigo Jones apparently did the best, 'having attributed almost all the pictures correctly'.[12]

On behalf of Cardinal Barberini, Panzani gave the queen at least three rosaries, of aloe wood, agate and buffalo horn, and gave devotional items to her ladies. George Conn met Henrietta Maria for the first time at Holdenby, in July or August 1636, in the middle of a hot and dry summer, and showed her a picture of St Catherine that he was planning to frame for her, but, 'declaring that she would take that trouble upon herself, she took away from me the tin case and the packthread with which it was tied, and gave orders that the picture should be fastened to the curtains of her bed; the applause of the assistants could not be greater'.

Henrietta Maria wore all the time a cross sent to her by Urban VIII, which was, she told Lady Savage, 'the most precious thing that I have'. She showed her husband this exquisite object, decorated with diamonds in the shape of bees – the Barberini badge – and he was very struck. He asked, 'Is it possible, my heart, that the Pope has given you this?' She said it was. The king then said, 'I am very glad of it, because I shall change the opinion I have hitherto held that the priests of Rome are always ready to take, but never give anything away.' Perhaps the Palatinate was on his mind.[13]

*

By December 1636, Inigo Jones's Catholic chapel at Somerset House was completed. The first Mass was the occasion for a Counter-Reformation assault on London. The queen's Capuchins were told 'to omit nothing that they could devise to render this solemnity august'. When the queen and her court arrived, they saw the east end of the church, where the altar stood, was concealed behind two vast curtains, falling from an arch, framed by two pillars, each one topped by the figure of a prophet from the Old Testament. The choir sang an anthem, and the curtains parted to reveal clouds of glory.

The display, designed by the (Huguenot) Fleming François Dieussart, was forty feet high. There were six steps leading to the altar, behind which the symbol of the Holy Spirit, a dove – known as the Paraclete, meaning 'the one who intercedes' – was 'raised above seven ranges of clouds, in which were figures of archangels, of cherubim, of seraphim, to the number of two hundred'.

The Holy Sacrament was displayed in the centre, lit by hidden candles, whose number somehow increased, so that the longer you looked the more you were dazzled and disconcerted visually, as though looking through a tunnel of light into a fiery vanishing point. The pyx, or box which held the host, sat on a golden base and was covered by a cloth, with an oval lamp above it of blood-red glass, with rays around it. Above and around the pyx were circles holding worshipping angels, winged children (putti), more cherubim and seraphim. 'Tears of joy seemed to trickle from the eyes of the queen.'[14]

This was the prelude to the celebration of the Mass, the core ceremony of Catholicism, which includes the Holy Eucharist, a miraculous transformation of the Communion wafer into the body of Christ. Mass at this time was celebrated according to the lengthy Tridentine rite, which used a Latin liturgy set to music. The spiritual experience of Mass was overwhelming for those who gave themselves to its mysteries.

*

Yet the tears of Henrietta Maria signalled more than holy rapture. She was always considered a strong, high-spirited person, yet there were times when melancholy possessed her. She did not and could not understand what was really going wrong in England during the years of her husband's personal rule, which was the alienation of the landed and business classes from all government decisions, especially decisions about finance and religion. However, she was sensitive to discontent and the news was disturbing.

In 1636 plague was resurgent in the south of England. There had also been a prolonged drought which ravaged the harvest – and caused famine. In early September Charles I had an accident when he was hunting. His horse fell into a concealed bog, and the king rapidly sank until only his head and shoulders were visible. At great risk to his attendants Charles was pulled out, but his horse disappeared beneath him. The king exchanged clothes with an unlucky courtier, jumped on another horse and continued the hunt, but he could easily have been killed, leaving his widow to secure the future of their children, five in the nursery and another one coming.[15]

The same month a man called Rochester Car, who 'hath been mad all this summer', broke out of the house where he was kept for safety, and told the people in the street that he would go to court and kill the king and marry the queen. When she heard the story, Henrietta Maria had a panic attack and could not breathe, so her dress had to be cut open to allow her more air.[16]

Gregorio Panzani made thoughtful comments about the woman he had been observing at fairly close quarters for almost two years. He knew that she was not the hedonist of Vatican and Puritan gossip. He knew she took her responsibilities seriously, and that sometimes they were too much. 'She suffers sometimes from melancholy, and then she likes silence; when she is afflicted, she has recourse earnestly to God. She thinks little of the future, trusting entirely in the king.'[17]

21

GOLD DAMASK AND THE BLOOD OF MARTYRS

In 1636, England was at peace. The royal finances were stronger every year. The nation's image overseas was bright thanks to investment in a fleet. The king's children promised his subjects stability forever. Charles I's power was confirmed by his unchallenged behaviour in Scotland in 1633, and by the success of the tall, dark and 'thorough' Viscount Wentworth. Lord Deputy of Ireland since 1633, and locally known as Black Tom Tyrant, Wentworth was steadily increasing royal revenues in the third Stuart kingdom while keeping the peace. Reigning without the help of Parliament was a success.

The lawyer Edward Hyde celebrated his twenty-seventh birthday this year. Thirty-five years later he was to write a history of the period describing England in the second half of the 1630s as a garden of Eden. 'This kingdom, and all her majesty's dominions ... enjoyed the greatest calm, and the fullest measure of felicity, that any people in any case, for so long time together, have been blessed with.'[1]

The court's culture provided publicity. When he ascended the throne in 1625, the king had already inherited the art collections of his brother Henry and his mother. Between 1627 and 1629, when he was trying to extract war finances from Parliament, he spent over £18,000 on nearly four hundred pictures and statues from the Gonzaga dukes of Mantua, who were selling everything they could. Between them Charles and Henrietta Maria assembled one of the largest royal collections of paintings and sculptures in Europe, placing the English royal family in the cultural vanguard.

The king's taste impressed the highly cultivated Rubens when he visited England in the late 1620s. The painter described the country as idyllic and the court as sophisticated.

> The island in which I now am seems a place well worthy of the curiosity of a man of taste, not only on account of the charm of the country, the beauty of the race, the outward appearance of luxury proper to a wealthy people, happy in the enjoyment of peace; but also on account of the incredible numbers of excellent pictures, statues and antique inscriptions by the court.[1]

Having agreed a peace treaty with Spain, which the famous painter was representing diplomatically, the king knighted Rubens (in 1630), and commissioned him to paint the ceiling of the Banqueting Hall at Whitehall with a series of works that celebrated his father, James I, as a unifying ruler of Great Britain, and sent him soaring into heaven. These paintings were installed in 1636 and are still there.

Rubens' pupil Anthony van Dyck was also knighted by Charles I (in 1632), and given a pension of £200 a year and a house at Blackfriars. He rewarded king and queen with iconic images, among them the 'great peece', the first royal portrait in which a King of England is portrayed with his wife and children as a family man. Painted in 1632, the picture includes the two children born so far. Charles and Henrietta Maria are both comfortably seated. The queen holds the baby Mary, while two-year-old Charles, Prince of Wales, stands at his father's side clutching at the king's knee. Two small dogs play between the royal couple. Two giant columns rise behind the relaxed, if luxuriously dressed, group, and a misty riverscape unfolds in the background, revealing, in the distance, Westminster Hall.

The new fashions have arrived. Charles wears a doublet of black silk trimmed with silver, and pure black breeches. His wide sleeves, only one of which, the right, is visible, are slashed, allowing a glimpse of a pale-blue silk undershirt. He has a starched ruff, and in the middle of his chest hangs a jewel on a sky-blue ribbon.

His black cloak, lined with pale-violet silk, is slung over his left shoulder covering that arm and sports the George of the Order of the Garter – the medal showing an image of St George, patron saint of England – held in the silver star which Charles himself added to the insignia. He wears stockings of violet silk, held at the knee with large blue ribbons tied in bows. His shoes are also silver, decorated with large pompoms.

Henrietta Maria sits beneath an immense swag of gold damask. Her full dress, narrow at the waist, is paler-gold silk trimmed with multi-layered starched lace at the cuffs. The neckline plunges but is decorous because of the wide and exquisite flat lace collar. A small cross is pinned to the lace around her neck, and a grey-blue ribbon is tied in a bow, covering the delicately concealed cleavage. She wears single-drop pearl earrings, a necklace of pearls, a single string – but the pearls are very big – and her dark-brown hair is pulled back from the forehead and secured with another row of pearls at the back of her head, leaving the pale oval face framed by a delicate fringe, and by clusters of softly curling hair falling free on each side to just below the ear. Her large, black eyes are fixed on her husband, who gazes at the viewer, as do both the children. By the king's side, on a table covered in red velvet, sit the mace, the orb and the crown.

The queen was a muse but she was herself responsible for major commissions. She paid for several van Dyck paintings and repeatedly sent family portraits to relations in France and Savoy. At Greenwich, where ambassadors were habitually greeted, Henrietta Maria in 1635 completed work on the classical building now called the Queen's House, which her husband's mother Anna of Denmark had started. Like the chapel at Somerset House it was a modernist work, whose revolutionary simplicity was highlighted by its position next to the early sixteenth-century royal palace Placentia. The architect was again Inigo Jones, who worked continuously for Henrietta Maria for more than ten years.[3]

At Somerset House Inigo fitted out and redesigned the queen's closet, the queen's cabinet room and the water stairs on the river, built a new cistern house and refitted the Cross Gallery. All this work brought classical French taste into London, and did so under the explicit direction of Henrietta Maria (Inigo's work for the king by contrast showed Italian influence). Drawings survive of his designs for a printed vertical panel, and a chimney piece featuring French motifs: grotesques, mask heads, swags, term figures. The vertical panel contains the queen's cipher, which combines the letters H and M into a single letter followed by R for 'Regina'. It is another piece of evidence that Henrietta Maria did not waste time thinking of herself as Queen Mary.[4]

The most spectacular work commissioned by the queen was the marble bust of Charles I by Bernini that was delivered to Oatlands in 1637, one of history's great lost works of art. While the king was passionate about art, so that his wife was moving with the tide, she made a distinctive contribution by promoting her native taste. It was also her approach to Rome that opened the door to Bernini, as well as producing the Barberini bonanza.[5]

*

Outside the royal court, life had another texture. When the plague epidemic was spreading through London in April and May 1636, gaolers were allowed to take their prisoners out of the cells to the country to save them from infection. However, John Bastwick, one of the inmates of the Gatehouse Prison, Westminster, was left in his cell, almost certainly on purpose.

Bastwick was there after being excommunicated, fined £1,000 and deprived of his licence to work as a physician, all as a result of his religious opinions. He was imprisoned until he recanted. Here he argued with the keeper of the Gatehouse, Aquila Wykes, who disliked Puritans.

An anti-Catholic pamphleteer in the 1620s, writing in Latin for an educated audience, Bastwick became increasingly convinced of Puritan doctrines, and was influenced by his fellow physician Alexander Leighton, whose English-language pamphlet *Sion's Plea Against the Prelacy*, published in 1628, urged the parliament of that year to abolish the bishops, and use their wealth to lead Europe in a Protestant crusade (he sent copies to all the Members, without realising the parliament had been dissolved). Leighton rejoiced in the assassination of Buckingham as a sign from God that 'removed the greatest nayl from all their tent', and railed against Henrietta Maria as a 'daughter of Heth'.[6]

When the pursuivants – the agents who tracked down religious dissenters – were investigating Leighton, they held a pistol to the head of his five-year-old son Caleb to persuade his wife Isobel to cooperate. The Star Chamber found the small, blonde doctor guilty of sedition. On 26 November 1630 Leighton was pilloried in a snowstorm for two hours; his left ear was then nailed to the pillory before being cut off, and he received thirty-six lashes and was branded with 'SS' (sower of sedition) on his face.[7]

In the Gatehouse in 1636, Bastwick thought he would catch plague. He had a vision from God, which persuaded him to write the *Letanie of John Bastwicke*, named as a parody of holy litany. This was written in English, 'peppered with lavatorial humour', and railed against the established church of William Laud: 'From bishops, priests and deacons, good God deliver us.'

The *Letanie* was published thanks to Bastwick's friend, a thin-faced, soulful man called John Lilburne who visited him in prison. The plague passed. Bastwick was still alive, and concluded that God was saving him for something more glorious, although probably just as painful, and meanwhile continued to live at the Gatehouse, where his wife and children joined him. Here he complained of eating roast meat only once a week.[8]

In 1637, the unrepentant Bastwick was put on trial by the Star Chamber on charges of libel and sedition, with John Prynne, the author of *Histriomastix* and shorter pamphlets, and Henry Burton, an ordained minister who had recently accused all bishops of the Church of England of being agents of Rome. The defendants were not submissive. The court found Burton, Bastwick and Prynne guilty and sentenced them to have their ears cut off, to be fined £5,000 each and to perpetual imprisonment. The maiming of the guilty men took place on 30 June 1637 in Westminster Yard in front of a large crowd.

Bastwick found his path to the pillory strewn with flowers. When the time came for his ears to be cut, he produced his own scalpel and offered that for use. After the mutilation he shouted, 'As I have now lost some of my blood, so am I ready and willing to spill every drop that is in my veins ... for maintaining the truth of God, and the honour of the king.'[9]

His wife Susanna picked up the severed ears from the ground, and cradled them in her bosom. Burton was cut so close to the head that his temporal artery was opened. Prynne had already had his ears lopped once, after publishing *Histriomastix*; this time the remains were removed. He was branded on the cheeks with the letters 'SL' (seditious libeller), then one of his ears was so crudely cut that part of his cheek was also cut off, and the other ear was partly severed and left hanging. The executioner had to be called back by the surgeon to finish the job.

The courage shown by the prisoners fanned the crowd's respect into hot admiration. Once these dreadful wounds were adequately healed, the three were sent to different gaols to keep them apart, Burton to Lancaster Castle, Bastwick to Star Castle in the Isles of Scilly and Prynne to the Channel Islands. The transfers of the famous criminals on three different routes were like royal progresses, open and visible to all they passed. Their story spread.

*

Oddly enough, Henrietta Maria had friends who were Puritan – or godly – sympathisers. Her confessor Fr Philip, of all people, told Panzani that 'the queen allies herself with the Puritans', and the French ambassador Fontenay-Mareuil said the queen was plotting with the Puritans behind the king's back. The most distinguished examples of godly sympathisers at the queen's court in the early and mid 1630s were the earls of Northumberland and Holland.[10]

In fact, it was not a Puritan plot by a Catholic queen; it was the Puritan grandees who were trying to make use of Henrietta Maria. She headed a faction at court, like any queen consort, which consisted of people whom she liked and trusted, and who looked for advantage from her. Puritan sympathisers could not hope for much from Charles I, who appointed Laud Archbishop of Canterbury, so they gravitated towards the queen, regardless of her Catholicism. What looks odd in the cold light of history was less odd at the time, since court politics was a mix of the personal, the material and, only then, if it figured at all, ideology.

The moves against Weston at the time of the Châteauneuf conspiracy came from the grouping round Henrietta Maria seeking to promote Holland. The same people in 1636 agitated for war with Spain, which seemed a possibility after the pro-Spain, anti-war Weston's death. In 1635 France declared war on Spain, at the same time that the embassy of Senneterre improved Anglo-French relations. In London Henrietta Maria was at the heart of these shifts, and it was now that she flirtatiously sent a message to Richelieu saying that, if they were to be friends, it was not up to her, but 'it was up to knights to pursue ladies all the time'.[11]

If war with Spain *had* been declared – for the usual cause, the Palatinate – Charles I would have been obliged to call a parliament to find the money. In other words, these factions were linked with the biggest question of all, whether Parliament would ever return, whether the personal rule would ever come to an end. Here was the Puritan plot, using the queen to support a war which would bring back Parliament, but the Spanish question disappeared when the fight returned to politics at home.

*

In the 1630s, Charles I raised finance through non-parliamentary means – that was precisely the point of the personal rule – with the result that people were not only asked for more money, but were asked in new ways. The means found by his ministers trod new ground by looking into the medieval past, for instance fining those who were entitled to become knights but had not done so, fining those who owned stretches of forest on the grounds that all forests in England belonged to the king. These measures were legal, but seemed to go against the spirit of the law.

Charles I also continued to take the revenues from tonnage and poundage (a tax on trade) although the Commons, when they were in session, never voted it to him for his entire reign. Was this legal, then? Legality therefore became an issue for those who disputed the king's right to rule and raise money without a parliament, and was tested by the 'ship money' case.

The king's shipbuilding programme was financed by money raised from all the counties of England for coastal defence whether or not they were coastal. John Hampden, from inland Buckinghamshire, challenged the legality of this highly successful tax by withholding payment of a very modest sum out of the total that he was due to pay. In 1637–8 the Court of Exchequer Chamber, in which twelve judges sat, heard a case brought against John Hampden for his refusal.[12]

The finer points of law only just led to a judgement in favour of the king, by seven judges to five, announced on 12 June 1638. Since judges were known to favour *force majeure* – were inclined to support the government – the fact that five senior judges ruled against the king made the verdict a moral victory for Hampden, a Pyrrhic victory, and encouraged others to refuse to pay ship money.

The hearing was meant to silence opposition, but instead increased pressure for the king to call Parliament. It was not a stunt. A number of courtiers and politicians were working for another meeting of Parliament. In Henrietta Maria's circle, Lords Holland, Leicester and Northumberland were among them – hence the attempt to coax Charles I into war with Spain. The Earl of Warwick, Holland's brother, and a still more prominent Puritan, was another.

Towards the end of the Christmas festivities at the beginning of 1637, Warwick had made an extraordinary personal appeal to the king. Face to face, he told Charles I 'he was as ready as anyone to sacrifice his blood as well as his goods for his Majesty' but he begged the king to have regard for his lesser subjects, who were anxious not to die 'having signed away the liberties of the realm'. It was an appeal to let his tenants off the payment of ship money.[13]

Warwick assured the king that Parliament would meet any of the Crown's financial needs to maintain the navy, to mount an attack on the Palatinate. He could also have made the point – was he aware of it? – that food prices were rising sharply, a further and frightening burden on ordinary people. He begged the king to summon Parliament.[14]

In the circumstances, Charles I reacted reasonably well.

His countenance remained smiling and composed at the end as well as at the beginning, although he said nothing to the earl in response except that he expected from the example of promptness shown by him that he should be obeyed by the others also.

There is no suggestion in our sources that Henrietta Maria gave thought to these scenes, even if she knew of them.

22

QUEEN MOTHER WEATHER

A delightful figure, the most charming face, big blue eyes, a mass
of fine, chestnut blonde hair, the most lovely breasts ... delicacy
and liveliness ... grace and passion...

The salient features of Marie de Chevreuse were not enough to
hide her endless desire to stir things up, which caused Cardinal
Richelieu to describe her as 'so dangerous a spirit'. The woman
who crossed to Dover in 1625 with the young Henrietta Maria was
worryingly homeless in 1637. With unique dash, she represented
everything that the parliamentary party in England least liked:
she was foreign, Catholic, a woman, an intriguer. She was what
Charles I needed not to have in Whitehall Palace and yet by the
end of 1638 it was in Whitehall that she was living.[1]

There was self-deception in Marie's character. She later said that
'she became interested in the affairs of the world, only in relation
to those she loved', but considering the circles in which she moved,
all royal princes and power brokers, and how many of them she
loved, that can be understood.[2]

In the mid 1630s Marie de Chevreuse was cut off from the great
world, living in Tours in internal exile as punishment for her part
in the Châteauneuf conspiracy. Here she drove the local women
to paroxysms of rage by her beauty, her bad reputation and her

wonderful clothes. In Tours she was known by names such as 'nun's belly', 'kiss me, darling' and 'constipated can't piss'. She stayed until 1637.[3]

Marie corresponded with her friend Anne of Austria, who also, at this time, wrote to her brother the King of Spain, through one of the English ambassador's secretaries. Anne complained of her treatment by her husband Louis XIII, and told Philip IV, and her other brother, the cardinal-infante Ferdinand (now governing Spanish Flanders), French military secrets. This was known as the Val-de-Grâce affair, after the convent where Anne wrote the letters. The queen and duchess had been shocked by the execution of the Duc de Montmorency in 1633, after they begged for mercy, and both regarded his death as the responsibility of Richelieu. They considered themselves morally justified when they attacked the cardinal in the correspondence.

Regrettably, after 1635 France and Spain were at war, so Anne's correspondence was treason. When she was discovered, the queen might be expected to survive – and did – but there was no reason to look for forgiveness of the dangerous spirit in Tours. Louis XIII himself put the blame for everything on Marie.[4]

On 5 September 1637, the Duchesse de Chevreuse rubbed a mixture of soot and ground brick on her face, which gave her a 'gingerbread complexion', put on a man's clothes and a blonde (masculine) wig, and put her fabulous jewels in her pocket with 10,000 livres' worth of gold. She jumped on a horse, which she rode astride, attended by two servants. On the way south she was given some help by her friend and lover the Prince de Marcillac, to whom she handed her jewels for safe keeping. Marie dismissed her servants. Marcillac instructed his man of business Malbâti to accompany her to the Spanish border.[5]

Apparently Malbâti really thought Marie was a man, an illusion which cannot have lasted terribly long. She told him she was the Duc d'Enghien, the seventeen-year-old son of the Prince de Condé, on secret business. She had her period and he saw there was blood on the saddle, but she said she had been wounded in the leg. Later in the escapade she admitted she was the Duchesse de Chevreuse, which must have impressed him far more.[6]

In early October Marie crossed the border with Spain, where she was welcomed by Philip IV as his sister's best friend. When she reached Madrid the entire court came out to greet her, although the Queen of Spain 'has fallen ill since this lady, who is a beauty, came to the palace'. Marie spoke Spanish, which made things easier. The promiscuous Philip IV probably became yet another lover of the thirty-seven-year-old *femme fatale*. Her time in Madrid was in fact a success, but even the King of Spain could not grant Marie's wish to become a lady-in-waiting at his exceptionally conventional court. The result was a trip to England, leaving behind her in Madrid 'a very great impression of her personality'.[7]

*

Marie de Chevreuse arrived in Plymouth on 14 April 1638 in lovely spring weather. Even in the north of England tulips flowered before the end of March, and there were 'apricocks and plum trees ... full of blossom'. Charles I and Henrietta Maria welcomed their old friend, who brought gifts from Philip IV. Her old flame the Earl of Holland was sent to accompany Marie to London, in a coach followed by twenty-five others filled with 'the young lords and gallants then at court' and with Sir John Finet, the Master of Ceremonies. In Hyde Park Marie transferred to a coach of the queen's which took her 'with a walking pace' to St James's Palace, where the king and queen awaited her, each greeting her with a kiss.

As a mark of unusual favour, the queen gave Marie the *tabouret*, which meant she could be seated (on a stool) in the queen's presence. This was designed as a snub to Richelieu and caused a row with the French ambassador, although Marie made very limited use of the privilege. At the outset Marie said she was merely passing through, on her way to join Marie de Médicis in Brussels.[8]

Things changed in France. Anne of Austria gave birth to a healthy boy on 5 September 1638, named Louis Dieudonné (Louis the gift of God). This transformed Anne's position at court and might help the exiled duchesse return to favour, but Marie felt safer in England, where she was provided with a royal pension, and rooms in Whitehall Palace and Greenwich.

Her presence was controversial. The Archbishop of Canterbury, William Laud, described her as 'a cunning and practising woman'. He told Lord Wentworth that 'we lose in France by courting her here' and was alive to the financial penalties, too. 'The Duchess of Chevreux is come hither out of Spain and spends as if our Treasury were infinite.' She lost no time in raising the royal blood temperature when she proposed a match between Prince Balthasar Carlos of Spain, Philip IV's son, aged eight, and Princess Mary, aged six. This was also aimed at Richelieu.[9]

*

The Duchesse de Chevreuse told the queen she was on her way to see Marie de Médicis, but the queen was already working on her mother's behalf. In autumn 1637, the Spanish authorities had ordered a search of Marie de Médicis' house in Brussels. It was done with a marked lack of courtesy to the sixty-three-year-old Queen Mother of France. The Flemish agents thought Queen Marie was in touch with the French government, spinning a web of intrigue against Spain, although this was so unlikely for a woman who had almost everything in common with the government of Philip IV that it is tempting to speculate that a false lead was given from the corridors of the Louvre in order to get her out of Brussels. Henrietta Maria was miserable when she heard of her mother's trials, and took to her bed.[10]

Marie de Chevreuse helped Henrietta Maria persuade Charles I to offer a home to Marie de Médicis. The king disliked this plan on grounds of cost alone. His mother-in-law's politics would be unpopular in England, and anyway she was not really homeless. She had another home available, if only she would return to Florence. Initially, therefore, Charles I offered his mother-in-law a couple of ships to take her to Spain or Italy, but Marie de Médicis did not accept.

Laud did his best to prevent this second, and worse, Catholic arrival. In the Privy Council, and behind the scenes, he argued against receiving Marie de Médicis for every reason possible. The archbishop knew she would be much more expensive than the Duchesse de Chevreuse, and he was becoming seriously concerned about the Catholic party at court nurtured by Panzani and Conn. He called the queen mother's arrival a 'miserable accident' and her supporters a 'seditious, practising train'. However, Henrietta Maria had no difficulty in outmanoeuvring the archbishop.[11]

In February 1638 she sent £20,000 to the Earl of Leicester,

ambassador extraordinary in Paris, to redeem her mother's pawned jewellery, planning to return it to her in person.[12] In September the Whitehall court heard that Marie de Médicis had suddenly abandoned Brussels, which started rumours flying of her imminent arrival. In fact she first went to visit the Protestant Dutch, partly to annoy the Flemish government. By courting Protestants, she may also have hoped to win popularity in England.

Marie de Médicis first went to The Hague, then on 1 September 1638 arrived at Amsterdam in the pouring rain. Here she turned down the offer of a seaborne entry into the city of canals and processed by sodden land. People climbed trees and the masts of ships to catch a glimpse of the famous Queen Mother of France. She stayed until 5 September, which was by coincidence the day when her grandson the dauphin was born.

The queen mother visited the gorgeous headquarters of the East India Company and watched a pageant on water, including a naval battle in which the combatants threw each other into the Amstel River to universal hilarity. A merchant vessel was named after her. Saturday 4 September was dedicated to shopping, when she was found to be a true Medici, good at haggling. In this way Marie de Médicis was celebrated as a great queen, which polished her image internationally, and the Dutch showed off their wealth and power, knowing that the queen mother would shortly be telling her daughter Henrietta Maria all about it.[13]

*

Marie de Médicis received more messages from her son-in-law, the King of Great Britain, which did not encourage her to cross the Channel, but on 18 October, after a choppy seven days at sea, she arrived unexpectedly in Harwich, where the winter storm had blown her flotilla. With her she brought six hundred French 'of no degree'. The storms continued, so that the watermen called it 'queen mother weather'.[14]

Charles rode to Romford, where he met his mother-in-law, and returned with her in his 'travelling coach'. At Aldgate a classical theatre had been temporarily built in the visitor's honour. Here they transferred to an ornamental state coach, and entered the city to a deafening cannonade from the Tower. They were greeted by the mayor and eighty aldermen. The city militia lined the road from Temple Bar to St James's Palace, where a large suite of rooms had been made ready, and there was a Catholic chapel.

Henrietta Maria, six months pregnant, was waiting with the children. With the two boys and two girls – Anne was left in the nursery – she came down to the courtyard, opened the door of the carriage herself and sank to her knees. Marie de Médicis raised her daughter from the ground, but the queen once more knelt, and once more was raised. The children were presented to their grandmother, and the royal party went inside.[15]

Henrietta Maria had not seen her mother for thirteen years, and was naturally struck by the fact that she had aged, but the famous exile settled down to daily visits from her daughter and her son-in-law, and received the Privy Council with *froideur*, remaining seated throughout the audience and saying very few words in reply to their respectful address. All her costs were borne by the Crown. Louis XIII was annoyed at the show of support for his mother, but pleased that she was an expensive burden.[16]

*

All in all, the Queen of England was on a high. Sincerely delighted though she was with Anne of Austria's pregnancy – she ordered fasts and special services in her chapel, praying for a full term, a healthy child, a dauphin – Henrietta Maria knew that she had herself trumped her peers by having a family of five royal children, soon to be six.[17]

The culture show went on. The queen had just (in the second half of 1637) sat for van Dyck for a triple portrait, two profiles and a full-face, to go to Bernini in Rome. The king wanted a companion piece to his own bust. As for building projects, Charles bought his wife the manor of Wimbledon in 1638, another large building she could expand and decorate, more work for Inigo Jones.[18]

Court theatricals continued. Shortly before the arrival of Marie de Chevreuse, on Shrove Tuesday 1638 there was a showing of the masque *Luminalia*, written by William Davenant, designed by Inigo Jones. In this production, 'noteworthy above all others … for the richness of the dresses and the subtlety of the inventions', the nine muses flee Greece, then Italy, to find a home in Britain, where the king and queen welcome them. As the title suggests, the entertainment was a celebration of the mystical power of light.

Although she had given up speaking parts, Henrietta Maria appeared in the ballet as an 'Earthly Deity' and goddess of light. The theme of the 'triumph of light' was married to a Catholic subtext.

Luminalia was first performed on 6 February 1638, four days after Candlemas, the Feast of the Purification of the Virgin Mary, which similarly was celebrated (for instance in the queen's chapel) with countless lighted candles. The masque featured the morning star, one of the symbols of the Virgin Mary, and proposed that the queen's beauty outshone the sun, as the Virgin did. When Henrietta Maria first appeared she was seated, and dressed in cloth covered with stars, and around her was 'a glory of rayes' on the pattern of so many Catholic depictions of Christ's mother.

It was a tribute, and a proclamation of Marian Catholicism, rather than a usurpation. Showing how much she valued this mystical message, the queen wanted to put the masque on again, for Marie de Chevreuse to see.[19]

*

It can only be seen with hindsight, but in these exuberant celebrations Henrietta Maria was overreaching.

There was a spate of conversions to Catholicism in her circle, even before the arrival of the two Maries. Wat Montague and Henry Jermyn converted in the mid 1630s, the former being ordained priest while he was abroad. Among the ladies who became Catholic was the Countess of Newport, who announced her conversion in November 1637. Her husband, the Earl of Newport, was furious because he thought his wife's new faith would compromise his career at court.[20]

The earl's protest (to Laud) triggered a confirmation of the penal laws against Catholics, although that was watered down after heavy pressure from Henrietta Maria. Laud also tried to persuade the king to expel George Conn from England in January 1638, but failed against the queen's defence. This was another argument between the queen and the Archbishop of Canterbury, who noted that Henrietta Maria was 'very angry and took exception to me … I am between two great factions very like corn between millstones'. His remark referred to Catholics on one side and Puritans on the other.[21]

Lady Newport alarmed her husband but repented nothing, indeed attending what looked like a celebration Mass in the queen's chapel, with the queen present along with other recent converts. Other notable Catholic women were the Duchess of Buckingham, the Countess of Arundel, Olive Porter (sister of Lady Newport) and the Countess of Roxburghe. Not all these ladies were recent converts. The scale of the scandal was exaggerated in the heat of the moment, but Henrietta Maria certainly allowed her people free reign in the battle for souls. We know that her grand almoner, the Bishop of Angoulême, and her confessor, Fr Philip, were actively promoting Catholicism in court circles at this time. Marie de Chevreuse could not be kept off the bandwagon, attempting, with no success, to convert the Earl of Holland, not a man given to spirituality.[22]

The Revd Mr Garrard, Master of Charterhouse, wrote to Viscount Wentworth in Ireland to keep him in the picture. He wrote about the Revd Dr Hayward's complaints that 'in a very short time a great part of his parishioners are become papist'. He told him of the 'horrible noise' about Lady Newport, Another time he said, 'Our great women fall away every day.'[23]

Stories now circulated that 'the king's majesty is a Catholic'. Charles I was in fact a convinced Protestant of the Laudian school but his toleration of Catholicism was visible in his friendship with Conn, and of course in the family. He was a known admirer of the Somerset House Chapel. His wife was Catholic, as his mother (Anna of Denmark) had been, also his famous grandmother (Mary, Queen of Scots). In addition, the Laudian reforms in the Church of England looked like Catholicism.[24]

The arrival of Marie de Médicis – her name alone was eloquent – polarised the argument. People, including members of the Privy Council, quite justifiably thought the cost of her maintenance prevented Charles I from giving financial support to his nephew Charles Louis of the Palatinate, who was trying to raise an army to win back his birthright. The same could be said of the Duchesse de Chevreuse. The king preferred the Catholics in his family to the Protestants. Naturally, the queen was considered responsible.[25]

In a contemporary memoir, written outside the court a few years later, the position of Henrietta Maria, goddess of light, is described by the intelligent and scholarly Lucy Hutchinson, the widow of a Puritan colonel, when she wrote,

> He [Charles I] married a papist, a French lady, of a haughty spirit, and a great wit and beauty, to whom he became a most uxurious husband. By this means the court was replenished with papists ... All the papists in the kingdom were favoured ... the Puritans more than ever discountenanced and persecuted ...[26]

If Laud was the loser from the confusions, since he looked so Catholic, so too was Henrietta Maria, who became identified, quite wrongly, as the force behind the mutilation and imprisonment of people like Leighton, Bastwick, Burton and Prynne.

PART FOUR

THE PRAYER BOOK

No bishop, no king.

James I of England, VI of Scotland

23

ROMISCH SUPERSTITION

According to Scottish legend, it was the market stallholder Jenny Geddes who struck the first blow against Charles I when she hurled the stool she had brought to sit on at St Giles' Sunday morning service – her 'fald stool' or 'creepie-stool' – at James Hannay, Dean of Edinburgh. What did Hannay do to deserve it? He had begun to read the collects out of the brand-new Scottish Book of Common Prayer. It was 23 July 1637. This attack would change the life of Henrietta Maria decisively and forever.

The week before, the Bishop of Edinburgh, David Lindsay, announced that a new prayer book would now come into general use in Scotland. The book had been in preparation for three years. A new book of canons (Church laws) was introduced to Scotland in January 1636. A year later, Charles I ordered a new translation of the psalms. The revision of Scottish worship was on course. Since the aim was to make Scotland religiously consistent with England, the prayer book was modelled on the English Book of Common Prayer, with slight alterations to take into account local sensibilities. No trouble was expected.[1]

Jenny, however, yelled, 'Daur ye say Masse in my lug [ear]?' and started a riot. Someone started the riot, in any case, and it was probably a woman. The congregation erupted, 'especially the women ... "Woe, woe!" some cried, "Sorrow, sorrow! for this doleful day, that they are bringing in Popery among us!" Others did cast their stools against the Dean's face.'[2]

Bishop Lindsay managed to complete the service, and preach his sermon, but he was attacked in the street afterwards. That afternoon he returned to St Giles for a second service, from which the women were excluded. He made it back to his lodgings in Holyroodhouse in the Earl of Roxburghe's coach, protected by footmen with drawn swords, while the crowd threw stones at him and shouted, 'Kill the traitour!'[3]

The result, on 29 July 1637, was the royal council's suspension of the new prayer book. The defence of the Kirk had only just begun, however. In August 1637, the Minister of Leuchars, Alexander Henderson, a man in his mid fifties, organised a popular petition which complained that the prayer book had not been authorised by the General Assembly of the Kirk, and also that it promoted a popish liturgy. It was true that Charles I did not consult the General Assembly when the prayer book was in preparation; he did not even consult many Scottish bishops.

Henderson was now following through from the secret meetings which conceived the St Giles protest. From the petition came a 'Supplication', which gave its name to the protesters, called the Supplicants. They organised a representative government structure for Scotland, one that did not depend on the Scots royal council. This was known as the Tables, there being four tables, one to represent the nobility, one the gentry, one the burgesses and one the clergy. A fifth was added to act as an executive. The protest was turning into a revolution, and not a revolution of stallholders but one encompassing all Scottish society.[4]

Charles I's fatal and historic reaction was to dig in his heels. In February 1638 he sent the Scottish Treasurer, the Earl of Traquair, who was briefing the king in London, back to Edinburgh with instructions to enforce the prayer book by proclamation.[5]

Henderson and the lawyer Archibald Johnston of Warriston, a man in his twenties, now drew up the defining document of the era, the National Covenant, which Warriston read out to a large gathering in the graveyard of Greyfriars Kirk on 28 February 1638, answering questions about the text and then watching as it was signed by the people who had come, headed by members of the nobility. Copies were sent throughout Scotland. The Supplicants were now the Covenanters. They were on record with their signed commitment to their faith.

The National Covenant included a section summarising the Acts of Parliament that supported Scottish Presbyterianism to show the legal basis of the protest. It concluded with an oath based on the 1581 King's Confession, binding the signatory to defend the true religion against innovation. In other words, it was like the king's coronation oath but with its own distinctive take. Warriston earlier recorded his thoughts about Charles I's prayer book when he wrote, 'If we licked up this vomit of Romisch superstition again, the Lord in his wrayth would vomit us out.'[6]

In April 1638, Henrietta Maria suggested to Charles that he could accept a peaceful compromise in Scotland. The queen knew it was hard to settle conflicts of this sort. Perhaps she was thinking of her mother's record in France. This was the time when she was preparing to receive Marie de Médicis in England. Her advice was not taken. Charles reassured her, and said he could force the Scots back in line. It was about this time that Henrietta Maria became pregnant again, for the seventh time.

Charles I did not brief the English Privy Council about Scotland until July 1638, a year after the St Giles riot, even though it was clear that the English Treasury would bear the costs of his chosen response. Instead he discussed Scotland with Laud and with the Scottish council, headed by the Earl of Traquair. Charles I was knocked flat by the Scottish rebellion. He did not go out hunting as much as before, nor 'play at mall, rackets and other sports'.[7]

By the summer of 1638, the king had appointed the Marquess of Hamilton as royal commissioner to Scotland. Hamilton could not find common ground when he went to Edinburgh. In reality both sides were preparing to fight it out, and everyone knew that talks were a front. He returned to England, made two visits to court, and was back in Scotland in September with the king's agreement to a General Assembly of the Kirk. The king also agreed to call a Scottish parliament. This did not blunt the will of the Covenanters, but had the unfortunate side effect of showing that through rebellion the Scots won what was forbidden the docile English.

*

Hamilton wanted to form a royal party in the Glasgow assembly, which he opened in November, but the project failed – there was no support for the king's opinions – so a week after it had convened, on 28 November 1638, the marquess dissolved the assembly by right of his status as king's representative. 'You have called for a free General Assembly,' he told the delegates, 'His Majesty hath granted you one, most free on his part … but as you handled and marred the matter, let God and the World judge whether the least shadow or footstep of freedom can be discerned in this Assembly.'

Alexander Henderson, the moderator, defended the assembly's procedure, admitting the king's rights but adding, 'Let God by whom kings reign have his own place and prerogative.' Hamilton told Henderson, 'Sir, ye have spoken as a good Christian and doubtful subject.' The assembly did not obey Hamilton, continuing in session after his rather undignified withdrawal (someone had locked the door and hidden the key, so the door had to be forced). The assembly sat for three weeks after Hamilton had withdrawn. The Earl of Argyll had attended as one of the assessors, a member of the royal council, in support of Hamilton, but continued his attendance after Hamilton withdrew, arguing that the assembly was still legal. Among other measures then passed was the abolition of Scottish bishops – the institution of episcopacy. Hamilton reported on the royal position. He was himself 'railled at in the streets, exclaymed against in the pulpits, and that in no other terms than that faggots is already prepared in hell for me'.[8]

*

In the seventeenth century the military campaigning season was spring to autumn, when the weather made it possible for armies to march across the countryside, supported by their supply trains and artillery, all dependent on horse-drawn transport. Bad weather and the lack of fodder, during the winter, made war difficult. For this reason, Charles I was looking to the following year, 1639, for his campaign.

The king was also keeping an eye on his wife. As her pregnancy came to term, Henrietta Maria was preoccupied with her health. She gave birth to Katherine at Whitehall on 20 January 1639. Since her mother was resident in St James's Palace, the queen could not enjoy the soothing ritual of preparation in the place where she felt secure. It was a very difficult labour, and the baby died soon after birth. Henrietta Maria thought she herself only survived thanks to the intercession of the Virgin Mary. She made a slow recovery, but refused to accept her doctors' suggestion of a trip to France to recuperate. Their advice shows serious concern.[9]

When Charles I left London on 27 March 1639 for York, he entrusted his wife to the care of the Earl of Northumberland, telling the Lord Admiral that Henrietta Maria was his jewel.

At York he administered a new oath of loyalty to the lords who were gathered with their followers, in preparation for the war, but lords Brooke and Saye refused to take it. They were imprisoned, then released, with the result that Saye, 'the oracle of those who were called Puritans in the worst sense', left York for the south of England, saying that his troops were his personal attendants. The people who wanted a parliament were beginning to come out of the woodwork.[10]

The king went on to Newcastle, arriving on 6 May, then to Alnwick, and to the border town Berwick, where the royal army took up a position on the River Tweed. The weather was very hot and dry. There was little water available for the troops, who were poorly provisioned and accommodated.

The Earl of Holland, general of the horse, led a cavalry troop across the border and found a Scottish infantry force drawn up near Kelso. Holland advanced with a thousand cavalry, leaving his three thousand infantry trailing behind. 'That day was the hottest that had been known.' Holland felt he was outnumbered – did the glare confuse him? – and that the Scots would mow down the cavalry with musket fire. He retreated and advised Charles I that it would be better to talk than to fight. He said a long campaign would be hard to run financially. This advice the king followed nonetheless, influenced by low morale among the English soldiers.[11]

The Earl of Holland had started his career as the queen's courtier, and owed his position as general to her support. He was allied to the Puritan side nonetheless, under the influence of his brother the Earl of Warwick. This was the first occasion during the Scottish crisis when a senior peer seemed to put his personal views before his allegiance to the king.

*

In the ensuing negotiations Charles I made a good impression on his antagonists, impressing them with his views on religion and also his cleverness. There was enjoyable badinage. The Covenanters claimed powers of excommunication for the General Assembly, whereupon Charles I asked whether the assembly could excommunicate him, the King of Scotland. 'Sir,' replied the Earl of Rothes, 'You are so good a King as you will not deserve; but if I were king and should offend, I think the Church of Scotland might excommunicate me.'[12]

An agreement with the Scots was reached on 19 June 1639, known as the Pacification of Berwick, which terminated the brief hostilities on 18 June 1639. The so-called First Bishops' War was therefore a war without a single battle. At Kelso Holland could have changed history with a successful engagement, breaking Covenanter morale. His loyalties became suspect thanks to the camaraderie he showed the Scots in the Berwick negotiations.

Charles I agreed to attend the Scottish parliament in the autumn, and also the next General Assembly of the Kirk. The next day General Leslie, commander of the Scottish troops, entertained a number of English lords, and gave them a tour of his camp, where every company had its standard stamped in letters of gold, 'For Christ's Crown and Covenant.' The soldiers were friendly, calling, 'God bless His Majesty and the Devil confound the Bishops.'[13]

24

SALMACIDA SPOLIA

Henrietta Maria did what she could. She asked her ladies to forgo a portion of their dress allowance and contribute the money saved to the king's military expenses. On 17 April 1639 she wrote personally to the Catholics of England, asking for a gift of money 'freely and cheerfully presented' for the king's costs on his Scottish expedition. Wat Montague and Kenelm Digby helped organise the appeal, under George Conn, and themselves wrote letters.[1]

Catholic priests were expected to ask their congregations for a contribution all across the country. At £14,000, a good part of which came from rich court Catholics, the response was much lower than the £40,000–50,000 that was expected, so the collection showed there was Catholic caution across the country. The Puritans naturally thought the appeal proved a royal Catholic agenda.[2]

After the Pacification of Berwick, the civilised relations between Charles I and the Covenanters fractured. The king insulted the Kirk by announcing that the 'pretended' General Assembly of 1638 was annulled by the new assembly that was coming, and by the new parliament. On 1 July the Scottish Treasurer Traquair announced the new General Assembly would include the bishops as delegates, a statement that caused rioting in Edinburgh. Traquair himself escaped the mob with difficulty. Charles I then decided not to include the bishops, but he did this as a trick – in his opinion, an assembly and a parliament without them would have no legal force. The Covenanting Lords – not all of them, and not Argyll – attended Charles I at Berwick only to be told to return in greater numbers, with the result they did not return at all.[3]

*

In September 1639 a Spanish fleet of seventy-five troop-carrying vessels was penned into the anchorage between Dover and Deal by a smaller Dutch fleet commanded by Admiral Maerten Tromp. They were on their way to Dunkirk, carrying Spanish troops for the increasingly futile Spanish attempt to return the Dutch Republic to its proper place as part of the King of Spain's empire. It was Tromp's job to put a stop to this.

There was a stand-off while Spanish and Dutch envoys petitioned Charles I for his support, and three fleets were stationed off the Kent coast: the Spanish, the Dutch and also the English, under Sir John Pennington, who had a watching brief. Charles I prevaricated. On 21 October Tromp opened fire on the Spaniards, starting an action, the Battle of the Downs, which ended in a decisive Dutch victory. The Spanish ships were either captured, or ran ashore, or were destroyed by fire, with about a dozen escaping.

In England the story spread that the Spanish ships were taking troops to fight against the Scottish rebels, with the implication that Charles I had a secret deal with Spain. The rumour showed the damage done by Chinese whispers and also by the activities of the pro-Spanish Duchesse de Chevreuse and queen mother. In addition (and contradiction) to this, the battle made Charles I look weak, since a sea battle in English waters between foreign powers, without English intervention, was like an invasion of English territory.[4]

A second piece of bad luck buffed up anti-royalist propaganda. Charles Louis of the Palatinate thought that peace in Scotland made it possible for his Uncle Charles to help him with soldiers and money. The young Elector Palatine sailed across the North Sea to talk to his uncle, found he was mistaken, and therefore returned to the Continent. He was thunderously saluted as he sailed from Dover by all three fleets anchored around the Downs, a week before the battle.

Outrageously, Charles Louis was then arrested in France. He was taken to Vincennes and held as a prisoner. Richelieu was about to secure an agreement for French occupation of the German stronghold Breisach, and did not want interference from Charles Louis, who also had his eye on Breisach. To make matters worse the second Palatine prince, Rupert of the Rhine, was already a prisoner in Linz, having been captured by imperial forces in October 1638. The problem was that Charles I was very visibly doing nothing to support his Protestant blood relatives. In the simplified terms of the era, he looked papist.

*

Henrietta Maria was busy with court appointments. On 17 January 1640 Sir John Finch was appointed Lord Keeper of the Great Seal, on her recommendation. Another success was the appointment of Sir Harry Vane as Secretary of State, on 3 February 1640, in succession to Sir John Coke, who was now seventy-six. Henrietta Maria and Hamilton successfully lobbied for the appointment of Vane, the Treasurer of the Household, a trusted royal servant, against the usually crushing opposition of Thomas Wentworth, who was the new power on the Privy Council.[5]

After six years as Lord Deputy of Ireland, Wentworth was called back to London in September 1639 to help on Scotland. He did not relish the challenge. 'The nearer I come to it, the more my heart fails me; nor can I promise myself any good by this journey.' Whether his fears were for the Scottish or the court opposition we do not know. As a close ally of Archbishop Laud, he was worried by the queen's faction.

However, he quickly won the king's confidence. Just before the appointment of Vane, Wentworth was made Earl of Strafford. His personal style can be seen in the subsidiary title that he requested with the earldom (and was given), that of Baron Raby. It was a finely calibrated insult to Sir Harry, since Raby Castle was the home of the Vane family. From this time Sir Harry possibly held a grudge against the king as well, for agreeing to the title.[6]

As well as making no bones about his contempt for Vane, Strafford was the enemy of Hamilton, whom he had prevented from obtaining a grant of lands in Ireland. As the pressures in Scotland increased, so did infighting at the court of Charles I.

While the court celebrated Christmas, plans continued to bring Scotland to heel. Strafford's contribution to history and to his own destiny was to persuade Charles I to call a parliament, so that money could be raised for war, because he thought the English Parliament could be managed – in the way that he had managed the Irish Parliament. His views on the Scottish rebellion chimed with the king's: rebels must be suppressed. This combination of views made a great appeal to Charles I. The writs went out in the last week of February summoning the first parliament since the rowdy sessions of 1628/9. At last the king's critics got what they wanted.[7]

*

On 21 January 1640 the most elaborate, and most explicitly political, of the Caroline masques was produced at Whitehall. *Salmacida Spolia*, by Davenant, designed by Inigo Jones, was originally a vehicle for Henrietta Maria, but was altered so that the king also appeared. In fact, he became the (silent) protagonist.

It was made into a visual statement of royal harmony, which also played on highly refined themes such as the essential hermaphroditic quality of sexual love: the man with his perfect woman – the woman with her perfect man – are one being of both sexes. Surrounded by the English elite, Marie de Médicis watched from beneath the canopy of state the last hurrah of her daughter's accomplished court, whose dreamy sophistication set it apart from the grinding reality of daily life for most of the inhabitants of Britain.[8]

The action begins with the arrival of the fury Discord who summons a number of grotesque anti-masquers, the agents of deception and chaos. The entry of King Philogenes ('lover of the people', played by Charles I) puts the demons to flight, and he is rewarded by the descent from above of a beautiful Amazon (Henrietta Maria) with her ladies. In this way both king and queen triumph over Scottish rebellion.

The final scene is an idealised London above which clouds float, containing 'eight persons richly attired representing the spheres' and ' a heaven opened full of deities'. The chorus hymns the royal couple with the optimistic words,

All that are harsh, all that are rude,
Are by your harnony subdu'd;
Yet so into obedience wrought
As if not forc'd to it, but taught.[9]

Beneath a bridge a river flows, sourced by the spring of Salmacis, after which the masque was named, whose waters could civilise barbarians according to the myth described in the choral text.[10] If any further indication were needed of the benefits that the Stuart marriage conferred on the British Isles, the queen was once more in the early stages of pregnancy, her eighth.

25

GOD CONFOUND THE QUEEN

Charles I opened his first parliament in eleven years on 13 April 1640 and dissolved it on 5 May, so it is known as the Short Parliament. At the opening, after Lord Keeper Finch asked for supply to support war against the Scots, Charles I handed Finch a letter from the leaders of the Covenanters to Louis XIII, intercepted by his agents. This appealed for help from the French king, for his protection. Finch read it out.

The letter was addressed 'au roy' – 'to the king' rather than 'to the King of France'. Charles I was enraged by these words, a treasonous recognition of his brother-in-law's sovereignty over Scotland according to the verbal conventions of the time. The English Parliament barely reacted. Why should they? They were not the Scottish Parliament.[1]

The Commons was intent on stating and apparently on receiving satisfaction for (English) grievances – their complaints against the king's government – before there was hope of supply, even when the king made an offer to abolish ship money. The one development from the Short Parliament was the prominence of John Pym, Member for Tavistock, a man who was about to start a revolution.

*

Pym was a landowner of the gentry class in Somerset and Hampshire who owed his Commons seat to the Earl of Bedford's patronage. 'A man of clear perceptions and patient resolution', Pym sat in every parliament since 1621. Born in 1584, he was alive when Elizabeth I defeated the Spanish Armada with the help of God, and, like many on the Puritan side, felt an attachment to the Elizabethan era. He thought the innovations of Charles I wrong morally and politically. He was pious and very hard-working. In the one image that survives from his lifetime we see a professional man dressed in expensive black, with a thick head of hair brushed neatly back from the forehead, sweeping down just below the ears. He is square-faced, beady-eyed, has heavy, gleaming jowls, a strong, sensuous nose and his moustache and beard are trimmed and orderly.[2]

In the opening debate of the Short Parliament, Pym followed his stepbrother Francis Rous with a comprehensive listing of grievances – the abuse of monopolies, the doubtful legality of ship money, and the rest – which he associated with Rous's claim that 'the roote of all our grievances I thinke to be an intended union betwist us and Rome'. From the start the complaints were financial or legal, but Catholicism was a target. From the start Pym led the campaign against the king's policies.

Unlike Rous, who earlier in his career described the Catholic Church as 'the mother of spiritual fornications', Pym avoided the language of fiery confrontation. The force of his attacks came from his meticulous preparation, and his mastery of Commons procedure, rather than oratory, but also from his supporters, the group of rich men, natural members of the English ruling class, with whom he had long associated.

'Pym's junto' included the earls of Bedford, Warwick, Holland and Essex, lords Saye, Mandeville and Brooke, Sir Benjamin Rudyerd and Oliver St John, men who wanted regular parliaments, something more like open government – at least open to themselves – and a religious practice that encouraged the extempore simplicity of Puritanism.[3]

*

They had reason to be afraid of royal absolutism. By the end of April 1641 no fewer than three ambassadors from Spain were in London for talks with Strafford. The earl's plan was to borrow cash from

Philip IV, possibly men too, and in that way both defeat the Scots and make Parliament unnecessary. The Duchesse de Chevreuse was part of the Spanish connection, trying to create an alliance which would reduce Richelieu to dust and ashes. She continued to pursue her original idea of a marriage between Princess Mary and the Spanish prince (which Henrietta Maria took seriously). It could not remain a total secret. Marie de Médicis weighed in on the Spanish side, holding meetings of French exiles, the enemies of Richelieu, at St James's Palace.[4]

The short life of the parliament also showed that the king was only half-sure that he needed it. It was Harry Vane who carried the 5 May Privy Council, arguing the Commons was not going to offer a penny of supply. The king dissolved Parliament that afternoon.

Provocation of parliamentarians continued regardless. In normal times Convocation, the Church of England synodal body, sat while a Parliament was sitting, not otherwise. This year, following the dissolution of Parliament, and protected by armed guards, Convocation continued in session. In May 1640 it imposed a new oath on all learned professions, who were to swear loyalty to 'the government of this Church by Archbishops, Bishops, deans and archdeacons etc, as it now stands established'. In no time the oath was called the Etcetera Oath, since its vagueness left all things open, including 'the curl'd lock of the Antichrist'.[5]

Soon after the dissolution, Warwick, Saye, Brooke, Pym, Hampden and others were arrested and searched, and their houses searched, to see whether 'protestations against the Scotch war' had been drawn up. The Privy Council wanted to see whether there was treasonous correspondence between the efficient Scottish rebels and Pym's junto.[6]

*

The pace in Scotland was accelerating. Edinburgh Castle, garrisoned by royal troops, was under siege by the Covenanters, who were also establishing positions on the English border.

There were protests against royal policy in London too. The aldermen of the City had been asked to lend Charles I £100,000 and refused, so they were told he now needed £200,000 from them, and, they were told, if they did not cooperate he would demand £300,000. Four recalcitrant alderman were put in prison. The men blamed for these actions were the king's leading advisers, rather than the king himself: Laud, Hamilton and Strafford, but mainly Laud.[7]

On 11 May 1640, a crowd gathered in the evening in St George's Fields, Southwark, and marched to Lambeth Palace looking for Laud, 'with the purpose of slaying him'. 'William the Fox' had taken refuge in Whitehall, which was well guarded. A nineteen-year-old seaman, Thomas Bensted, tried to break in the door of Lambeth Palace with a crowbar. For this he would be put on trial and found guilty of treason. He was hanged and quartered. His head was put on a spike on London Bridge. The dangerous precedent was set of a young life ruined. Was it really treason to hit the door of Lambeth Palace?[8]

These crowds were young, mainly city apprentices boiling with energy and frustration, fuelled by a passionate commitment to the Puritan God, railing against authority. On 14 May larger crowds gathered. Some went all the way to Croydon where Laud had a country palace, which they attacked; others went to release those imprisoned as a result of the earlier disturbance, and did so with great violence to anyone standing in their way. They 'knocked down the gates, slew the keepers, and released all the prisoners, especially those in custody for the riot of Monday'.[9]

The young men hoped for more. Two days after this, the apprentice Richard Beaumont told members of the Privy Council there were plans to 'pull down the Queen-Mother's house, Somerset House Chapel, and Arundel House'. While Richard said that Arundel House was targeted because of ordnance mounted there against the apprentices, in fact all three were papist, the Earl of Arundel being a crypto-Catholic and his wife being Catholic.[10]

The gatherings were advertised by placards in the streets bearing suspiciously Scottish language, for instance 'urging every class to preserve their ancient liberty and chase the bishops from the kingdom'. In Whitehall someone scratched a terrible prayer on a windowpane in the king's ante-chamber: 'God save the King, God confound the Queen with all her offspring, God grant the palatine to reign in this realm.' The king smashed the glass with his fist.[11]

There was trouble outside London. Across the country, levies of men for the next campaign against the Scots were resisted. Leominster, Hereford, Marlborough, Warwick, Oxford, Cambridge and Uttoxeter all suffered a breakdown in public order. Both

Somerset and Dorset levies killed officers who were Catholics. One was clamped in the pillory when he was dead.[12]

*

The heavily pregnant Henrietta Maria was the loser. Laud insisted that the king must turn on the Catholics. A public show was made by searches of Catholic houses, burning of Catholic books, confiscation of devotional images and the arrest of forty-seven priests, and of any Catholics attending the queen's chapel, or those of foreign ambassadors. The effect was miraculous. The rioting aimed at the king's ministers 'entirely ceased', although specifically anti-Catholic agitation continued. The imprisoned aldermen had already been released.[13]

On 8 July 1640 the new royal baby was born, a boy named Henry. St James's Palace was still occupied by her mother, so Henrietta Maria went for her labour to Oatlands in Surrey. Henry was born with no complications for mother or son, and placed in the care of the (Catholic) Countess of Roxburghe. Charles I stayed with his wife through this period, returning to London to deal with the crisis that just kept on getting worse.

Just after giving birth the queen felt her vulnerability. It was not just the politics. George Conn had died in Rome, in January 1640. A new papal envoy was sent, Carlo Rosetti, who took over from Conn in August 1639, but this was the death of a good friend and ally. The queen also carried the burden of her baby Katherine's death eighteen months before, and Anne, three years old, was constantly ill. Henrietta Maria also felt responsible for her mother, who was now struggling because Charles I, very short of money himself, had cut her revenues by half.[14]

Delighted with Henry, Charles I made another reversal by celebrating with a relaxation of the penal laws for the month of the queen's lying-in, and the release of imprisoned Catholics. Of course he remembered the difficult labour of Henrietta Maria when she gave birth to poor Katherine, when she too came close to death, and saw that her faith had helped her then, and was helping her now. His see-saw moves of course convinced his critics that he could not be trusted.[15]

*

On 20 August 1640, the Covenanter army crossed the border with England and headed for Newcastle. England was invaded by a foreign power.

On 28 August the Scots crossed the Tyne at Newburn, easily overcoming the English troops of Lord Conway. When the news reached Newcastle the remaining garrison fled, so the city surrendered two days later. As the Scots marched into Newcastle, 'universal acclamations ... became ever louder'. It seemed 'the cause of the invader was the cause of the invaded as well'.[16]

During these days there was a weird equivalence of timing in England and Scotland. On 20 August, the same day that the Scots entered England, Charles I left London heading north; and on 28 August, as the ford at Newburn was contested, the *Petition of the Twelve Peers* was published in England calling for another parliament (a call supported within the Privy Council). The coincidence of dates was chance, but there was collaboration between the invading Scots and the English parliamentary lobby.[17]

A pamphlet that urged the rights of the Scottish invaders, *Information on the Scottish Nation*, was printed by the Scots and distributed in London where it was popular reading. The grandee opponents of the king were busy in meetings where they discussed next steps. Warwick, Brooke, Saye, Pym and Hampden were released from the Tower, and met with Bedford and Essex.

Henrietta Maria sent her husband a warning about their plans to present him with a remonstrance or protest against him for which signatures were being gathered. On 1 September 1640, the minister Calybute Downing preached a sermon to the Artillery Company that blamed the Jesuits for separating the king from his people – not even Henrietta Maria had time for the Jesuits – but said a subject people could be entitled to resist an unjust sovereign. On 15 September Edinburgh Castle capitulated.[18]

*

In order to decide what to do after the occupation of Newcastle, the king called a Great Council of Peers. This was not a parliament. His advisers found a precedent for Charles I – from the time of Edward III three hundred years before – to provide a constitutional forum for the decisions that needed to be taken, one that would preserve the king's shredded authority.

At the council, which assembled at York on 24 September 1640, Henrietta Maria and Parliament featured in one and the same breath. Charles I told the peers that his wife had advised him by letter to call a parliament, and he would take that advice. It was a mistake to confirm so publicly that the only person's opinion he truly respected was his wife's, but he raised the queen's profile as a conciliatory force.[19]

Charles I was not in a position to pay the costs of war, so he could not fight battles. Instead he appointed fifteen commissioners from England to negotiate with their Scottish counterparts at Ripon. Because he had to accommodate his (English) enemies, the commissioners included senior members of the Pym circle: Bedford, Essex, Mandeville and Brooke. The terms signed at Ripon on 14 October 1640 were that hostilities would cease, the Scots would continue to occupy Northumberland and Durham (charging Charles I £850 a day for their costs), England would reimburse Scotland for the costs of the war so far, and the treaty would be ratified by Parliament. No Parliament, no treaty.

The Treaty of Ripon made a second parliament inevitable because of the money that would be needed, but the explicit link between peace and Parliament trapped Charles I. The second parliament of 1640 was called in circumstances that were totally different from those of the Short Parliament. The king's negotiations with Spain failed thanks to a rebellion in Spanish territories – the Catalan revolt – so Philip IV could not offer men or money to his brother Charles I, who therefore was stuck.

Henrietta Maria also featured at Ripon. Here the Scots spoke 'in confidence of the excess of the queen's power, which, in respect of her religion and of the persons who had most interest with her, ought not to prevail so much upon the king as it did in all affairs'. It was not so much a new note as a louder one.[20]

*

At the Council of Peers, Strafford bore the brunt of criticism of the war strategy. Nonetheless the earl was down but he was not out. Instead he was considering whether to bring charges of treason against the Members of Parliament who were working with the invading enemy to corner the king.

As viceroy of Ireland, Strafford had in reserve an Irish army of

9,000 Catholics awaiting orders and – if they could be arranged – transports to invade Scotland. It would also be possible if the word were given, always in the king's name, to land in England.[21]

When the second parliament of 1640 opened in Westminster on 3 November, Strafford was with the army in York, but at the king's request he came to London. He took his seat in the Lords on 11 November, without once rising to his feet. It was unusual for him to delay. Pym and his friends realised they must act quickly. The same day a committee of the House of Commons accused Strafford of treason and started proceedings for his impeachment with the House of Lords. Strafford at once returned to Westminster, but the opportunity was gone; he was arrested on the spot. Having forced Charles I to recall Parliament, the opposition politicians were now using Parliament to take away the people who supported the king.[22]

26

THE HOUSE OF ORANGE

The children were growing up. In 1640 the black-haired Charles
was ten, Mary eight and pretty, James nearly seven – ages which
at the time qualified them for treatment as small adults. Elizabeth
was nearly five, Anne three, Henry six months. What would
their future be? For the girls it was all marriage. After the arrest
of Strafford, the initiative stayed with Parliament which, during
the closing months of 1640, continued attacking the king's chief
ministers to isolate Charles I, who therefore needed allies.

In addition to the negotiation with Spain – proposed by Marie
de Chevreuse – marriage talks had started with the Protestant
Dutch, whose unlikely champion was the Catholic Marie de
Médicis. She had discussions in Amsterdam in 1638. Once she
was established at St James's, she spoke to her daughter about the
proposal.

The Dutch United Provinces were a republic, but there was a
Dutch prince waiting to be married: William, son of the Prince of
Orange. The not-quite-royal House of Orange was a noble family
of great wealth, holding vast Dutch and German estates, holding
also Orange, a territory north of Avignon in the Rhone valley
studded with Roman ruins, surrounded on all sides by France
itself. Orange gave rank – the Prince of Orange was a sovereign –
but his international standing came from his powerful position in

the Dutch Republic. Frederick Henry, Prince of Orange, was the Dutch 'Stadholder' (Governor) and the head of the Dutch armed forces.

This unique position arose from the leadership given by William I of Orange – William the Silent[1] – when the Dutch rebelled against Philip II of Spain in 1568, starting the war of independence that was still being waged in 1640. In 1625 William's youngest son Frederick Henry became Prince of Orange, the third of his family to lead the Dutch as their Stadholder and Captain- and Admiral-General. Frederick Henry's position was powerful, but he was not quite a king. He depended on the support of the States (representative assemblies) of each of the seven Dutch provinces.

Perhaps a belief in predestination made it easy for the princes to live lives of riot. Frederick Henry married the beautiful Amalia van Solms, a German noblewoman in the household of Elizabeth of Bohemia, because his elder brother Maurice threatened, otherwise, to legitimise his own bastard children. Amalia's resulting son, William, was born in 1626 (his father was forty-four at the time), and therefore was fourteen in 1640.

Stuart marriage plans were mainly influenced by the collapse of Stuart peace at home, but they fed into the European war machine. Both the Dutch and the German wars looked as though they would last forever. The Palatinate had become a Swedish Protectorate.[2]

The Dutch backed William in order to keep Balthasar Carlos out, while for Charles and Henrietta Maria the question was the effect of a royal marriage on the situation at home. Spain's own difficulties made a Spanish match less attractive, and in addition the proposer of Balthasar Carlos, Marie de Chevreuse, made another of her sudden exits when she left London on 1 May 1640, arriving a week later in Dunkirk. She in fact left because her husband was on his way to fetch her back to France himself, and she wanted to avoid him.[3]

*

While these plans were discussed and dreamed of, the Scots commissioners arrived in London at the end of October 1640 to continue the Ripon talks. It was an open secret that both sides planned to spin things out in order to strap Charles I into a straitjacket. Godly ministers throughout London preached that the Scots were 'angels sent by God to deliver the people from idolatry and tyranny'. For Henrietta Maria it was all danger, because her husband's enemies whipped up anti-Catholic frenzy.[4]

The Commons heard terrifying revelations that 'the Papists of Lankeshire have prepared all this summer more armes than the Protestantes'. Internal sedition was linked to Strafford's Irish army, with its Catholic troops, which was never intended for use against the Scots, but only to invade England and suppress Parliament. So it was argued in the Commons. Never mind that *they* had disobeyed their king, invaded England and were occupying two of the northern counties; it was politically incorrect to refer to the Scots as rebels. 'Sir William Witherington called the Scots rebells. Mr Hollis and Mr Glyn moved either for explanation or for punishment.'[5]

These fears and threats and distortions were part of the great work of the Commons, which was to build a case against Strafford. Strafford had to be found guilty because the Scots believed that he wished to treat them as he had so effectively treated the Irish, and reduce them to a subject race. He had to be found guilty to prevent him from calling on his Catholic Irish army. So intent were the Commons on their business that the members failed altogether to notice how uncomfortable the chamber had become, with many of the windows broken over the years when it was not in use. Not until 4 January, when the winter was well advanced, did they order the broken windows to be replaced.[6]

*

The Christmas season of 1640/1 was a bumpy downhill ride for Henrietta Maria. On 15 December Princess Anne died from tubercular infection, the third child that Henrietta Maria lost. Her parents were overwhelmed with grief. In this period child mortality was high, so the queen was fortunate to have five children in good health – and the toddler, having been baptised, would fly to heaven – but the death of a small child can only be a torment. It was a severe blow when so much was crumbling.

The Hispanophile Secretary of State Sir Francis Windebank fled to France, 'preferring to experience the rigours of justice from a distance rather than to implore in vain the clemency of his judges as a prisoner'. He was desperate to avoid impeachment by the Commons for signing warrants that released Catholic priests from custody. With his nephew Robert Read, who had tried to defend him in the Commons, he rode at night from London to the coast and bribed a man to row them across the Channel.[7]

On 18 December the Commons accused the Archbishop of Canterbury of high treason, and started work on his impeachment articles. Although he must have known what was coming, it did not occur to Laud, now sixty-seven years old, to run away. One of the articles of impeachment that was eventually produced was that 'he hath traitorously and wickedly endeavoured to reconcile the Church of England to the Church of Rome', and this included the charge 'that he was an instrument of the queen's', a pathetic reversal of the truth. On 22 December Lord Keeper Finch, who presided over the House of Lords and the Star Chamber, sailed 'in the cold and dark' to the Dutch coast to take refuge at The Hague.[8]

The king looked to his wife for advice. Henrietta Maria wrote to Cardinal Barberini to ask for a loan of £125,000 to bribe the king's opponents. She had hardened – 'she never ceases to urge him [the king] to throw himself into desperate courses'– but then she was herself under open attack.[9]

In December 1640 Henrietta Maria received a message from Parliament that she must dismiss her Catholic servants, to which she replied that she would only do so if at the same time she dismissed her Protestant servants as well. This unprecedented assault on the royal household by Parliament broke international law – the marriage treaty – but now Pym and the others needed total victory, because anything less signed their own death warrants.

The pressures on her mother added to Henrietta Maria's worries. In January 1642 Marie de Médicis reduced her household to twenty, and sold her carriages, horses and plate to raise cash. The entire royal household was being starved of funds.[10]

*

When the Stuart marriage was announced by Frederick Henry in The Hague on 12 December 1640, Europe was astonished: marriage between the Stadholder's son and a Stuart princess gave the royal seal of approval to the Dutch Republic.

Charles and Henrietta Maria suddenly had a lifeline. Having previously said she had lost the power to protect him, the queen told Carlo Rosetti that he should stay in London. She was also buoyed by the expectation of a new ambassador extraordinary from Louis XIII, who was expected to guarantee the terms of her marriage treaty. Charles I, too, showed new confidence.[11]

Three ambassadors sent from The Hague to finalise details survived an attack from Dunkirkers during the crossing to arrive for a formal audience with Charles I on 7 January 1641, and the next day they had separate and informal audiences with the king and queen. They went on to audiences with the children, which took place at Somerset House, Charles and James at one meeting, then Mary – who was suffering from a fever – and Elizabeth at another, at which the lead ambassador, the Lord of Somersdyk, spoke with baffling complexity and at astonishing length.[12]

By the beginning of February the details were settled, including a dowry of £40,000 and, more surprisingly, something that might have been decided earlier: the identity of the princess to be married. The Dutch wanted Mary, the 'first princess'. Charles and Henrietta Maria were thinking of other husbands for their elder daughter, whether Balthasar Carlos or the Elector of Brandenburg. They preferred to give Prince William the second princess, Elizabeth, as more suitable for his regrettably modest rank. But they gave in, and Mary became the Dutch bride.[13]

At four o'clock on 6 February 1641, all the Dutch ambassadors returned to Somerset House for another audience with the nine-year-old Mary, who received them with her governess Lady Roxburghe. Other ladies stood about the room in the normal way.

This time it was ambassador Aersens who paid their respects more briefly, saying, 'Madam, the last time we came to your royall highness, it was from the States of the United Provinces and the Prince of Orange as to the Princess Mary eldest daughter to the King of Great Britayne, but now, Madam, we come to your royall highness from the King, your father, not only as to his eldest daughter but as to the mistress of the young Prince William of Orange.'

Lady Roxburghe was flummoxed how to prompt her charge to reply, but she managed something, leaving the ambassadors free to depart with honour satisfied. They did not see that Henrietta

Maria was all the time standing in the corner of the room, concealed behind a mask.[14]

*

The fourteen-year-old groom landed at Margate on 17 April 1641, and sailed on to Gravesend on 19 April. William made a good impression. He wore his curling, dark-blonde hair long as any English cavalier and was well brought up. He made a ceremonial entry to London in the royal coach, followed by those of the nobility, driving straight to Whitehall. Here the crowds made it hard for the carriages to get through. Inside the palace, too, hundreds of people wanted to see the Stadholder's son. William was met on the staircase by the Prince of Wales and Duke of York, who escorted him to the queen's privy chamber, where Charles and Henrietta Maria waited.[15]

The young prince was received with affection. Henrietta Maria took him by both his arms, told him he was much taller than she expected, and said she would be a second mother to him, but did not allow him to kiss her. There was gossip about the lack of kissing, attributed to the prince's status as the representative of a republic. Nor, when he met her, did Mary permit a kiss but Mary was still sick. The two of them spoke in French, in which William was fluent but Mary less so. William also went to visit Marie de Médicis in St James's, and on this occasion the old lady behaved with grace and charm.[16]

With four hundred gentlemen in attendance, William stayed at Arundel House, where he could see the famous collection of paintings and sculpture. He brought with him presents for the royal family, not just the lavish jewels he gave his bride and her mother but also a large sum of money in gold bars for the king, rumoured to be over a million ducats. Some of this Charles I sent to the troops in the north of England, a wise move since the political situation in London was now very difficult thanks to street demonstrations against Strafford.[17]

The wedding was a low-cost private ceremony on Sunday 2 May at Whitehall, where the chapel was decorated with cloth of gold and spread with carpets. William came in first, attended by the ambassadors and others; then Mary arrived, escorted by her brothers and Lady Roxburghe, followed by a train of more children, the bridesmaids, daughters of noble houses. She was a miniature bride in silver tissue and pearls, wearing a large diamond which William had given her.[18]

With the chief officers of his household, the king arrived after his daughter. Henrietta Maria could not keep away from her daughter's Protestant wedding but did not join Charles I in the chapel; instead she watched from a gallery above, together with Marie de Médicis. They were the last to arrive. The king led both his daughter and her groom to the altar, where Matthew Wren, Bishop of Ely, Dean of the Chapel Royal, officiated, following the service in the Book of Common Prayer. William made his responses in English, and was surprised that the ring he had to use was unadorned gold. The service lasted roughly an hour and was finished by two.[19]

Feasting afterwards was for family only, in the king's withdrawing chamber at Whitehall. There was a dinner immediately, then the queen and the children went for a walk in Hyde Park, then, except for Elizabeth and Marie de Médicis, they met again for supper in the evening. The ghost at the banquet was Charles Louis of the Rhine, who had hoped to marry Mary himself, or at least to be party to an Anglo-Dutch treaty supporting his restoration in the Palatinate. He was in a furious sulk, having achieved neither.[20]

'The non-appearance of the Prince Elector in that company was wondered at.' He made his point by refusing to call on the groom in the days before the wedding, and boycotting the service itself. This show of temper unfortunately undermined the case that Charles I had made to Parliament, that the marriage was destined to help his sister, the Queen of Bohemia, 'and her orphan children'.[21]

The Elector Palatine also missed the formalised consummation of the marriage, when the children lay together on a bed while adults watched, including the Dutch ambassadors. All that was required was for flesh to touch flesh in the presence of witnesses, but the whole business took an hour and a half as the prince, suitably attended by the king among others, undressed in one room and Mary lay on a bed in another, with her mother seated at her side. William joined his wife, kissed her on the forehead and tried to loosen her nightshirt so that he could touch her leg, which was all that was needed, but the nine-year-old was swathed in a nightshirt far too big for her and William couldn't find the leg. Jeffrey Hudson made the decisive intervention, by stepping forward with a pair of scissors and handing them to Prince William with a bow. The groom cut the gown, the two legs touched, the deed was done.[22]

27

HENRIETTA MARIA IN THE LIMELIGHT

While the finishing touches were put on the marriage agreement, Parliament started to attack the queen. Her position was vulnerable because she stood for Catholicism, a faith she had proclaimed in her chapel, in her patronage and in (many of) her friends. She was not, however, the cause of the sudden collapse of her husband's position; that happened because he was intent on making the Scots worship in the same (Protestant) way that he did. Nor was Catholicism a terrorist plot against England, despite the foolish *Regnans in Excelsis*. As later events would show, English Catholics were by nature both peaceable and intensely loyal.

On 27 January 1641, the Catholic contribution to Charles I's 1639 expedition against the Scots was revealed to the Commons in a work of 'fowre folios' and furiously debated. 'This was a Catholike cause ... this was done for the Queene's sake.' Wat Montagu and Kenelm Digby both gave evidence to Parliament which may have obscured things, but nonetheless Henrietta Maria was given her new dramatic role of evil genius.[1]

The Puritan heroes Burton, Bastwick and Prynne had been released by Parliament at the end of 1640. Prynne and Burton returned to London together on 28 November, through Brentford. They were accompanied by more than a hundred coaches and a crowd of thousands. Bastwick returned through Blackheath a few days later, to be escorted by twenty-seven coaches and a thousand horse. The godly faction was triumphant.[2]

There was an uproar about a Catholic priest arrested and condemned to death for treason – by hanging, drawing and quartering – but reprieved by the king. It was Henrietta Maria who asked her husband for mercy for Fr Goodman. Charles concealed the queen's request when he sent a message to the House of Lords in explanation. The king said that Fr Goodman was guilty of being a priest but of nothing more, and was therefore being spared a horrible death at his, Charles's, will, but nevertheless 'the King was still readie to punish him by imprisonment or banishment'. He reminded Parliament of the risk of repercussions abroad for English Protestants if Goodman were tortured to death. After a stand-off – the sovereign's prerogative of mercy had not been challenged before – Charles I agreed that Parliament should decide Goodman's fate. Divesting himself of an ancient power, he aimed to protect Henrietta Maria from investigation. The Lords blocked the execution but the Commons won their point.[3]

Although for the time being it came to nothing, the Scottish campaign against the bishops also hit England. A petition to abolish the episcopate and to reform the Church of England – on Puritan lines – 'roots and branches' was signed by thousands of Londoners and presented to the Commons in December 1640. Not only did this menace William Laud's vision of the Church of England, it would also take from the House of Lords a block of royalist votes.

*

The king and queen launched a charm offensive. On 19 February 1641, Charles I appointed seven of his opponents onto the Privy Council: Bedford, Bristol, Essex, Hertford, Savile, Saye and Mandeville. They accepted. This alone might have shown the way to an orderly settlement.[4]

Soon there were projects of marriage that promised the essential family ties between the court, the court's noble opponents and the Covenanters. Bedford considered marrying his daughter to the Marquess of Hamilton. Hamilton offered his daughter to the Covenant leader Argyll's son.[5]

A few months later, under Bedford's direction, ideas emerged on financial reform, setting royal finances on a secure basis by the introduction of a general tax on exports, and making the efficient Pym Chancellor of the Exchequer. The junto seemed to respond to the king's offer to bring his critics into government. Such moves were not binding on Charles I, however, since the taking away of these positions was in his power as much as the giving. There remained the future of Lord Strafford and there remained what went with it, the issue of trust.[6]

*

On 4 February 1641 Henrietta Maria sent a message to the House of Commons which confused the Members. They were amazed by the things she said. The queen asked the Commons to forgive her for her part in the Catholic contribution in 1639, making the perfectly fair point that 'it was only to joine in advancing his Majesties service with divers other persons Protestants that did contribute at the same time to the furtherance of the same service'.

She reminded them she had urged Charles I to call Parliament in the first place. She promised to control attendance at her chapel, and to ensure that illegal Catholic priests would leave the country, and she would also send Carlo Rosetti away.[7] She asked the forgiveness of the Commons. She 'concluded with great expressions of her goodwill to us and her readines to perform all good offices to his Majestie on our behalfe'.

After the message was read out by Thomas Jermyn, 'there was a generall silence'. Some Members called for the House to return to its business, while others asked for the message to be read again, this time by the Clerk of the House. It was not personal hostility which produced this reaction, although the House was suspicious of the queen; it was a feeling that the queen had no business sending messages to the House of Commons. They were amazed not by the message, but by the fact that it had been sent at all. It was misogyny.

When Sir Simmonds d'Ewes reminded the Members that the position of a Queen of England was different from that of an ordinary woman – that she 'had the same power of the dispositon of all matters concerning her estate as if she were a widow' – he found some support and managed to persuade his colleagues that Henrietta Maria was not entirely out of order. The House voted to send their thanks to her for her message, although they did so with reluctance.

The final words in particular, when Henrietta Maria offered to intercede with the king on behalf of the Commons, were very badly judged, since it was the prerogative of the Commons to communicate directly with the king. Nobody wanted a Catholic princess speaking to the sovereign in their place. The message was well intentioned but counter-productive, because it conveyed to the men of Parliament a sense of the queen's hold on Charles I.[8]

In short, the royal tactics did nothing to relax the House of Commons, which did not let up. 'At present nothing is left to him but the title and the naked shows of king, and he does not know how to conceal the passions which naturally torture him.' On 16 February Charles I gave the royal assent to the Triennial Bill, which ensured a parliament every three years, regardless of the sovereign's will. He had resisted this strenuously, because he knew it would reduce to a fraction the power he inherited in 1625.

A noxious side effect was that the more Charles I ceded powers to Parliament, the less attractive he became as an ally, with the result that Louis XIII, to whom Henrietta Maria had appealed for help at the end of 1640, had less and less incentive to help his sister.[9]

The Commons forced the king's signature to the Triennial Bill when they 'loudly threatened the most extreme designs'. So heady was their sense of victory – Parliament had broken the royal veto – that the Commons ordered bonfires to be lit throughout London in celebration.

By giving in, Charles I bought time for the accomplishment of Mary's marriage, and for saving the Earl of Strafford. However, the pressures against a peaceful settlement increased when the Scots published a paper on 24 February 1641 in which they insisted on the abolition of episcopacy in support of the English petitions and demanded the execution of Strafford. Alexander Warriston noted that, in reaction, 'the king hes run starke mad'.[10]

*

In February Henrietta Maria thought of travelling to France, theoretically for her health's sake though in reality to drum up support for her husband, but Richelieu put her off. Now she turned her attention to the domestic front.[11]

During the weeks leading up to Strafford's trial, Henrietta Maria later recalled holding meetings with members of the opposition in the most extraordinary way. She told a friend that she used to go at night through the Whitehall corridors, holding a torch, to the apartments of one of her ladies, who was away in the country, and there, alone, she would meet her husband's enemies to bargain.

It is probable she met the Earl of Bedford, who stood for moderation, and possibly Pym, whose patron Bedford was. Maybe she met others. In addition to this direct intervention, the queen became aware of disaffection in the army because the soldiers had not been paid by Parliament.[12]

28

THAT FATHOMLESS ABYSS

During the early weeks of March 1641, Westminster Hall was prepared for Strafford's trial with the construction of benches all around, ten tiers high. There were public benches, benches reserved for the court and for the commissioners from Scotland and for Members of the Commons and the Lords. Every day of the trial, every seat would be taken. People stayed in their seats all day to keep them, which meant that the detritus grew as time passed, along with a pervasive stench. Outside, crowds gathered. The trial was a national sensation which took precedence over all other business in the law courts and much of the trade of London.

On Monday 22 March 1641, at seven in the morning, Strafford left the tower of London by the Traitors Gate and travelled upstream to Westminster in a barge escorted by five other barges, each carrying twenty soldiers. When he entered Westminster Hall he stepped up on to a raised platform. Behind him, in ascending order, were the spectators, the Members of the Commons, the Scots commissioners, other reserved seats and then the seats open to all.

He faced the court of peers, who were dressed in red and wearing hats, as the highest-ranking people present. In front of the peers sat the judges. Dressed in black, and wearing only the garter star as decoration, Strafford knelt at the narrow bar separating the peers from everyone else, then stood. Later he was provided with a chair.[1]

The king's throne was empty throughout. Charles I and Henrietta Maria watched from a curtained alcove in a gallery overlooking the hall, the queen's ladies taking notes. For some of the time at least they had their older children with them. The trial presented a microcosm of Caroline society, with every rank present, excluding only the most senior clergy, the bishops, who decided to stay away rather than cause controversy by attending. Their absence provided a problem for the defence, because they would be expected to vote for Strafford's innocence.[2]

The procedure was cross-examination of witnesses by the prosecution (the House of Commons, represented by John Pym, John Glyn and John Maynard) and the defence (Strafford conducted his own defence), while the judgement was for the Lords. The chair was held by the Earl Marshal, the Earl of Arundel. Perhaps it was a surprise, in the first week, that Strafford's defence went well – much too well from the point of view of his accusers, who knew that failure would return Black Tom Tyrant to the political arena, where he would be relentless.

Those who framed the articles of impeachment overplayed their hand, both in the number of articles (twenty-eight), and in their publication three weeks before the opening. The scale of the attack and the publicity were deliberate, to build momentum, but the publication created resentment in the House of Lords, always jealous of the honour of any peer. As for image, the appearance of Strafford in Westminster Hall excited sympathy. He was coming up to his forty-eighth birthday, but was stooped and grey-haired, wrapped in a warm cloak and wearing a fur-lined cap against the cold. Members of the general public were heard to say, 'Poor soul.'[3]

*

However, he was articulate and quickly became forceful. His powerful intelligence found inaccuracies and discrepancies in the charges and he acquitted himself with clarity, even humour. Strafford was impeached on a charge of high treason, but his actions in Ireland and England were done in the royal service, and it could not be shown that they damaged the security or welfare of England. There was only one article which had the promise of conviction: article twenty-three, in which the earl was accused of intending to bring an Irish army into England to suppress the English people. This could be considered as treason against England. On 5 April 1641 this was the charge that the trial examined, a difficult charge because intention is difficult to prove.

The attention of the crowds in Westminster Hall was now drawn to a conversation eleven months before, on 5 March 1640, when the Privy Council discussed the dissolution of the Short Parliament. At this meeting Strafford talked about the army he had just raised in Ireland, but what exactly did he say?

Sir Harry Vane was happy to tell the court that the earl had advised Charles I to remember the Irish troops which could be used 'here to reduce this kingdom'. The question was, which kingdom? In Sir Harry's testimony, if that was the advice of Strafford, he was telling the king to use Irish troops against the English, but it was a big if. Might not 'this kingdom' more probably refer to Scotland, where there was an armed and organised rebellion in progress against the king? The charge lost force when Strafford questioned Hamilton, Cottington and Juxon, all of them present at the meeting, all of them disagreeing with Vane, all denying that Strafford advised the king to use Irish troops against the English.

Five days later, on 10 April, the Commons prosecutors returned to article twenty-three to submit fresh evidence, that is to say the copy of a copy of the notes taken by Vane at the critical meeting.[4] Strafford at once informed the court that he had new evidence too, in respect of articles twenty-one and twenty-three. The Lords decided that Strafford too was entitled to submit new evidence, and the earlier charge, twenty-one, would need to be revisited first.

The prosecution's case was losing direction but also credibility. The 'precise part' of the Commons yelled, 'Withdraw, withdraw!' The session descended into chaos, and was adjourned by the Earl of Arundel. The Earl of Strafford 'could not hide his joy' and the king was seen to be laughing.[5]

*

The king laughed too soon. That same afternoon of 10 April 1641, Sir Arthur Haselrige introduced a Bill of Attainder against Strafford on the floor of the House of Commons, in order to by-pass the trial. The Bill of Attainder implied that the normal arguments of law were not relevant. All that was needed was for the Members of Parliament to vote for the Bill – which simply declared that Strafford was guilty – and the 'poisoned arrow of treason' would be lodged in his breast. Attainder did not appeal to the principle that a man was innocent until proven guilty, it appealed to the prevailing mood in Parliament.

The law-minded Pym was desperate enough to agree to the nuclear option. When the occupants of Westminster Hall listened to Strafford's summing up in his defence on 13 April, the earl's sheer good sense was beginning to sound convincing. 'My Lords,' he said, 'do we not live by laws and must we be punishable by them ere they be made? ... These gentlemen tell me they speak against my arbitrary laws. Give me leave to say that I speak in defence of the Commonweal against their arbitrary treason.'[6]

On 21 April 1641, the Commons closed their ears to Strafford's persuasive voice and passed the Bill of Attainder by 204 votes to 59, after a debate in which only one person, George Digby, bravely spoke against the motion. The Bill went to the Lords, who disliked the precedent.

If attainder were accepted, anyone might be hauled before Parliament as a traitor, with no process of examination and judgement to protect him. It seemed also to undermine the Lords, since it side-stepped the process of impeachment, in which the House of Lords stood as judge. Although many lords detested Strafford, that did not mean they would all vote for the Bill of Attainder. There was hope for Strafford still.

*

On 1 May, the day before the wedding of Mary and William, Charles I addressed Parliament in a joint session. He denied ever planning to use the Irish army against his English subjects, and said that no minister had ever advised him to do so. He told Parliament he did not see evidence of treason by Strafford, although there was evidence of 'misdemeanours' for which the earl should be punished. Strafford was not fit, he said, to serve him as a minister in the future. These were effective points to make in support of the earl; they allowed for punishment short of execution.

Unfortunately, the king went on to appeal to the lords not to put pressure on him by voting for the attainder, since 'no fear or respect [for Parliament] will make me go against my conscience'. By this Charles I meant that he would not sign a Bill of Attainder if Parliament passed it. This appeal catastrophically undermined the rest of his speech. It urged on the Lords the judgement of the king rather than the judgement of the law. Even worse, Charles's speech absolved the Lords of responsibility. He was telling them that, regardless of their vote, he would not sign the Bill of Attainder into law.[7]

Meanwhile the street organisation of the godly was unleashed. The City of London told Parliament they would not supply the loan of £120,000 they had promised unless Strafford were found guilty. Lists of the Members of the Commons who had voted against the attainder were put up in public so everyone knew the 'Straffordians'. Street demonstrations at Westminster continued up to the day when the Lords voted on 7 May 1641, with a mob outside 'threatening the most violent actions against the state and against his Majesty's own person and all the royal House'. Above the din the word 'Justice!' was heard again and again as the lords' coaches struggled to get through. Of the forty-eight lords present for the vote, eleven had the courage to vote against the attainder. The Bill therefore passed. Parliament voted Strafford a traitor.[8]

*

What started as a political trial, deftly challenged by Strafford's defence, had become a situation of great complexity, thanks to the actions of the king and also, more especially, of his wife. Before the Lords voted, another scandal had erupted.

Four days before the vote, the Commons voted to send supplies and pay to the army. This was not just administration. An army which was not fighting a campaign was a worry in itself, and if the soldiers were unhappy because of arrears of pay, the risks multiplied.

Stories of atrocities in the German wars were well known in England, perhaps the most famous of which was the massacre of 20,000 citizens of Magdeburg ten years earlier by a Catholic army, but that was at least the result of a siege and a strategy, whereas disaffected, unoccupied soldiers might harry the people without any form of control. The fear of Strafford was also the fear of his Irish army, which Charles I had failed to disband despite repeated requests that he do so. If the unpaid, unhappy English army in the north combined with the Irish army in a descent on London, something much more horrible might be expected than Magdeburg.

There was more. In the Commons, Lenthall said that 'ill-affected persons have endeavoured to make a misunderstanding in the Army of the intentions of Parliament towards them'. He was telling his colleagues there was a plot to turn the army against Parliament. Who were these people? A committee was put together to investigate. It seemed they were friends of the Queen of England.[9]

On 5 May (two days before the vote), the Commons sent for a number of officers whom they wished to question: Henry Percy, Henry Jermyn, Sir John Suckling, William Davenant and the Earl of Carnarvon. Two were cavalier poets (Suckling and Davenant). Jermyn was a senior member of the queen's household, her Master of the Horse. He was accused of more than sedition; he was also accused of 'too great an intimacy with the queen'. This smear recalled the fate of Anne Boleyn and Katherine Howard, both executed for adultery. The others, Percy and Carnarvon, were members of Henrietta Maria's inner circle. All at once disappeared, either across the Channel or to safe houses in England, which was tantamount to admitting guilt.[10]

There was more. Charles I attempted and failed to reinforce the Tower of London, where Strafford was held, with loyal soldiers. Sir William Balfour (a Scot), the Lieutenant of the Tower, refused to accept them, or to hand the key to the munitions store to the king's officers. Sir William also refused the enormous bribe of £20,000 that Strafford offered, to allow him to escape. The actions by the king and Strafford were clearly concerted; in short, it was evident that Charles was ready to use force to save Strafford. The details came out later in public but were known earlier within the inner parliamentary circle.[11]

*

As for the 'Army Plot' itself, the embarrassing truth was that both king and queen knew about it before Strafford's trial began. It had two very different strands. The Earl of Northumberland's brother Harry Percy formed a plan which was both legal and constitutional, whereby army officers would sign a petition showing their support for the king in return for a peaceful settlement of the politics and of their arrears.

Henrietta Maria's Master of Horse Henry Jermyn, with the fervent support of the poet Suckling, proposed something illegal and much harder to deliver, hare-brained in fact, exactly the kind of project that was feared: an armed assault on Parliament coordinated between the army in the north and the garrison of Portsmouth (under its governor George Goring), where foreign troops might also land.

Percy discussed his project with Charles I, while Jermyn talked to Henrietta Maria. The two groups were brought together, but unhappily so. The Percy plan failed when it became evident that there was little support from army officers to sign his petition. The Jermyn plan remained on the table, but its dangerous – treasonous? – ambitions were elusive if army officers were not even prepared to sign a petition.

Goring decided, probably in April 1641, that too many people were involved. There would be a leak. He protected his position by moving first, telling his friend the Earl of Newport. Newport passed the information to his fellow peer Bedford and also to Pym, who did nothing about it until the beginning of May (at which time Bedford fell seriously ill). Historians have taken the view that Pym stage-managed revelations of the plot in May to influence the Lords' vote on Strafford.

*

The impact of Lenthall's statements, and of the flight of the officers, was certainly dramatic. Like a firework display, rumours exploded across London of French invasion, of an attack on the House of Commons, of the king selling Portsmouth to Louis XIII. Crowds gathered.

On the same day that the House of Lords voted on the Strafford attainder, a London mob advanced on Whitehall Palace 'to secure the royal persons'. Who was behind this freakish idea? Perhaps nobody. There were earlier stories about the king joining the troops at York and the queen taking refuge in Portsmouth, stories that seemed to validate every hysterical rumour. Charles and Henrietta Maria panicked, and prepared to abandon London, but

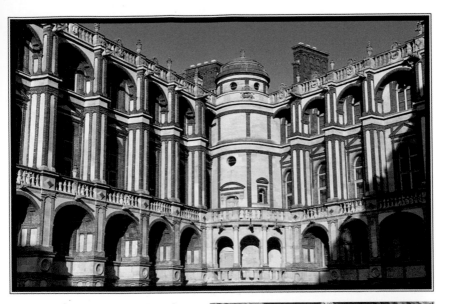

Above: 1. St. Germain-en-Laye, the fortress palace where Henrietta Maria lived as a child, in the royal nursery. (British Library)

Right: 2. The young Henrietta Maria. Engraving by Pieter Claesz Soutman. (Rijksmuseum)

3. The Louvre, the Paris home of the kings of France. Etching by Jacques Callot, 1629. (National Gallery of Art, Washington DC)

Left: 4. The parents of Henrietta Maria, with their eldest son Louis. Henri IV is shown as Mars, Marie de Médicis as Pallas Athene. Gilt bronze medal by Guillaume Dupré, 1603. (National Gallery of Art, Washington DC)

Right: 5. Charles I, when Prince of Wales. Miniature by Peter Oliver. (Yale Center for British Art)

Above: 6. Dover Castle, where Henrietta Maria spent her first night on English soil. (Author's collection)

Right: 7. George Villiers, 1st Duke of Buckingham, famous for his beauty. (Private collection)

8. The Fyndon Gate, St Augustine's, Canterbury. Henrietta Maria's wedding night was spent in the state bedroom above the entrance. (Author's collection)

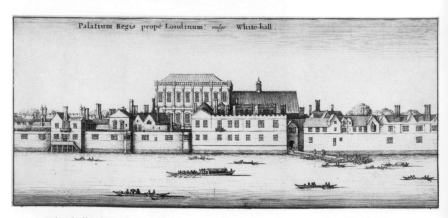

Palatium Regis propè Londinum: *vulgo* White-hall.

9. Whitehall Palace, the royal headquarters in London. Engraving after Wenceslaus Hollar. (Yale Center for British Art)

10. The Queen's Chapel, St James's Palace. One of Henrietta Maria's Catholic chapels in London, designed by Inigo Jones. (Author's collection)

11. The Queen's House, Greenwich. Another Inigo Jones building, begun for Anna of Denmark and completed on Henrietta Maria's instructions in 1635. A number of changes were made under Charles II and in the nineteenth century, including the addition of flanking colonnades. (British Library)

12. Henrietta Maria and Charles I. Engraving by Robert van Voerst, 1634. (Rijksmuseum)

13. Henrietta Maria felt happiest at St James's Palace, when she gave birth. In 1638 the palace was placed at the disposal of her mother, Marie de Médicis. (Author's collection)

14. The Princess Royal Mary, with her husband William of Orange. Gerard van Honthorst, 1647. (Rijksmuseum)

Left: 15. The Diana Fountain, commissioned by Charles I for his wife, and originally placed in the garden at Somerset House. The statue is by the Huguenot Hubert le Sueur. The fountain is now in Bushy Park. (Author's collection)

Below: 16. Stadholder Frederick Henry, who helped Henrietta Maria raise money and arms for Charles I in 1642–3. Dish, 1654. (Rijksmuseum)

17. Henrietta Maria with her adored Jeffrey Hudson. Next to him she seems rather tall. Anthony van Dyck, 1633. (National Gallery of Art, Washington DC)

Left: 18. Charles
I – poised and
withdrawn. Daniel
Mytens. (Private
collection)

Below: 19. Marie
de Médicis visits
Amsterdam in
September 1638.
Engraving by
Salomon Savery.
(Rijksmuseum)

· TRIUMF POORT AAN DE VERKENS SLUYS ·

Above: 20. Greyfriars Kirkyard, Edinburgh, where the National Covenant was first signed on 28 February 1638. (British Library)

Right: 21. Marie de Médicis at the time of her move to England. Engraving by Salomon Savery, 1638. (Rijksmuseum)

Sic ivit noſtram grandis MEDICEA per Vrbem.
Sceptrorum Mater ſuſpicienda trium.

22. Charles I, at St Margaret's Westminster. (Author's collection)

23. Merton College, Oxford, where Henrietta Maria lived in 1643–4, and where she became pregnant with her last child, Henriette Anne. (Author's collection)

AFBEELDING van de VISITE van Haare MAJESTEYT van GROOT BRITTANIE HENRIETTA MARIA, met haare Neef PRINS WILLEM van NASSAU,
Gegeven aan den HEERE ADRIANUS PAAUW, Heere van HEEMSTEDE-OP 'T SLOT te HEEMSTEDE den agtsten September 1644.

24. In Holland in 1642, Henrietta Maria makes a visit. Anonymous engraving.
(Rijksmuseum)

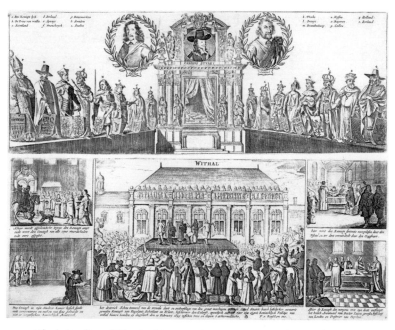

25. The beheading of Charles I in 1649. Anonymous engraving. (Rijksmuseum)

26. Oliver Cromwell closes down the Rump Parliament in 1653. Anonymous engraving. (Rijksmuseum)

27. Henrietta Maria as a widow. Miniature by David des Granges. (Yale Center for British Art)

28. Despite the defeat of the royalist cause in the civil wars, Charles II was restored as king in 1660. Silver medal by John Rhoettiers. (National Gallery of Art, Washington DC)

Ciahou aen de landtsi buyten Parijs.

5

29. A view of Chaillot, where Henrietta Maria set up a convent of the Order of the Visitation, and where she wanted to retire. Engraving by Rainer Nooms. (Rijksmuseum)

FOUNDED 1634

MARYLAND

WELCOMES YOU

ENJOY YOUR VISIT!

IT'S THE LAW
IN OUR STATE

30. Maryland in the United States was named after Henrietta Maria, and founded as a place of religious tolerance. (British Library)

were persuaded to stay by the French minister (this news alone caused the Londoners to disperse).[12]

The queen's friend Lucy, Countess of Carlisle, was summoned before a committee of Parliament to explain what she knew of the Army Plot. Lucy was the sister of Harry Percy and famously political, but it was extraordinary for a woman to be questioned in this way. Whether or not she was in the picture – she probably was – her experience before the Commons led Lucy to another important act eight months later.[13]

On the orders of Parliament, the queen's court was searched and her correspondence read, so that Henrietta Maria asked the Venetian ambassador to send at least one letter concealed in his despatches, which were not read (he did). Her carelessness in failing to check Jermyn and Suckling was repaid with humiliation. Her mother asked for a special guard against the London crowds at St James's Palace, which she received, but Parliament made it clear that Marie de Médicis would have to leave England.[14]

*

It was in these terrifying circumstances that the words of Charles I came back to haunt him. With the Lords vote against Strafford, he must decide whether to follow or deny his conscience. After all, would he sign the Act of Attainder into law and therefore kill his loyal minister?

The king consulted the judges and five senior bishops. Was it legal, was it moral to sign such a Bill? Bishop Williams of Lincoln produced an answer worthy of the detested Jesuits, that a king had both a private and a public person, and that public morality differed from private morality. The king's responsibility to his people was a duty superseding personal conscience. Failure to sign would have consequences for all the English, which could not be predicted but which must be violent. Experiencing an intense personal crisis, Charles I accepted the bishop's impressive, if doubtful, distinctions and signed the Bill of Attainder into law in the evening of Sunday 9 May.

Of all the actions of the king's life, it is this that most vividly illustrates the ringing phrase of his advisor Edward Hyde, 'that fathomless abyss of reason of state'. His abandonment of Strafford haunted Charles I for the rest of his life.[15]

In no condition to protest, the king also signed an emergency Bill which Pym rushed through, which prevented the current parliament from being dissolved without its own consent. This made the so-called Long Parliament a historical institution which would later – inadvertently – show up the hypocrisies of the age.

The third great event of that extraordinary day, 9 May 1641, was the death of Francis, Earl of Bedford, of smallpox. The House of Commons adjourned all its committees so that its Members could attend Bedford's funeral at Chenies, the only time under the Stuarts that Parliament showed such respect to any Member of Parliament. Bedford was a dreadful loss. He was the conciliator, working for a settlement within the inherited political system. His advice to Charles I might have changed the king's speech to Parliament and the Lords' vote. However, even Bedford must have struggled to persuade the Commons to drop their tight collaboration with the Scots – and the Scots were bent on the death of Strafford, to preserve their independence.[16]

*

On 10 May, Charles I's consent to the Bill of Attainder was given to Parliament. He declared his loyal servant Strafford a traitor. On 11 May, the king sent his son the Prince of Wales (aged ten) to the House of Lords to make a plea for the earl to be punished by 'close imprisonment' rather than execution, but this was ignored.

On 12 May 1641, Strafford was executed on Tower Hill. It was normal for the condemned man to make a speech just before he died, and this Strafford did with composure. 'I am at the door going out, and my next step must be from time to eternity ... I do solemnly protest before God I am not guilty of that great crime laid to my charge.' He then waved aside the cloth that was offered to cover his eyes.[17]

Henrietta Maria did not share the king's guilt over Strafford. She did not advise him to sign the Bill. Everything we know about her suggests she must have been opposed, since her strongest instinct was to protect loyal servants. However, she could not be free of the consequences of Strafford's execution at a time when Bedford's wisdom and sense of restraint were also lost.

PART FIVE

CIVIL WARS

Sadness was not made for beasts but for men, but if men feel too
much sadness they turn into beasts.

Cervantes, *Don Quixote*

29

POURING RAIN

In 1641, Sir Theodore Mayerne was a white-bearded physician of sixty-seven, still running his practice from St Martin's Lane, where his house was frequented by his favoured companions, immigrant artisans. A man of the intellectual and professional elite, Sir Theodore was born a Huguenot in Geneva, godson to Calvin's successor, Theodore Beza. On 14 July the doctor addressed a committee of the House of Commons on the queen's health. Despite her Catholicism and his Protestantism, he had been her trusted personal physician since she arrived in England in 1625. He told the gentlemen of the committee, 'The queen is sick in body and minde and shee thinks she cannot recover.'[1]

Mayerne had been asked for an opinion on Henrietta Maria's plan to visit Spa in Flanders to take medicinal waters. It was her second attempt to get out of England on health grounds. 'He says she is dangerously ill, both in minde and body.' Mayerne considered that Spa water was potent, and should not be taken by anyone who had sunk beneath a certain level of physical resilience. Henrietta Maria, he advised, was too weak to go to Spa.[2]

Sir Theodore had examined his patient and listed, in his private notes, no less than twenty-three symptoms, or conditions. They included '*hypochondriaca affectio*'. He noted that Henrietta Maria had a naturally melancholic temperament. This was a medical opinion about the preponderant 'humour' in her metabolism, however it was consistent with Panzani's remarks about her need for silence and prayer, and confirms that her gutsy high spirits were sometimes a front. As well as a congenital condition, scoliosis of the spine, the queen had suffered severe weight loss, plus kidney stones, a repetitive cough, headaches and cold sores. She could not bear to put anything on her head because it felt so hot. She could not sleep, so he was doping her with syrup of poppies. In short, the queen's health had collapsed.[3]

At the beginning of June, Prince William and his men returned to The Hague without taking Mary (by agreement). At the same time Marie de Médicis left England, sailing to Dunkirk on her way to Cologne, and from there she would go to Florence. Henrietta Maria lost the company of her mother and would soon lose that of her daughter, since the Prince of Orange was pressing to have his daughter-in-law with him in The Hague as soon as possible.[4]

At first Henrietta Maria did not even tell her sister Christine that the marriage had taken place. It was only on 8 August 1641 that she wrote to her sister, saying, 'I am sorry not to have told you about my daughter's marriage with the Prince of Orange [William]. I hope that marriage will be helpful to us, and although he will not be a king, I have no doubt she can be just as happy, because I know well that it is not kingdoms that bring happiness.' What was behind the queen's reticence? She could not be entirely comfortable with a marriage which was guaranteed to keep Mary Protestant, but really it was just the pace of events, one thing on top of another.[5]

The queen was stunned by the preliminary report of the committee on the Army Plot, made on 8 June, which accused Henrietta Maria as its mastermind and also as the tactician behind the plan to release Strafford from the Tower. This was a further public attack on a woman who was accustomed to official protection. Many people believed the report was slanted, but the queen was incapable of hiding her misery. 'The queen is tortured by cruel distress and even her spirited nature has not been able to prevent her eyes from performing their tender office.' It was also revealed publicly that the plot was betrayed by her friend George Goring, a further shock (it did not turn her against George).[6]

Henrietta Maria's resulting plan to take Mary to the Prince of Orange in The Hague, then go to Spa for the waters, was questioned by Parliament because they thought it was all cover, and she wanted to raise money for her husband abroad. The consultation with Mayerne supplied an honourable reason to report that the cost of the trip could not be justified, another blow, which the queen accepted with a telling message to the committee.

'I hope you believe I have so much interest in the good of this kingdom that I shall never wish any thing to the prejudice of it,' wrote Henrietta Maria, followed by the astonishing rider, 'You will pardon the imperfectness of my English; I had rather spoke in any other language, but I thought this would be most acceptable.' Not only does this show how, sixteen years after her first night at Dover, the queen was still far happier in French than in English, it also shows innocence, since the gentlemen of Parliament would hardly enjoy being told she would have preferred any other language than English. However, it was not her nature to hold things back.[7]

*

Not that the Queen of England was entirely open with the gentlemen of Parliament. Her true sentiments were communicated to Christine at this time. 'I swear to you that I am almost crazy with the sudden change in my fortune, because from the highest degree of happiness, I have fallen into unimaginable misery of all sorts.'[8]

Following Henrietta Maria through these months is like trailing through a gloomy labyrinth lit by distant flashes of lightning, filled with dead-ends and surprise turns, stuck between the entrance – or exit – and the unreachable holy grail of the sanctuary at the centre. With Strafford dead, Laud in prison, Finch and Windebank in exile, the army hotheads in hiding or exile, the bishops under attack and the queen prevented from travelling, it seemed Charles and Henrietta Maria had nothing to hold on to. But there was something: Scotland.

Peace was, after all, agreed with the Scots. It sealed the failure of the prayer book crusade, but the failure was obvious and Charles I accepted the terms, everything, taking back every statement he had made against the Covenanters, making no protest against joint consultations – yet to occur – between the foreign invaders and the

English Parliament, to supervise changes in the Church of England (so that it would mirror the Kirk).

In the post of Governor of the Prince of Wales, he replaced the cavalier Earl of Newcastle, discredited by association with the Army Plot, with the Earl of Hertford, who was brother-in-law of Essex. He allowed the queen's confessor, Fr Philip, to be questioned about the Army Plot, and agreed that Carlo Rosetti, the tenacious papal envoy to Henrietta Maria, should leave England. Then he announced that he would visit Scotland, as its king, since there were appointments to be made, and so that he could address Scottish Parliament.[9]

A beam of golden sunlight shone through the thick cloud cover. It was suddenly apparent that the reformed Charles I was perfectly positioned to build support in Scotland, where there was a great attachment to the Stuarts, provided they fitted in. In fact his plans very quickly included asking Scottish Parliament to raise funds for an army for the Calvinist cause of his nephew the Elector Palatine, which would reclaim Protestant credibility and provide an army.[10]

On 10 August 1641, Charles I went to Westminster Hall to sign a group of Bills into law and was surrounded by several hundred petitioners begging him to stay in England. These were not spontaneous demonstrations, but Charles I had regained his confidence. He told the people he was pleased to be so much desired in both his kingdoms and disappeared into Westminster Hall. The next day, in the company of his Palatine nephew, he set off north.[11]

To the king's delight, Pym's Anglo-Scottish alliance was creaking at the seams. The Scots commissioners in London were in a position to witness first-hand the attempt by the Lord Mayor, with the support of his aldermen, to prevent payment of the indemnity to the Scottish army, an attempt astonishingly supported by the Commons (but blocked by the Lords). The Commons proposed Ten Propositions which aimed to purge Henrietta Maria's court of Catholics, and to control the king's advisers and disband the army, but Charles I was feeling more confident.[12]

*

It was a hot, dry summer. There was an outbreak of plague in London. Henrietta Maria was not allowed to go with her husband to Scotland, as she asked. She complained to Christine that she was held in the south 'like a prisoner'. While Charles was in Scotland, the queen had a succession of nightmare experiences over the next three months as, with the help of his secretary Edward Nicholas, who risked staying at his post in Westminster, she tried to build royalist support by writing to friendly peers.[13]

With the children she went to Oatlands, only to receive a demand from Parliament that the children stay in the custody of parliamentary officials. The queen did not return her family to London, but did send them away from Oatlands, probably to Richmond (fifteen miles away).

One evening, a neighbouring gentleman came to the palace to warn Henrietta Maria that he had received instructions from Parliament to summon and arm a group of his tenants, and to be ready with them on the edge of Oatlands Park at midnight, where he would receive more instructions. Henrietta Maria sent to her friends in London to ask for help, and armed every one of her household with whatever came to hand, ready for action. She walked up and down outside the house in the dark, but nothing happened, although twenty or so men were seen, poorly mounted, riding in the park during the night.

The queen organised relays of horses on the road to Portsmouth in case a sudden flight was necessary and briefed George Goring, still commander of the Portsmouth garrison. She asked the Earl of Denbigh to send a guard of a hundred gentlemen to be with her at all times. She moved to Hampton Court (closer to the children), then returned to Oatlands.[14]

The threat against her, and against the Prince of Wales, was repeated when the Earl of Newport said they should be taken hostage for the good behaviour of Charles I, until the king returned. Henrietta Maria seems to have brought the children back to Oatlands, then sent the boys to Richmond to appease Parliament, which instructed their new governor, Hertford, not to allow them to visit their mother. These instructions were harsher than anything yet attempted, but there was news from Ireland.[15]

*

Because of the plague, the House of Commons was thinly attended on 1 November 1641, when Members received a visit from the lords of the Privy Council, headed by the Lord Keeper Littleton. The king's men came to warn the Commons of 'a great Treason, and general Rebellion, of the Irish Papists in Ireland'.[16]

A rebellion had indeed broken out. Under the leadership of the O'Neill family, the Irish of Ulster were attacking English settlements, taking prisoners and killing those who resisted. The attacks quickly spread to Munster in the south, so that the royal government of Ireland, no longer under the iron will of Strafford, found itself facing a coordinated revolt throughout the country. The recently (and only partly) disbanded army of Strafford mainly joined the rebels.

Adding to the shock, Sir Phelim O'Neill shone a brilliant light on the position of Charles I, when he jubilantly told his men (and his prisoners) that he was acting as a loyal subject of the king. It was the king, he said, who ordered the rebellion. Sir Phelim produced a commission under the king's Great Seal, copies of which were distributed all over Ireland.

Phelim's commission was an obvious forgery. If Charles I had commissioned the rebellion, he would not have made it an official instruction with his Great Seal. The king reacted calmly and correctly to the news of the Irish rebellion as it first reached him when he 'was playing his customery round of golf on the links at Leith'. He ordered it to be reported at once to Scottish Parliament. The rebellion was truly a rebellion against his authority, as was widely understood.[17]

Even so, there was subliminal damage from Phelim's claim of loyalty to Charles I. The English people's deep fear of Irish troops came back – they really were now killing Protestants – and the royalist connection with them. On parliamentary orders, all foreign mail was opened and read. The queen's confessor, Fr Philip, was summoned for questioning by Parliament, then imprisoned when he refused to swear an oath on a Protestant bible. Catholicism was back in the frame.[18]

*

On 25 November 1641, back from Scotland, Charles I made a formal entry into London. With Charles, Prince of Wales, at his side, and Henrietta Maria following in a coach, the king rode through streets filled with crowds who shouted, 'God save the king!' The royal family, with attendants, were treated to a feast at the Guildhall, where the king promised to do everything in his power to support the City of London. He made the mayor a baronet, and he knighted the aldermen. The king was returning to his capital to protect his people. Charles I had turned the corner.[19]

As far as anyone in England could see, he had left Scotland at peace, having appointed a number of his former opponents to the Scottish council, and now here he was welcomed, applauded, generous in London. The resurrected Charles hoped the Irish rebellion would open the hearts of the people to the king, and he had made up his mind that he was strong enough to face down his enemies in Parliament. Was he? The events which followed show the difference between forming a plan – including forming a good plan – and carrying it out.[20]

There was plenty to face down. While Charles was away, Pym had been busy with attacks on the episcopate and on the king's rights to control the army – alarmingly highlighted by Ireland – and was drawing up a 'Grand Remonstrance', which listed the complaints of the people against the king throughout his reign, a list that would justify everything that Pym and his supporters had achieved over the previous fifteen months.

Rain poured down across the south of England through December 1642, and the storms at sea prevented the arrival of foreign mail. In these wet, cold, isolated weeks Charles and Henrietta Maria redoubled their attempts to persuade royalist members both of the Commons and Lords to attend debates, while on 1 December 1641 the king coolly accepted the devastating Remonstrance, with its 204 separate grievances, its revolutionary demands that bishops should be expelled from Parliament and that Parliament should have a veto on all Crown appointments. He merely said that he would consider these requests (a reply was later made which did not accept them). On 22 December, Charles I replaced William Balfour as Lieutenant of the Tower with the thuggish royalist Col Thomas Lunsford, and on 24 December he dismissed the Earl of Newport from his position as Constable of the Tower, taking custody of it himself.[21]

The fickle Londoners took to the streets to rail against Lunsford, bishops, Catholics and the king's show of power. Charles I dismissed Lunsford, replacing him with Sir John Byron, but did not back down. Crowds invaded Westminster Hall – the unpopular Lunsford was one of the officers who fought them off – and appeared outside Whitehall Palace, but were driven off by armed courtiers and troops from the north. The crowd invaded Westminster Abbey and attacked the high altar and the royal tombs. A guardhouse was built outside the Whitehall gatehouse in Scotland Yard to keep the city apprentices at bay, and more gentlemen registered as members of the royal militia.[22]

The counter-attack continued from the lords of religion. Eleven bishops, led by John Williams, Archbishop of York, petitioned the king and the House of Lords against all legislation passed during the king's absence, proposing that it was void. They were at once accused of treason by the Commons, who said they were 'endeavouring to subvert the being of Parliament'. Williams and his followers were arrested.[23]

The Commons then asked the king for a bodyguard. It was a curious request if one considers the Commons was arguing that the king should not control any troops at all, yet the Commons really did feel under threat and really did want its own guard, and asking the king was the legally correct way. It was also a test. Would the king support his Parliament by sending troops? Charles I gave an unclear, delaying answer.

*

On 1 January 1642 a committee of the House of Commons met, not at Westminster but at the Guildhall, a mile and a half away, in the City of London, where the Members could rely on the City apprentices for protection. The Members who attended staged their own propaganda coup by riding through the streets fully armed, implying that the Commons was in danger of attack. Their discussion was therefore very publicly advertised and, although what was said was neither witnessed nor recorded, the outcome was clear.

The committee – perhaps it was not really tantamount to the House of Commons itself, but in the heat of the moment that was how it seemed – decided that the king's evil counsellors had to be tackled in the most decisive way possible. They would accuse the queen of treason.[24]

30

THE WALLS AND SINEWS OF THE PARLIAMENT

The queen was innocent of treason. She had not conspired with the Irish rebels. Her hostility to the Pym faction could not be considered sedition, unless you belonged to the Pym faction (many Members of the Commons and Lords did not). She had definitely – most constitutionally – encouraged peers to attend sessions of the House of Lords; she had discussed, perhaps with Pym himself, almost certainly with the late Earl of Bedford and other peers, a compromise solution to the worries of Parliament; she had possibly offered naked bribes, but a bribe was not treason. It was not Henrietta Maria who conspired with an invading foreign army to force the King of England to his knees. It was not Henrietta Maria who subverted the ancient English constitution by stripping Charles I of the royal power divinely conferred on him.

The charges against her were the opposite of the truth, except in one respect, and that was her support for, or interest in, Harry Jermyn's part of the Army Plot. The merits of this were arguable. Interest was not treason. Was support treason? What kind of support? The queen could say that defence of the king against a faction was the highest patriotism, and many Englishmen – many lawyers – would agree. However, objective guilt was neither here nor there. In the equations of power, neither truth nor justice appeared. Charles I had to defend his 'dear heart'.

On 3 January 1642, the Serjeant at Arms was admitted to the House of Commons and called to the Bar, where he stood without holding the mace which showed his office (it was potentially a weapon), and here he spoke.

> I am commanded by the King's Majesty, my Master, upon my Allegiance, that I should come and repair to the House of Commons, where Mr. Speaker is; and there to require of Mr. Speaker Five Gentlemen, Members of the House of Commons; and, that these Gentlemen being delivered, I am commanded to arrest them, in his Majesty's Name, of High Treason. Their Names are, Mr Hollis, Sir Arthur Haselrig, Mr Pym, Mr Hampden, Mr William Strode.

On the same day, Lord Keeper Littleton gave a similar message to the Lords about Lord Mandeville, who heard the news 'with a great deal of Chearfulness'.

The news of the king's accusations against six Members of a sitting parliament caused crowds to gather for a time in the City. The Londoners were in fact frightened.[1]

So the Commons proposed a charge of treason against the queen, and the king counter-attacked by actually making charges of treason against Pym and colleagues. They could not both be right. The king accused the 'five Members' on seven articles, including 'that they have traiterously invited and encouraged a Foreign Power to invade His Majesty's Kingdom of England', and that they 'Raised and Countenanced Tumults against the King and Parliament'.[2]

On the face of things, the king would find it easier to support his charges with evidence, after months in Scotland where he had found more evidence of collusion between the English Parliament and the Scots. However, Parliament, like Lord Mandeville, was hard to unsettle. The five Members of the Commons and one Member of the Lords were not delivered to royal custody.[3]

Instead, both houses continued their joint campaign for an armed guard of Parliament and argued that the troops around Whitehall Palace should be dispersed. They voted for the disbanding of the queen's Capuchins, and voted for every servant of the king and queen, and their children, to take the Oaths of Supremacy and Allegiance, something Catholics could not do. A party of men burst into Somerset House while Henrietta Maria was in the chapel at prayer, threatening 'to kill everybody; but this I confess did not greatly frighten me', the queen later told Mamie St George.[4]

*

Both houses appointed committees to look into the king's accusations, including precedents – was it legal for the sovereign to accuse Members of a sitting parliament of treason? – while the Commons instructed the five Members to attend every day. As for Lord Mandeville, he did not mind what was threatened, and was in no way bound or instructed.[5]

The Commons stated its case in poetic words.

> That the House of Commons apprehend the Parliament to be the Great Council and the Representative Body of the Kingdom; and both Houses are but as One Body of the Realm: The Privileges are as the Walls and Sinews of the Parliament; which being cut, Destruction will speedily follow.[6]

The privileges were the rights of Members of Parliament, the protection of their persons and property. Charles I understood the force of these words but his royal honour had been degraded to nothing for fifteen months by these self-aggrandising subjects, whose pursuit of his wife was coming to its terrible climax. Did such people have any rights at all?

Already he had sent Sir William Killigrew and Sir William Flemming to seal the studies and the trunks of the five (with Mandeville, six) Members, so that they could be searched for evidence, but this only gave Parliament the chance to accuse him of assaulting their privileges.

Instead of delivering up the men – nobody wasted time reminding the Commons that Strafford had *at once* been taken into custody, Laud too, when accused of treason – Parliament ordered the arrest of Killigrew and Flemming, men guilty of nothing more than obeying orders. Parliament could make arrests, could challenge legally binding international treaties – the Catholic provisions of Henrietta Maria's marriage treaty – but its Members could not be touched.[7]

The events of Tuesday 4 January are famous in English history. After the midday dinner which he ate with Henrietta Maria, the king set off that Tuesday from Whitehall Palace for the House of Commons, in the nearest coach he found in the courtyard outside – that of a 'private individual' – with his nephew at his side, the Elector Palatine. They were protected by a large body, maybe four hundred armed men – the king's guardsmen, his courtiers, officers from the recently disbanded army of the north, some of the queen's gentlemen.[8]

Henrietta Maria stayed at Whitehall, where she prayed for success. After his rushed start Charles I found himself blocked. A number of petitioners stood in his way, taking advantage of their king's sudden appearance to plead their various causes. Instead of driving on through, Charles I stopped and listened. The royal cavalcade was visible to everyone in in the vicinity. There was plenty of time for the news of his impromptu visit to reach Parliament.

When he arrived at Westminster, about half-past three in the afternoon, the king committed constitutional sacrilege by walking into the chamber of the House of Commons. He left his armed escort outside, bringing only Charles Louis with him, but hundreds of his men were nearby, pistols and swords at the ready, primed for action.[9]

It was precisely this that Parliament feared, an armed attempt by the king. Parliament as an institution existed as an instrument of peace, a body representing the nation, so that king and nation could talk, not fight. The sovereign could summon and dissolve Parliament, but he could not attack Parliament with his soldiers and consider himself to be acting constitutionally, or legally.

Charles I, characteristically, had come with an exact and narrow plan. He wanted to make a personal arrest of the five Members of the Commons, Pym, Hampden and the others, whom the House had refused to give up. Unfortunately, before the arrival of Charles I they left. William Strode had to be pulled out physically, so keen was he to stand his ground, but there was, when the king arrived, nobody to arrest.[10]

The king bowed to the Members as he walked in, they bowed back. He took his hat off, they took theirs off. To the Speaker of the Commons, William Lenthall, he said, 'Mr Speaker, I must for a time make bold with your chair.' He asked where the five Members were. With great deference, Lenthall asked the king's pardon, and said that he (Lenthall) could not speak unless directed to speak by the House. The house was silent, from shock, from caution, and, procedurally, because the Speaker was not sitting in his chair. The king made a speech, assuring the remaining members than he would make his arrests in time, and promised he would do nothing to harm the privileges of Parliament. With his nephew, he then walked out, returned to the coach and to Whitehall.[11]

What the Commons had just witnessed with bated breath – they could have been massacred – was a king who threatened violence but went no further, because he was determined to stay within legal bounds. He did not want to be a tyrant. His men stood near the open door of the house, disarming the attendants of some Members, and saying, among other angry things, 'A pox take the House of Commons, let them come and be hanged.' But the king retreated without doing anything worse.[12]

The fatal flaw of Charles I – tactically – was his commitment to legality. He thought the law allowed him to arrest sitting Members of Parliament, if he had made a formal accusation against them, and therefore when he went to the Commons he was only prepared for success.[13]

*

For the rest of her life, Henrietta Maria thought this appalling flop her fault. There is a story that she hectored her husband, as he wondered whether to go to the Commons in the first place, forcing him into decisive action by crying, 'Go you coward!' Although we see from her letters how forthright she could be with her husband, it is improbable that she accused him of cowardice (and especially not in front of anyone else). She certainly thought the plan was a watertight secret, until, some time after he had left Whitehall, she exclaimed to Lucy Carlisle, 'Rejoice! By now I expect the king is master of his realm', adding that the five Members would have been arrested and on their way to prison.[14]

Why did she blurt it out? The queen knew that Lucy, cousin of the parliamentarian Earl of Essex, sister of the wavering Earl of Northumberland, had parliamentary friends. Henrietta Maria must have felt safe to tell the secret, not realising how the king was delayed. Although the queen and countess were old friends, there is the hint of a competitive edge. Both Lucy and the queen inspired the poets, but Lucy's admirers cannot be described as platonic. John Suckling, the man involved in the Army Plot, was lyrically frank about his feeling for the beautiful Countess of Carlisle when he wrote,

I was undoing all she wore
And had she walked but one turn more,
Eve in her first state had not been
More naked or more plainly seen[15]

These were not compliments one could pay to the queen. Perhaps it did not help that Lucy was ten years older than Henrietta Maria.

At any rate, Lucy slipped out and sent a note to the Commons to warn … whom exactly? The gossip was that she sent the note to Pym, but it was probably to her cousin Essex in the Lords. Like her friend Marie de Chevreuse, Lucy lived and breathed politics and knew the players. To frequent the royal court and at the same time support her friends in Parliament was part of the analogue flow of aristocratic existence for Lucy, it was no conflict of loyalties. After her questioning by Parliament over the Army Plot, she also surely thought she must show that she was not their enemy.[16]

Lucy's alarm call was not the only one. Captain Hercule Langres, a French officer, was told by the French ambassador to run to the Commons and tell the five Members that the king was coming to take them into custody. Langres actually had to push his way through the royal troops as they marched to Westminster, but he made it before they did.[17]

As well as these two known personal warnings sent to the Commons, Whitehall Palace was flashing red lights all day long, buzzing with a 'multitude of gentry and soldiers who flock to the court' so that the citizens of London were afraid. Something was obviously coming, and there were certainly spies watching the palace gates. Probably the petitioners were deliberately stationed to delay the king. It was not Henrietta Maria's fault that the five Members escaped, and nor did the king blame her when she told him about the unreliable Countess of Carlisle.[18]

*

Six days later, on 10 January 1642, the king and queen left London for Hampton Court, with their three eldest children, the Elector

Palatine and a small retinue. Essex and Holland, parliamentary moderates, made desperate attempts to find someone to talk Charles and Henrietta Maria into remaining at Whitehall, as did Lucy Carlisle. They realised how defiant the flight of the king and queen would seem. However, the reason Charles and his wife decided to leave so quickly was that they thought that within a day or two, if they stayed at Whitehall, the queen would be arrested.[19]

They left Elizabeth (five) and Henry (eighteen months) behind at St James's, perhaps because of the rush, but also because the king thought he was in a position to come to agreement with Parliament. He had tried to smooth the waters with a friendly visit on 5 January to the City, where he addressed the Lord Mayor and aldermen, but it achieved nothing. The king had to put up with more shouts of 'parliamentary privilege', as well as the insult of men refusing to take their hats off in his presence. Hiding in the City, the five Members were not betrayed.[20]

On Saturday 8 January, Pym and the others appeared to join another large committee meeting of the Commons in the Guildhall, where it was resolved that anyone arresting a Member of the Commons or Lords with that house's consent would be declared a public enemy. Londoners in their thousands rallied to defend the City and Parliament from the royal assault they thought was coming. Henrietta Maria received a message to say the Commons was about to launch her impeachment.[21]

*

It did not strike the queen she might lose her head as a traitor, but she did think she could be imprisoned. She had already come to the view that the king would have to fight for his crown. The Elector Palatine urged his uncle to find middle ground with Parliament but 'the queen would not hear of it'. The French ambassador offered to mediate with Parliament but 'the queen in particular has refused'. She told one of the Dutch envoys that 'everything was preparing for a rebellion' and that in the City people were declaiming the Old Testament text from the Book of Kings: 'To your tents, O Israel ...'[22]

In these weeks Henrietta Maria's actions helped secure civil war, but she was reacting to ferocious attacks on her husband and herself, and to an implicit threat to their children. She saw that Strafford's death had raised the stakes beyond the hopes of compromise for both sides.

The royal departure from London was decided to protect Henrietta Maria. Nothing was ready for the royal party. No beds had been sent to Hampton Court, so the entire family had to sleep together in one bed. They spent two nights at Hampton Court then continued to the more-or-less impregnable Windsor, a much bleaker fortress than it is today, crossing with difficulty the swollen Thames and its tributary streams, which were increased by floods to several times their normal size.[23]

Nearly a month passed, the queen spending several days exhausted in bed, during which ambassadors and courtiers travelled from London to Windsor and back again trying for normality. On 8 February, Sir Theodore Mayerne passed a crucial message to Baron Heenvliet, the Dutch envoy whom king and queen trusted. The physician said that the time had come for Henrietta Maria to take the waters of Spa – 'it is impossible that she can endure these difficulties and troubles' – and he added that he was sure Parliament would approve such a trip this time. It was therefore Mayerne who offered the queen a safe exit.[24]

While Charles and Henrietta Maria cast around for ideas, Parliament passed legislation depriving the bishops of their seats in the House of Lords. The king, to buy time, signed the Bill into law, losing votes in the Upper House. London celebrated with bonfires in the streets. The next piece of legislation deprived the sovereign of control of the militia, or trained bands, which went to the heart of the matter – as recent events showed – and on this the king delayed. Without the power to command troops, Charles I would hardly be king at all.[25]

In short, even with his temporising response on the Militia Ordinance, Parliament was winning ground. Pym and his colleagues now changed their view of the queen's position, deciding that it would be better to have her out of the country, to isolate Charles I. The arrest of the resolute Henrietta Maria would insult her brother Louis XIII, and England's other powerful neighbour on the Continent, the Stadholder Frederick Henry, who had made it plain that he wanted Princess Mary in his household. The Commons told the queen they had no idea why she thought they planned to impeach her, and she replied she must have been mistaken.[26]

On 9 February 1642, Charles and Henrietta Maria returned to Hampton Court, where the eleven-year-old Prince of Wales and eight-year-old Duke of York remained, so as to make it clear that nobody was trying to smuggle them out of the country. The king and queen went on to Greenwich with Mary, then to Canterbury and Dover. At Greenwich the Venetian ambassador, Giovanni Giustinian, came to pay his respects to Henrietta Maria before she left. She told him that 'to settle affairs it was necessary to unsettle them first'. The ambassador also noted how unhappy the court was at the queen's departure.[27]

At Dover ships were loaded with the queen's possessions, including some of the Crown Jewels – fetched from Westminster by Sir Edward Nicholas – six coaches and 120 horses. Henrietta Maria would travel in the *Lion*, and the others were the *Entrance*, the *Mary Rose*, the *Providence* and the *Grayhound*. The party was delayed by the weather until 25 February 1642. It was at this time, in Dover, that Charles told his wife that he would never come to an agreement with Parliament without her consent.[28]

Now ten, Mary was saying goodbye to her father forever. The queen and her daughter embarked, attended by a small number of people including the Duchess of Richmond, the Earl of Arundel, the Countess of Roxburghe, Fr Philip and Jeffrey Hudson.[29]

Although she was travelling almost like a private person, the queen was also escorted by fifteen Dutch warships sent by the Prince of Orange. Charles I rode along the shore, keeping the ships in sight while he could, before wheeling off to fight his battles. It was more than a romantic flourish.[30]

The marriage was rock solid and the parting was filled with pain.

31

GETTING HELP

I was ... surprised to discover that the queen, so beautiful on canvas,
was actually a short woman (despite the extra-high heels of her
Liège-style chopines) with long wizened arms, crooked shoulders,
and teeth protruding from her mouth like ravelins from a fortress.

In this way, Princess Sophie of the Rhine debunked the Henrietta
Maria myth when they met after the queen's landing at Brill.[1]

Elizabeth of Bohemia was despatched that early spring of 1642
from her borrowed palace in The Hague to greet her sister-in-law,
and took her youngest daughter as a friend for Mary. The eleven-
year-old Sophie saw a woman of thirty-one exhausted by the English
power struggle, then punished by a rough crossing of the Channel.
The more telling part of her memories was what happened next.[2]

Henrietta Maria told Sophie that she was rather like Mary, a
risky compliment, since girls of eleven seldom like comparison
with girls of nine. Miraculously, the remark changed Sophie's
mind entirely. She decided Henrietta Maria was truly beautiful:
'I found that she had very beautiful eyes, a well-formed nose, and
a lovely complexion.' Here we glimpse the ability of Henrietta
Maria to apply an irresistible charm.

*

The queen could not understand the difficulty her presence in the United Provinces caused her host, Frederick Henry of Orange. We see Frederick Henry today as painted by Gerard van Honthorst and others, usually wearing armour, round-faced, pigeon-chested, big blue eyes, thin lips, an almost Grecian nose, a mass of hair, moustache and beard elegantly trimmed. The Calvinist soldier-politician had survived his self-indulgent youth to enjoy a successful marriage, and in some ways he had common ground with the Queen of England, for instance in the splendour of his court and his artistic patronage, practised in partnership with his wife Amalia. But his hands were tied.

Frederick Henry's job was to defeat Spain and preserve Dutch liberties, not to give shelter to the sister of Spain's queen. He wanted his daughter-in-law Mary in Holland within his household, but he did not want her controversial mother, whose character he knew from Baron Heenvliet. The opposition of English Parliament to Henrietta Maria's trip suited the prince. When this opposition evaporated, however, Frederick Henry accepted that the queen would come with her daughter, and ordered an appropriately republican greeting committee, consisting of six deputies to represent the states of the republic. He sent his son and also went to meet her himself, supported by Elizabeth of Bohemia. He made sure the towns the queen passed through would celebrate their exotic guest, and that people would line the streets (which probably needed no prompting).[3]

Henrietta Maria went first to The Hague, where Frederick Henry lived in the Binnenhof complex, and where Mary would now be housed under Orange protection. However normal in the world of the time, it cannot have been an easy thing to hand over her child. Later the queen moved to Breda near the border with Flanders, and would also visit Amsterdam, the real centre of Dutch power – because of its trading wealth – and here she travelled on the canals in a barge drawn by swans.[4]

For a time Henrietta Maria was celebrated with swans and other entertainments, but she was an oddity in the Dutch Republic. Except for the refined members of the Orange court, the Dutch thought the Queen of England just another colourful foreigner. They would sit in her presence – unheard of – would keep their hats on their heads – worse – and sometimes they just stared at her without saying a word. Her Catholicism was an advertisement of the wrong sort. An English visitor said that he thought the queen out of place and noted that she was watched by agents of the Dutch state – and was not permitted to travel to Cologne to see her mother. He thought she would be back in England by Easter 1642. He was wrong. Actually, she stayed with the Dutch for nearly a year, because, once she had delivered Mary, her mission was to find help for Charles I.[5]

*

When the queen arrived at Brill it was a time of phoney civil war in England. Having seen Henrietta Maria off at Dover, the king refused to return to London, riding instead to Theobalds, then to Newmarket and ultimately to York, but neither he nor his opponents had raised their armies, so there was no formal breach. There were clashes nonetheless. Charles I wanted to occupy Hull for its large arsenal, but was defied by the military governor Sir John Hotham, this being the first time the king's authority was challenged in person. It was the failure to win Hull that made it important for Henrietta Maria to buy arms (as well as raising cash).

She succeeded. The jewels she brought to trade were not the main regalia – the crown, mace, orb and so forth, which were not permitted to leave Westminster Abbey. Still, there were massive pieces including several strings of pearls – two weighing in at eleven ounces, one at eight and a half ounces – plus two large necklaces of rubies and pearls and a jewel called the 'three sisters' consisting of three large rubies and two large pearls. It was easy to sell or pawn the smaller jewels, such as a beautiful string of pearls which were once the king's buttons, because they were clearly privately owned, but the larger pieces belonged to the English state, and Parliament published a declaration that they had been taken outside the country without authorisation, so the Dutch merchants were not confident in lending on their security.[6]

The merchants did well on the transactions, being professional traders. 'You may judge how, when they know we want money, they keep their foot on our throat,' she told her husband. She cast about for different markets, sending George Goring into the Spanish Netherlands, to Antwerp, to pawn the king's 'ruby collar' in June, and made enquiries in Denmark to see whether anyone would lend on the 'largest collar', but what applied in The Hague, Breda and Amsterdam applied in Antwerp and Copenhagen. Francis Windebank, John Finch and Harry Jermyn joined Henrietta Maria, also Harry Percy and Wat Montagu. She wrote to Charles to tell him how much these men did to help and certainly she did not act without advice; nonetheless, it was her shoulders that bore the weight.[7]

Frederick Henry complained about the cost of entertaining the Queen of England but gave money to the royalist cause. When the Dutch army failed to supply Henrietta Maria with the six promised cannon (four were provided) he made sure cash was found for two more. He advised the queen to send arms across the Channel anonymously, under the name of a merchant, and pay duty, instead of petitioning for freedom from the duty, which would publicise her efforts, so Parliament would hear. He allowed his name to be used to help with the sale and pawn of the jewellery, which was probably critical for the money that was raised.[8]

At the end of August 1642, Parliament sent Walter Strickland as ambassador to the States-General. Strickland at once demanded the seizure of the vessels which the queen was sending to England loaded with arms – if the Dutch really were neutrals, as they claimed – but Frederick Henry made sure that every such boat was arrested, which included two belonging to Parliament. The queen's was returned to her. The Prince of Orange also considered a stronger tie with the royal Stuarts when the queen suggested a second marriage, between Charles, Prince of Wales, and Frederick Henry's daughter.[9]

Frederick Henry did not stop there. He made a bid for peace in England by sending Dutch ambassadors to London to mediate between Charles and Parliament, a project that failed when Parliament suggested the queen herself might like to mediate. However unlikely this was, the idea was repeated by others, a dreamy return to the vanished Neoplatonic Henrietta Maria. However, the queen had her fun when the ambassadors came to take formal leave of her, and one kissed the hand of Jeffrey Hudson, thinking he was the Prince of Wales.[10]

*

Henrietta Maria did buy arms and did raise cash, and hired officers and also some skilled men, including at least one engineer (the Dutch were the most advanced engineers in Europe). These reinforcements made it across the North Sea in several shipments, one when princes Rupert and Maurice of the Rhine crossed to England in August 1642 to join their uncle, who was on the verge of declaring war on his Parliament. The navy, loyal to Parliament, watched shipping as best it could, and the North Sea was lashed by westerlies, so the Palatine princes had to turn back at least once. They finally arrived at Newcastle in the second half of the month, bringing money and arms, including gunpowder, for the king's armies.[11]

In October another shipment made it through, landing either at Newcastle or in the Humber River. The third transit was when the queen herself returned to England, in spring 1643, bringing supplies with her. Two more ships carrying arms arrived shortly after she did.[12]

Henrietta Maria sent other vessels which were intercepted by Parliament. In October one ship was captured, perhaps part of a larger consignment. To spread the word about the queen's disgraceful behaviour, a fake letter was published for general consumption in England. The letter was addressed to Charles, beginning, 'Most Royal and Illustrious Monarch of Great Britain, my great, my good and worthy liege' – when Henrietta Maria invariably addressed her husband as 'Dear Heart' – and exulted in the fact that the Crown Jewels were in pawn to 'some certaine Jews of Amsterdam' when the whole problem was that they were not.[13]

All in all, his wife's efforts made a material difference to Charles I. She probably raised enough cash to arm several thousand men, when the king had about 20,000 men under his command by the early autumn.[14] However, arms and money intercepted by Parliament armed hundreds of enemy troop, maybe more.

While she was in the United Provinces, the queen also tried to find diplomatic support for her husband. She made approaches to Denmark and France without success. She also did her best to obtain the release of English troops fighting in Germany, and those employed by other Continental rulers, so that they could return and fight for their king in England.[15]

*

On a field behind Nottingham Castle, Charles I raised his standard on Monday 22 August 1642. The flag featured his arms overlaid with a hand pointing to the crown above and the motto, 'Give Caesar his due.'

There were nearly three thousand troops, horse and foot, in attendance. A herald was instructed to read out the king's proclamation, which appealed to the people of England to support him in the struggle against the Earl of Essex, the man who was leading Parliament's troops. At this critical moment of history Charles I had second thoughts. The king took hold of the proclamation for a final check, and, 'seeming to dislike of some passages therein, called for Penne and Inke, and in his own hand crossed out and altered the same [the proclamation] in diverse places', with the result that the herald, when he was given the amended text, struggled to read it at all. On each of the following two days the same ceremony took place – the herald now knew the lines – and after this it was agreed that a state of civil war obtained in England.[16]

Not long after, on 23 October 1642, the first pitched battle of the war was fought at Edgehill in Warwickshire, with inconclusive results. The royalist cavalry under Prince Rupert showed guts and flair with a devastating charge on the right flank, but they were not disciplined. Rather than regrouping to attack the main army again, they chased the soldiers who broke before them, and galloped off to find Essex's baggage train. Otherwise the king might have destroyed much of the parliamentary army on the first encounter. The aftermath of Edgehill was an advance by Charles I on London, but he was blocked at Turnham Green, and retired to Oxford.

*

Throughout her time with the Dutch, Henrietta Maria and her husband wrote to each other. The letters were sometimes intercepted, although they were often (not invariably) written in a cypher which obscured meaning by replacing names, for instance, with a series of numbers. The correspondence did not always go smoothly. 'Be careful how you write in cypher, for I have been driven well nigh mad in deciphering your letter ... I remind you to take care of your pocket and not let our cipher be stolen, ' wrote Henrietta Maria in March 1641.

The queen did not mince words. Repeatedly she told her husband to be resolute: 'You have already learned to your cost that want of perseverance in your designs has ruined you'; 'That letter ... which you sent me concerning an accommodation [with Parliament], is so insupportable that I have burnt it with joy'; 'Lose no time, you have lost enough already'; 'Delays have always ruined you.'

Henrietta Maria was pressing on the need to take Hull. Sir John Hotham refused to allow the king into the city, even when the nine-year-old James, Duke of York, was sent to ask for admittance. The king did not have the resources for a siege. Henrietta Maria told Charles, 'I have wished myself in the place of James in Hull; I would have flung the rascal [Hotham] over the walls, or he should have done the same thing to me.'[17]

She would then apologise, explaining her zeal was for her husband's love: 'Pardon once again my folly and weakness; I confess it...'; 'I beg your pardon if I have said anything in my letters a little passionate; it is the affection I have for you, which makes me do it.'[18]

In the autumn of 1642, when she had been away for six months, Henrietta Maria wrote a remarkable passage, when she told her husband that she did not mind if anyone else read her words; her letter would never be published by Parliament because the royal cause was just.

> JUSTICE suffers with us. Always take care that we have her on our side: she is a good army, and one that will at last conquer all the world, and which has no fear ... She is with you, and therefore you should not fear; you will both come out together, and will appear more glorious than ever. I am very sure of it ...

In the same letter she went on to mention the 'melancholy solitude' that she sometimes felt, but said that 'no ill humour' could have any power over her. The letter concluded with a declaration of total love. 'I am yours after death, if it be possible.'[19]

Separation from her husband and children was a burden, but the queen's complaints were few, about toothache, about her eyesight (attributed to too many tears), about a cold. In July 1642 Marie de Médicis died in Cologne, news which reached her daughter a week later. Henrietta Maria wrote to Charles to say that she was upset, and that he, the children and the court must wear mourning, but this came at the end of a letter that first dealt with Prince Rupert, then with Parliament's plan to appoint judges, then with her recommendation that Charles appoint James, Duke of York, admiral and then with the need to remember those who had been loyal to him, if he was to offer an amnesty to those who had not.[20]

The queen confronted rumour briskly. 'They have made you dead, and Charles a prisoner; although I see your letters, you may imagine this pleases me not. As to Prince Rupert, there are men who have touched his dead body and that of Prince Maurice. For battles, there is not a day in the week in which you do not lose one,' she wrote to Charles at the end of November 1642. She passed on to him any news she thought helpful, as when a 'poor woman' from Portsmouth told her that she had heard Essex and his officers discuss a plan to capture the king. She closed another letter on a practical note: 'Adieu my dear heart, I am going to take my supper, and as it has cost money, I must not let it be spoiled.'[21]

Parliament castigated Henrietta Maria as a foreigner using her position as queen to subvert the English constitution to Catholic despotism. Her letters from the Dutch Republic show her as a superb product of the royal system, a woman devoted to her husband and to his country. In September she wrote, 'I wish to share all your fortune, and participate in your troubles, as I have done in your happiness, provided it be with honour, and in your defence; for to die of consumption of royalty is a death which I cannot endure.' As Christmas approached she wrote to say, 'I need the air of England ...'[22]

*

At the worst possible time for sailing, in January 1643, Henrietta Maria set off to rejoin her husband. Her eleven ships were at sea nine days in a storm before they could make it back to the Dutch coast. During this horrible experience, the queen and her ladies were tied into their beds. Her ships never came close to landing in England. Two of the boats went down, losing eighteen people and twenty-eight horses, and the state of the survivors was appalling.[23]

The queen's clothes, and those of everyone else, were so filthy they were burned – there being no possibility, in the bucking ships, of using a chamber pot or close stool, everything going everywhere. 'I confess I never expected to see you again,' wrote Henrietta Maria to her husband, and indeed confession was the word. She and her ladies were so sure they were about to die that, at the height of the storm they all – including Henrietta Maria – shouted out their sins in an unexpectedly public set of confessions to their accompanying priests, to be absolved before they faced the judgement of God. It was a time when secrets came out.

The memory of these near-death confessions entertained the queen when she looked back, but at the time she was literally stunned. 'I am so stupefied that I cannot easily write more, for I have not slept during nine nights.' Nobody could stand for long when they were back on shore. The Capuchin priest who celebrated a Mass of thanksgiving for their survival had to be held up physically by two men as he did so. She returned to The Hague exhausted. Not that the experience put her off. On 27 January she wrote to Charles, 'I hope to set out again when the wind is good.'[24]

*

Henrietta Maria waited a few weeks before trying once more, with a Dutch escort under Admiral Tromp. The crossing was trouble-free, although the wind changed so that the queen's ships did not sail to Newcastle as planned, but had to put in at Bridlington on the Yorkshire coast, where they landed on 14 February 1643. Cottages were commandeered for the royal party from the fishing families. Unloading was left for the next morning.

The next day, at first light, the lookout saw four parliamentary ships had arrived on the high tide, tracking the queen. There was a rush to unload the precious cargo in case the enemy came onshore, but their commanding officer instead gave the order for a bombardment. One of the parliamentary ships was moored opposite the house where Henrietta Maria was staying, which was by the quay, in order to have a good aim. It was a well-planned attack, with reconnaissance in advance. They wanted to kill the queen.

'Before I could get out of bed, the balls were whistling upon me in such style that you may easily believe I loved not such music,' Henrietta Maria reported to Charles, writing later the same day. Throwing a cloak over her nightgown, she was rushed out of the cottage by her ladies towards safety – then she remembered Mitte, 'an ugly dog that she really loved'. Henrietta Maria ran back to her house, rescued Mitte, and with the other women took refuge in a ditch outside the village, where they continued to be targeted, 'the balls passing always over our heads'. Later she said there were more than two hundred shots taken at the cottage where she was staying. One of the queen's servants was killed twenty paces from her.[25]

At great personal risk, the men, including Jeffrey Hudson, went on saving the precious ammunition. The tide turned, so the parliamentary vessels had to sail out to open sea to avoid being beached. The Dutch admiral now sent a message to the parliamentarians warning that, if they did not retreat, he would fire on them as enemies (Tromp's excuse for not intervening earlier was a haze on the water). The cargo of arms anyway survived, and so did Henrietta Maria, who was showing extraordinary resilience against the forces of nature and man.[26]

32

THE IMPEACHMENT OF HENRIETTA MARIA

When the queen returned to England, the English Civil War was six months old. Parliament controlled the navy, but there was a balance between the two sides on land. The king's support in the north was strong, also in the west, in large tracts of the West Country as well as Wales. If Ireland were to become calmer, royalist troops could be released to land on the Welsh coast to add to the king's forces in England. Having lost London, Charles I established himself with his court at Oxford, where he occupied Christ Church College.[1]

People who lived in towns often supported Parliament, London being the leading example of a parliamentary/puritanical urban population. Parliament also controlled the south-east of the country, and East Anglia. The Midlands were disputed as a new border country. This was the geographical pattern, but loyalties were divided at every level of society and within families. There were plenty who worked on the land, close to subsistence, prepared to change sides or turn against both, particularly as time passed.

*

After Edgehill it was the king's side that won ground. On 19 January 1643 the royalist Sir Ralph Hopton defeated Colonel Ruthven's men at Braddock Down, the engagement that secured Cornwall for

Charles I. The battle was won by an uphill charge of Hopton's men. Prince Rupert captured Cirencester at the beginning of February, which protected royalist lines of communication. At the end of February, a parliamentary attack on Newark was repulsed.

Parliamentary forces were successful in capturing Leeds, Lancaster and Stratford-upon-Avon. Peace proposals were made by Parliament at the beginning of the year. In support, commissioners from Scotland asked to see Charles I in Oxford in February. The king granted the Scots an audience but told them they had no business interfering in England. He did not accept the parliamentary proposals.[2]

When the queen landed at Bridlington, she added to her husband's hopes by supplying him with arms and pepping up royalist morale. Since she was very nearly killed twice on the way, it was hard not to be cheered by Henrietta Maria's determination. No other pampered princess of Europe put herself in the front line like this.

From the coast Henrietta Maria travelled to York, where she arrived at the beginning of March 1643, and stayed three months in lovely spring weather. In the most beautiful city in England, whose famous minster was surrounded by winding medieval streets, with spreading orchards and gardens beyond, all enclosed by the encircling defensive wall, the queen held court under the protection of the Earl of Newcastle. Her intention was to increase the numbers who declared for the king, which she did, attracting real, practical assistance, men and arms from Sir Hugh Cholmley and declarations of loyalty from the Earl of Newport (who previously thought she should be held hostage) and the Hothams, father and son (who earlier denied Charles I entry to Hull).[3]

Hamilton and other Scottish lords came to pay their respects. The ultra-loyal Earl of Newcastle had a sick wife who died in April, and at this difficult time he somehow aroused the irritation of the king, but Henrietta Maria stepped in – 'you are not the only person who has been chid, I have had my share of it …'; 'I give you no advice I have not taken myself …' – to assure him of her friendship.[4]

The queen was involved in military discussions, for instance on tactics for the siege of Leeds, and she was always pressing for action. When Parliament asked her again to influence the king to agree terms – asked her to help calm things down – she appeared to agree, but only to buy time for the convoy of arms and money to reach the king. Much of the arms and equipment that she brought from Holland she gave to Newcastle's men, or to the Earl of Derby in Lancashire. She would lead these men to her husband – an army, rather than the munitions alone – when the time came.[5]

*

'This is not written in anger,' she wrote to Charles I, who was upset at her protests against the Oxford peace talks, 'but comes from a mind very resolute, and not frightened by our affairs; for had I to suffer a thousand times more than I have done, which is I think impossible enough, I should not be rebuffed; on the contrary I should strengthen myself against misfortunes.' Henrietta Maria was eloquent on persistence. Nor was she short of ideas. She advised her husband to transfer the Shetland and Orkney Islands to the King of Denmark for arms.[6]

Having tested the water, Parliament realised there was no hope of the queen changing her spots. She truly wanted peace in England but on royal terms. 'Certainly I wish a peace more than any ... but I would the disbanding of the perpetual parliament first.' Once again her enemies took aim. On Maundy Thursday 1643 (2 April) her Capuchins in London were arrested and the beautiful chapel of Inigo Jones at Somerset House was sacked. The iconoclastic mob destroyed the peerless Rubens altarpiece and shattered the image of Christ crucified.[7]

Pym and his supporters took up what was threatened before. On Tuesday 23 May the Commons voted to impeach Henrietta Maria of high treason. Her refusal to be crowned in 1626 was used as a reason for treating her as an ordinary woman, rather than the Queen of England (nobody knew whether a queen consort really could be impeached legally, especially since her crime was to assist the king). The Lords did not immediately respond to the Commons vote. It was an example of the difference between the houses and the ever-present risk of disputes. After their vote, it was left open how the Commons would proceed, although everything depended on securing the agreement of the Lords first. They probably favoured a trial rather than a Bill of Attainder: Sir Henry Ludlow pointed out that this was one Bill that would not receive the king's signature.[8]

Pym and his supporters, among whom Oliver St John, Harry

Vane (the younger) and Oliver Cromwell were coming forward, argued that the queen was responsible for the king's determination to fight the war. It was a misreading of Charles I, although his wife was certainly bent on rejoining him with an army behind her, and in every way she added fire. The fear of being put on trial was unknown to Henrietta Maria, who told Hamilton (recently made a duke), 'God forgive them for their rebellion, as I assure you I forgive them from my heart for what they do against me.' In this way the threat of being impeached fell rather flat, although it did mean that Henrietta Maria, if she fell into the custody of the Parliament, would be vulnerable to a trial or a vote in Parliament.[9]

On 14 May 1643, Louis XIII died after a long wasting illness. To the queen, her elder brother was a bit like someone of an earlier generation. They had clashed politically and were never close personally. Henrietta Maria wrote to Hamilton that 'from France (except the death of the King my brother) I have very good news, as likewise from Denmark'.[10] Richelieu died five months before the king, and was succeeded as First Minister by his trainee the Italian Cardinal Mazarin. Henrietta Maria became more hopeful of help from France.

*

She left York at the end of June, taking with her a large force of men: three thousand infantry, thirty companies of cavalry, six cannon and two mortars, with supplies of cash in addition.

She rode on horseback – not in a carriage – ate in company with the men, and treated them as part of her extended family, which was certainly how she thought of them. It is easy to forget what this leadership meant to the soldiers, to whom the queen was the closest thing they would ever see to Aphrodite or Artemis.[11]

Harry Jermyn commanded the troops, but Henrietta Maria was leading the army. From Newark on 27 June 1643 she wrote to Charles I to explain the situation, calling herself 'her she-majesty, generalissima, and extremely diligent'.[12]

On 13 July 1643 Henrietta Maria at last rejoined her husband, and their two eldest sons, at Edgehill. From Stratford-upon-Avon she was escorted by Prince Rupert on the most risky part of the journey, but there were no serious encounters. The queen brought her army through in triumph. The next day the royal party entered the royalist capital, where Henrietta Maria was lodged in Merton College, next to Christ Church.[13]

*

The king's successes continued, the most brilliant of which were the destruction of Sir William Waller's army at the Battle of Roundway Down in Wiltshire by Henry Wilmot (13 July), and Prince Rupert's capture of Bristol (26 July). On 15 September the Marquess of Ormond signed a one-year ceasefire in Ireland with the Irish Confederacy (the Irish rebels), which released troops to come to England for Charles I. It was not the huge Irish army always devoutly wished for but they were extra men. There were divisions on the parliamentary side, for instance with Essex being criticised as commander-in-chief.

On the other hand, factionalism broke out in Oxford. The success of his most dashing general, his nephew Rupert, made others around Charles I jealous, such as Harry Percy and the now tried-and-tested Henry Wilmot, and most of all of George Goring. While Henrietta Maria presided over the Oxford court, the quarrels of young noblemen were managed with skill and tact. The queen was a subtle court politician and the only person who really had the trust of Charles I. The royal double act which ran the radiant Caroline court of the 1630s also ran wartime Oxford well. But the queen did not stay in Oxford.[14]

*

Two developments started to tip the military balance to Parliament. The first was the defiance of Gloucester, under Colonel Massey. On 5 September 1643, parliamentary Gloucester was relieved from a royalist siege of nearly a month by the Earl of Essex, a huge boost to parliamentary morale, and strategic, since a Gloucester garrison disrupted royalist communications in the west. General Essex returned to London in triumph, surviving the First Battle of Newbury on the way, where Charles I commanded his forces in person (16 September). The relief of Gloucester was later seen as the moment when everything changed, yet the decisive event was the return of the Scots.

The leaders of Parliament returned to their risky friendship with the Scottish government, after Harry Vane the younger negotiated a deal in Edinburgh. The 'Solemn League and Covenant' was an agreement between Parliament and the Tables which promised to safeguard Scottish religion, and to reform English practice in line with that. This agreement reopened the conflict in the north, since the Scottish army could challenge the royalist Lord Newcastle there. It was again an argument of numbers, adding a new army to the parliamentary cause.[15]

Before these advantages became evident, Parliament was only slightly troubled by two plots whose ambition was a sectarian or tolerant settlement under the king's leadership. The first was the Ogle Plot, the second the Brooke Plot, named after Sir Thomas Ogle and Sir Basil Brooke respectively. Both were easily discovered by Parliament, but the second, which was supported by Henrietta Maria and the Duchess of Buckingham, encouraged the Lords to move towards the queen's impeachment. By bringing the Scots back, Parliament supported a Presbyterian settlement – one that insisted on a single, defined form of Calvinist Christianity. These were signs of a Protestant division that would soon become serious.

It took time for the Scots to mobilise. They would enter Northumberland in January 1644. Their toughness can be seen from this date. They started with a winter campaign. Meanwhile, Parliament was hit by the death of Pym on 8 December (from stomach cancer as Sir Theodore Mayerne's autopsy showed). St John, Vane and Cromwell took over the leadership in the Commons.[16]

*

In the holiday camp of wartime Oxford, Henrietta Maria became pregnant. Officers and men slept in the streets, taking advantage of the hot summer weather, while the ladies were crammed into small rooms above shops. There were parties and love affairs and teasing of the locals. The earls of Bedford, Holland and Clare, disturbed by the increasingly hard tone of Parliament, came to declare their loyalty to the king. But sickness developed in the overcrowded city since the sanitary habits of the cavaliers did not – in the circumstances *could* not – match their charm and swagger. There were quarrels about lodging, and about foraging. The lack of discipline seen at Edgehill continued among groups of young men who were energetic, proud and competitive, and the cavalier adventure became less exciting in winter weather.[17]

At thirty-four, the queen had a difficult pregnancy. Although the Earl of Essex did not set out from London until May 1644, it was clear before then that Parliament might assault Oxford itself when campaigning started, so her presence would be a distraction as well as a risk to mother and baby. In February she wrote to Christine in Savoy, 'I am the only one who is miserable, because I am pregnant, and do not know where to go for safety ...' Henrietta Maria decided, at any rate, not to stay in Oxford. On 17 April 1644, with Charles I at her side, she travelled to Abingdon, where the king and queen took leave of each other.[18]

In removing the queen from Oxford, her 1643 pregnancy determined the course of the rest of her life, and perhaps determined the course of the English Civil War. Once she had gone, Charles I struggled with the management of his senior generals, notably the spiky Prince Rupert.[19]

In May Essex led his army to Oxford to trap the king. Charles I broke out and avoided battle. On 6 June the parliamentary generals decided to split their forces, with Sir William Waller pursuing the king, who defeated him decisively three weeks later at Cropredy Bridge in Oxfordshire (29 June). Meanwhile, Essex marched west to relieve Lyme Regis in Dorset, which Prince Maurice was besieging, and to capture Henrietta Maria. This would put an end to the war, since Charles I would do anything to protect his pregnant wife.

*

The queen was wracked by physical pain. She went first to Bath, then moved to Exeter where she stayed in Bedford House. Both king and queen wrote to Theodore Mayerne begging him to attend her in Exeter, the king saying simply, 'Mayerne, for the love of me, go to my wife' – and this the overweight sixty-nine-year-old doctor did. From France, Anne of Austria again sent the midwife Mme Peronne, plus money and linen.[20]

Attended by highly experienced professionals, Henrietta Maria gave birth to a girl on 16 June 1643. Resting after the birth, she hoped that she would start to feel better, but she felt worse and concluded that she was sick with something entirely separate from the pregnancy. On 28 June, Henrietta Maria wrote to Charles, 'Instead of finding relief [after giving birth], my disease has increased, and is so insupportable, that if it were not that we ought not to wish for death, it would be too much longed for, by the most wretched creature in the world.' She suffered from attacks of paralysis, especially in the legs; her guts and stomach were swollen and felt very heavy, so much so that at times it was hard to breathe. She lost feeling in one of her arms, and lost vision in one eye. She was probably suffering from puerperal sepsis. At this impossible time, she received intelligence of the approach of Essex's army.[21]

The day after Cropredy Bridge, the king wrote to his wife, congratulating her on the birth of his youngest 'and prettiest' daughter – attractive words, considering Charles I had seen many newborn babies – and asked for her to be christened in Exeter Cathedral as a Protestant. He also suggested his wife send a letter to the Earl of Essex offering the king's pardon if the earl laid down his arms, or brought his soldiers over to the king.[22]

This letter was intercepted, but Charles no doubt wrote several times. Henrietta Maria does not seem to have written to Essex, but followed her husband's instructions on the christening. On 21 July 1644 their youngest child was christened Henrietta in Exeter Cathedral in a Protestant service. The queen herself did not attend.[23]

*

Although her friends thought she was taking more risks by leaving Exeter than staying, she was sure they were wrong. Entrusting the tiny baby to the nurses under Lady Dalkeith, Henrietta Maria abandoned Exeter in order to avoid being taken prisoner by Parliament. She was right to go. Lord Essex did not in fact occupy the city, but that was because the queen's departure devalued it. It was later believed that, after leaving Exeter, the queen had to lie hidden under a pile of rags and refuse, listening to soldiers walking past, talking about the reward they would receive if they found her.[24]

Anyway, she was not found. Carried in a litter, she travelled to Falmouth with a group including her secretary Sir John Winter, Harry Jermyn, Jeffrey Hudson and Theodore Mayerne, with an armed escort under a Captain Brett.[25]

Henrietta Maria now wanted refuge in France. On 9 July, from Truro, she wrote to her husband, 'I am giving you the strongest proof of love that I can give; I am hazarding my life, that I may not incommode your affairs.' Those who met her were shocked at her condition. Sir Francis Barrett wrote to his wife on 3 July to tell her that 'here is the woefullest spectacle my eyes yet ever beheld on; the most worn and pitiful creature in the world, the poor queen, shifting for one hour's life longer'.[26]

Nonetheless, she made it to the coast. At Falmouth five royal vessels were docked, on one of which the queen and her friends embarked. There were parliamentary ships patrolling the waters outside Falmouth, including one, the *Vice-Admiral*, which had fifty-eight pieces of cannon. At this even Henrietta Maria baulked, but her captain pointed out that the longer they waited, the more likely the parliamentary boats were to find reinforcements.

Always decisive, the queen told the captain to set sail. Leaving Falmouth, he steered directly for the *Vice-Admiral*, which shot five rounds of cannon at the queen's ship. There was one hit, but the damage was slight. The captain wanted to return fire. Henrietta Maria forbade this, ordering him to sail on, making for the French coast at full speed. She also gave him the unwelcome instruction to set fire to his store of gunpowder, in other words to blow up the ship and everyone on it, if they were overtaken.[27]

Henrietta Maria and her friends were pursued by three parliamentary vessels, the *Vice-Admiral*, the *Warwick* and the *Paramour*, but thanks to the risk-taking Cornish captain, her ship was ahead, and she made her escape, landing on the Breton coast the next day (26 July).[28]

33

UNREPENTANT

Soon after their arrival in France, Theodore Mayerne gave a brusque reply to his queen and employer. Bloated, in pain, half-blind and desperate for her baby, for her husband, the queen told her doctor she thought she would go mad, and without hesitation he said, 'You need not fear that, Madam, you are already mad.'[1]

After anchoring off the coast, the Cornish captain handed the queen into a longboat, which took her with her immediate attendants to the shore. Here they clambered across the rocks to a fishing village. When they learned who their visitor was, the people here looked after her – the legend of Henri IV was powerful – amazed though they were at the bizarre courtly troupe.

Mayerne, Jeffrey Hudson, Harry Jermyn and others had also faced the *Vice-Admiral*'s cannonballs, then the threat of death by self-inflicted – Henrietta Maria-inflicted – explosion at sea, and then they had to help their mistress across the rocks – difficult for every one of them, Mayerne being old, Hudson being small, Jermyn being fat – and still then they had to convince the local people of the queen's identity. Then, after all their efforts, there they were in a fisherman's cottage miles from civilisation. It is not surprising the physician thought Henrietta Maria deranged.

Local landowners came to pay their respects, to house the

Queen of England more appropriately and to send word to Paris. Henrietta Maria was quick to ask for two Parisian doctors, either because she had lost the ability to deal with Sir Theodore, or he had lost the ability to deal with her; regardless, he wanted the next boat home. She headed for the spa waters of Bourbon in central France, nearly two hundred miles away, a journey in an unsprung carriage on the rough roads of the seventeenth century, which damaged her further.

Harry Jermyn was sent to Paris to ask for help. He returned with 10,000 pistoles for her expenses and the patent for a large monthly pension, the gift of Anne of Austria. The Paris doctors met her at Ancenis, between Nantes and Angers, and agreed that she should continue to Bourbon. As she travelled across France, crowds came to stare at the daughter of Henri IV, and those who glimpsed her saw that she was weeping.[2]

Henrietta Maria's progress was also followed by people anxious for bad news. As she made her way through France, disappointing the agents of Parliament with her stamina, the 'Perfect Occurrences of Parliament' in London reported that the queen was heading towards Bourbon for the waters. 'But will the Bourbon waters cure her? There are other waters set open for her to drink, in the Protestant Church, the waters of repentance.'[3]

Mad, half-mad or worn to a shred but not remotely repentant, it was the same Henrietta Maria who, on 25 August 1644, arrived at Bourbon and was greeted by a group of Jesuit fathers. They presented her with salutary verses, respectfully hoping that the waters would cure her physical problems and ... help with? ... her other problems. She thanked them, saying, 'This is very well done but do still more', meaning provide some money for Charles I. Henrietta Maria never showed a great affection for the Jesuits.

At Bourbon an abscess in her breast was lanced, and she drank the waters and bathed in them. She started to recover, and wrote to her husband asking for Charles, Prince of Wales, to be measured so that she could order him a suit of armour. As her health improved she benefitted from the attentions an intelligent French lady-in-waiting sent to her by Anne of Austria, this being Françoise de Motteville, who later wrote memoirs of the French court.[4]

*

More courtiers slipped away from England to join the queen, including William Crofts, her Captain of the Guards, and his brother Charles. Their nerves were stretched in exile. In October, at Nevers, the cavalier youth entertained themselves by making fun of Jeffrey Hudson, who snapped, and challenged Charles Crofts to a duel. This was thought hysterically funny by Charles, who arrived at the appointed place with a large syringe filled with water as his weapon. Jeffrey came with pistols and shot his opponent dead.[5]

It was appalling and it was embarrassing, since Henrietta Maria and her small court were guests in a country whose new government – the regency of Anne of Austria, run by Cardinal Mazarin – was trying to eradicate the tradition of duelling. Jeffrey's duel was illegal and he was now a murderer. This happened about the same time that Henrietta Maria received the upsetting news of the death of her sister Elizabeth of Spain.

She wrote to both Anne of Austria and Mazarin to ask permission to settle the matter herself, since all the participants were English and servants of hers. Permission was given. For his own good, she banished Jeffrey from France.

Sailing back to England, the court dwarf moved into a new phase of life when he was captured by Barbary pirates, and spent the next twenty-five years as a slave, probably in Algiers. In the course of this experience Jeffrey grew another eighteen inches. It is likely that his condition was caused by growth hormone deficiency, with the result that a new, hard-working life as an agricultural labourer stimulated his pituitary gland. He would not come home until 1669.[6]

*

In early November 1644, Henrietta Maria entered Paris, a city she had not seen for almost twenty years. The beautiful, warm, generous Anne of Austria and her second son, the Duc d'Anjou (aged four), came to meet her outside the walls. At last Henrietta Maria was in the hands of friends.[7]

When she was a girl – when she was Madame Henriette – she was not kind to her sister-in-law Anne, a young bride with a difficult husband. Henrietta Maria had joined her mother Marie de Médicis in a series of sniping attacks on Anne to keep her in her place. The older and infinitely wiser Henrietta Maria had every reason to thank her kind sister-in-law, therefore, who, in addition to the pension, provided her with the Louvre as a residence and the old nursery palace St Germain-en-Laye as a country retreat. The welcome given by Charles I in the 1630s to the Duchesse de Chevreuse, Anne's ally against Richelieu, helped build bridges.[8]

France honoured the daughter of Henri IV, but would not provide money, weapons or men for Charles I. This was firstly because a weak England was good news in Paris. Secondly, France was governed by a foreign woman, the Regent Anne, who relied on her Italian First Minister, exactly the arrangement that led to grandee rebellions under Marie de Médicis thirty years earlier. Third, and most important, France's war with Spain continued, so the country was stretched. Becoming involved in the English Civil War was impossible for the government of Anne of Austria.

Even so, Henrietta Maria tried everything possible inside France to find help for her husband. Outside she tried the Prince of Orange, the King of Denmark and the Duke of Lorraine, but increasingly she looked both to Catholic Ireland, where she planned to go herself, and to Scotland.[9]

*

The king and queen of Great Britain wrote to each other, using a new cypher (which the queen entrusted to Harry Jermyn) and suffering from the interception of letters by Parliament. 'I know not whether you have received any of my letters ... '; 'It is a cruel anxiety to know nothing of you ... '; 'I do not cease to labour for your affairs.' As before, the queen gave her husband advice and urged resolution above all things on Charles I. 'You are not resolute in your designs; for the thing of all others that has most injured you here [Paris] was your having this reputation.' Whatever the truth was, the strategic position of Charles I was on a downhill slide.[10]

In 1644 a major battle at last took place, in Yorkshire. As Henrietta Maria attempted to recover from the birth of her youngest child in Exeter, royalist York was besieged by the joint armies of the Scottish Covenanters and of Parliament. By a brilliant manoeuvre which deceived both enemy armies, Prince

Rupert relieved York without attacking the enemy. He received a message from Charles I which appeared to instruct him to engage the two armies directly. Although this message was ambiguous, it probably was the king's intention that Rupert should fight.[11]

The Battle of Marston Moor started at 7.30 in the evening of 2 July 1644. It was partly fought by moonlight. The royal army was totally defeated by the Scots and parliamentarians, who included the newly trained, disciplined 'ironside' cavalry of Oliver Cromwell. The north of England now came under the control of Parliament and its Scottish allies, a huge setback for Charles I.[12]

This damage was masked by the king's equal success in the west of England, when he destroyed the army of the Earl of Essex (the same army which had threatened Henrietta Maria in Exeter). Essex was defeated at the prolonged Battle of Lostwithiel in August 1644. He escaped capture by abandoning the field and his men, sailing away in a fishing boat. Essex had marched into Cornwall believing that local people would support his troops, but they did not. After the battle the locals threatened and harried his disarmed men as they marched back to Plymouth.[13]

At the same time, with great dash the Marquess of Montrose was fighting a royalist campaign in Scotland. The king's two English victories at Cropredy Bridge and Lostwithiel, plus the fire of Montrose, compensated for Marston Moor and led to a new set of peace negotiations at Uxbridge in the beginning of 1645.

All this was deceptive. Parliament was resurgent. The Uxbridge talks failed. The parliamentary army command was cleared out by the 'Self-denying Ordinance' which required Members of both Lords and Commons to lay down their military commands so that weak commanders such as the Earl of Manchester (previously Lord Mandeville) no longer held things up. The parliamentary troops were reorganised into the New Model Army.[14]

*

On 10 January 1645, William Laud was executed after being found guilty of high treason. The vindictive execution – the seventy-one-year-old was harassed up to, and on, the scaffold by two unusually unpleasant men, Sir John Clotworthy and Hugh Peters – gave the king a conviction that God, who had been harsh because of his abandonment of Strafford, would now look on him with favour.

'This last crying blood being totally theirs,' he wrote to Henrietta Maria, 'I believe it is no presumption hereafter to hope that his hand of justice must be heavier upon them and lighter on us.' On 8 June Charles told his wife, 'Since this rebellion my affairs were never in so fair and hopeful a way.'[15]

At the Battle of Naseby in Northamptonshire, on 14 June 1645, the royalists shouted out 'Queen Mary' as they charged. They were outnumbered and destroyed by the New Model Army under the command of Thomas Fairfax and Oliver Cromwell. Soon after, on 10 July, at the Battle of Langport in Somerset, the last royalist army under George Goring was defeated by Fairfax. This time it was the royalists who, after the battle, were harassed and attacked by local people, called clubmen. On 11 September Bristol fell to Parliament, a final disaster blamed on the defending Prince Rupert.[16]

Quarrels between Prince Rupert and George Goring were part of the reasons for the royalist catastrophe. For instance, the division of the royalist troops before Naseby, which led to Charles I fighting against far superior numbers, was due to Prince Rupert wishing to divide his troops from those of George Goring. Parliament fielded between 14,500 and 17,000 men against the king's 9,000–10,000. In another version of history the queen might have stayed in Oxford and reconciled the generals. Could Charles I, with a larger army, have won the alternative Battle of Naseby?[17]

It was a cruel irony that the queen played a part in her husband's defeat in the country. Parliamentary propaganda won hearts and souls when the king's coach, captured after Naseby, was found to include her letters to Charles, which were published to show how she was planning to use foreign and Catholic troops to invade England. An anonymous author, with notes accompanying the letters, described Charles I as entirely in thrall to his wife, whose counsels were 'as powerful as commands'. He said that 'the Kings Counsels are wholly managed by the Queen, though she be of the weaker sex, born an alien, bred up in a contrary religion ... as harsh and imperious towards the King ... as she is implacable to our religion, nation, and government'. Parliament liked the idea of Charles I being henpecked. Henrietta Maria's direct and clear way with words made a bad impression on the men on the other side of the argument.[18]

34

MAN OF BLOOD

From the Louvre, Henrietta Maria threw herself into Irish diplomacy. An agreement with the Irish Confederacy (the Catholic rebel government) could lead to that Irish army again and again dreamed of – and dreaded – to be sent to England to rescue Charles I. The Marquess of Ormond was trying to obtain exactly this agreement in negotiation with the Confederacy, while Kenelm Digby was sent to Rome to ask the Pope for help.

Unfortunately Pope Innocent X took his own initiative by appointing a nuncio to go to Ireland, Giovanni Rinuccini, Archbishop of Fermo. On his way to Ireland in May 1645, Rinuccini arrived in Paris, about a week before Naseby was fought. He was instructed to confer with Henrietta Maria, and to obtain from her an agreement to the surrender of Dublin to the Confederacy before assistance to Charles I was discussed. Dublin at this time was held by Ormond for the king.

The deadly weapon of etiquette was deployed. The queen could not see Rinuccini because his status as nuncio to Ireland had not been agreed with Charles I. However, if he took his hat off in her presence she would see him. The uncovered head would signify acceptance of the authority of Charles I. Rinuccini countered that there was no formal diplomatic relationship between the Pope and the King of England, so the hat had to stay on his head. No meeting took place.[1]

These flourishes betrayed the insoluble problem that, on the one hand, Henrietta Maria thought the nuncio would undermine her husband's authority in Ireland, while, on the other, Rinuccini (and Pope Innocent) distrusted Charles I. Both were right. The Pope and his envoy were familiar with the king's record on Catholicism, which looked alarming to the English but pathetic to the Holy See. Innocent simply did not believe that Charles I would ever introduce real concessions for the English Catholics. He preferred an independent Catholic Ireland.

Even so, Henrietta Maria successfully played on Rinuccini's vanity. The archbishop stayed much longer in Paris than instructed. This allowed Ormond to make progress with the Confederacy, but he found himself undermined by the Catholic Earl of Glamorgan, sent to Ireland by Charles I with instructions that are still not understood. Whatever his instructions, Glamorgan pursued a parallel negotiation with Ormond's, and, benefitting from the trust between co-religionists, he signed a secret treaty with the Confederacy on 26 August 1645, which gave wide concessions to the Irish Catholics, abolishing the penal laws in Ireland, removing them from the jurisdiction of Protestant clergy and securing in return an army of ten thousand for the king. This was the agreement but it was not implemented.

A copy of the Glamorgan treaty was found in the luggage of the Archbishop of Tuam when he was attacked by a Scottish raiding party in October 1645, and sent to the English Parliament. Here was proof of the king's dealings with the Irish rebels after all. Parliament was thrilled by its own outrage. To show he was not collaborating with the Confederacy – to show that he was no papist – Charles I repudiated the treaty in early 1646. On his arrival in Ireland Rinuccini, who seemed to think he was papal viceroy in Ireland, also disavowed it, since he thought Glamorgan did not have the authority to carry it through. In fact, Rinuccini was successful in blocking any progress between the Confederacy and the king from then on.

In Rome, Innocent X decided that the extravagant behaviour of Kenelm Digby could only be explained by insanity. There was at least one heated exchange between Christ's representative on earth and Henrietta Maria's chancellor, when Digby 'grew high and hectored with His Holiness'. Innocent sent 20,000 crowns to

Henrietta Maria even so – the first time she managed to extract money from the papacy – because he was impressed by the military plans of the Earl of Arundel, and hoped to persuade the queen to agree to a treaty which would restore Catholic churches and Church land in Ireland – something, however ardently she might wish it, she knew was impossible. With this and the Glamorgan fiasco, the plans for an Irish army evaporated.[2]

Henrietta Maria's reputation in England took another beating when more of her letters were discovered among the papers of George Digby in October 1645. Here were attempts to find help from the Prince of Orange and from Denmark, who were Protestant, but also from the Catholic Duke of Lorraine, the Catholic Irish and the Pope – 'the very Romish Antichrist'. Whether she could sink any lower in the English imagination is debatable.

*

The battles of Naseby and Langport convinced another Catholic, Cardinal Mazarin, that the time had come to act. He concentrated on Scotland. The cardinal sent Jean de Montreuil to broker a deal which would return Charles I to his throne. This intervention was partly due to Henrietta Maria's ceaseless campaign for action, but was not exactly altruistic, since Mazarin hoped for English neutrality in return when France attacked the Spanish Netherlands.[3]

The bare narrative conceals politics of great complexity. The Scots supported the English Parliament in Pym's day when there was shared ground, but a religious fault line opened that split the Puritans of Britain. On one side were the Presbyterians, such as the Scottish Kirk, who wanted a unitary Calvinism true to one theology. On the other were the new devils: the sects, varied groups – Quakers, Anabaptists, Brownists – with different interpretations of Christ's gospel, not only religiously but politically radical. These were the Independents. The Kirk first feared William Laud, but now feared the Independents more, since the New Model Army under Fairfax and Cromwell was a sectarian hotbed, and was becoming politically active, and inevitably very powerful.

To protect the discipline of their own religion, the Scots were prepared to fight in England for a third time in order to impose a

Presbyterian settlement on England, as they had long wished – but this time it would be through the king. All Charles I needed to find an army at his back supported by France was conversion to the Presbyterian cause. It seemed a long time since the English were worried he would convert to Catholicism.[4]

In Paris, Henrietta Maria agreed the project and tried to persuade her husband to accept it. What did it matter if the king, if only he were king, were one sort of Protestant or another? She encouraged him always to be resolute, but now he was resolute against her. In January and February 1646 Charles I, whose options in Oxford had reduced to almost nothing, being without money and without soldiers, made it clear to his wife that he would never support the abolition of the bishops (on which the Scots always insisted).[5]

Military reality overtook theology. By May 1646 Charles I was boxed in at Oxford, and had to choose between three courses of action: surrender to Parliament, surrender to the Scots or leave the country. It was hard to reach the coast without interception. Parliament was not attractive and Montreuil reassured him about his reception by the Scots. On 2 May 1646, the king delivered himself to the Scottish army at Newark. They took him up to Newcastle. He was their king, but, despite Montreuil, who seemed to have secured no guarantees at all from the Scots, he was also their prisoner.

Here was the opportunity. By hectoring him with Presbyterian lectures given by Alexander Henderson, the Scots did their best to convert Charles I to the Kirk, but he stuck to the views he had already expressed to his wife. He would not take the Covenant and he would not agree to abolish the bishops (she agreed on the former). The result was that in January 1647 the Scots decided to return to Scotland, and handed Charles I over to English parliamentary troops in return for a payment of £400,000, which prompted the king to remark that they had sold him cheap, and exposed the retreating Scottish soldiers to the abuse of the women of Newcastle, who called 'Judas!' after them.[6]

In the custody of Parliament, the king was now taken to Holdenby in Northamptonshire. From his point of view it was quite an encouraging journey. Crowds came to see the king, cheering him, many of them keen to be touched for scrofula, a reminder of the semi-divine status that Charles I had in the eyes of countless subjects. At Holdenby he was so clever in making his appeals to populist royalism that his captors called him the 'stroker'.[7]

Another coup took place in June 1647. Cornet Joyce, with a posse from the New Model Army, arrived unannounced on 2 June at Holdenby and told Charles I that they would be leaving together the next day. Early on 3 June, the king amused himself with the improvisations of his opponents.

'I pray, Mr Joyce, deal ingeniously with me, and tell me what commission you have?' the sovereign asked the former tailor.

'Here is my commission,' replied Joyce.

'Where?'

'Behind me,' said Joyce, indicating his soldiers.

'It is as fair a commission, and as well written,' replied Charles I, 'as I have seen in my life, and a company of handsome, proper gentlemen as I have seen a great while.'[8]

The cornet, of course, had no official commission at all. Nonetheless, he conveyed the king via Newmarket to Hampton Court. Charles I had handed himself over to the Scots for safety. In despair at his stubbornness, they handed him over to Parliament. Now he was in the hands of a third grouping of his enemies, the most dangerous. Cornet Joyce represented the sectarian army Cromwell's men. This third capture of the king marked the end of the First English Civil War.[9]

*

Surprises continued when conditions for the king, now that he was in the hands of Satan, improved. In Newcastle there were restrictions on correspondence between the king and his wife, but now he could receive Henrietta Maria's letters more freely. In fact, against every expectation the situation was very much better than it seemed. Because of the divisions between his enemies, amazingly the king was better placed to win the peace than he had been the war. The weight of the king's mystical – and legal – authority could secure one or other faction in power. Desperate for a settlement, desperate for her husband, Henrietta Maria sent first John Berkeley and then, in addition, John Ashburnham to support him with advice at Hampton Court.[10]

However, Charles I did not want a deal. Perhaps he had listened too much to his wife's opinions about resolution. The king wanted to unleash war again, a war that he would win. In this way his honour would be satisfied, his principles vindicated, his opponents defeated. On 12 November 1647, the king escaped from Hampton Court to Carisbrooke Castle on the Isle of Wight. The king's flight was a shock to Cromwell, who in the Putney Debates (28 October to 11 November) was supporting a settlement in which Charles I would play his part as king, albeit with vastly diminished powers.

These debates were internal to the army, and showed there was a large body of military opinion, including the emerging social equality doctrines of the Levellers, opposed to further negotiations with Charles I, that even wanted the permanent abolition of royalty in England – a thus far unimagined revolution. Cromwell's earnest maxim for the debates – 'Let us be doing but let us be united in our doing'– wore thin and the timing of Charles I was shocking. By running away he destroyed his credibility with the army command.[11]

He was an appealing figure, on the other hand, to the English people, who had endured five years of conflict, including humiliation by the Scots and the dissolution of the royal court, an institution that was part of the national and economic fabric. People longed for peace and they longed for legitimacy, and they feared the New Model Army. Public opinion, even if it was not unanimous, was turning to the king.

Charles I found the governor of Carisbrooke loyal to Parliament, so after his escape he was once more in prison, but nonetheless he could correspond and he had visitors. The king tried to escape from Carisbrooke at least twice. Instead, he finally secured agreement to an attempt at a comeback. At the end of 1647 he was able to negotiate an 'Engagement' with Scottish Parliament. Under the Engagement, a Scottish army would fight in England but now it would fight for the king. In May 1648 part of the English fleet defected to Charles I, and in the south of England and Wales there were uprisings against Parliament, most notably in Kent and Essex.

On 8 July 1648 the Duke of Hamilton led the Scottish army across the border, but he was late. By this time the New Model Army was on top of the English rebellions. With his highly drilled troops, Cromwell confronted Hamilton at Preston in Lancashire on 17 August 1648 and inflicted an overwhelming defeat. The

Battle of Preston marked the end of the Second English Civil War, yet another vindication of Cromwell's discipline, but it was not the most distressing event of the short war.

When the city of Colchester sheltered royalist troops, it underwent an eleven-week siege, which ended on 28 August.[12] The siege was conducted with great harshness. After the surrender, two of the royalist leaders, Sir Charles Lucas and Sir George Lisle, were executed – a penalty very rarely demanded of officers who offered their surrender. They became royalist martyrs, but the army propaganda machine found its own hero in the Leveller Thomas Rainborough, who had led the arguments in the Putney Debates, had fought at Colchester and was killed in Doncaster on 29 October, resisting a party of royalist officers.

These and other deaths resulted from the determination of Charles I to inflict war on his people for the second time, when it was open to him to work in peace with the parliamentary side. Not only the Levellers but also the army grandees headed by Cromwell and his faction now believed the king was a man of blood, prepared to sacrifice any number of English lives in his unquenchable thirst for power. They saw one solution only: the death of Charles I.

35

30 JANUARY 1649

To Henrietta Maria it was disappointing that the Scottish plan failed, but civil conflict, she knew from France, rolled on. Kings and queens survived, provided they survived the fighting, until God decided otherwise. There was no reason to think Charles I was in real danger. She therefore worked on plans to help him.

The court of France, like Sophie of the Rhine, was surprised at the difference between their battered princess and her van Dyck image. However, her lovely eyes and complexion drew admiration and her lively conversation was popular, as was her natural generosity. Sources refer to her 'endless style and wit ... pleasing in company, honest, sweet, straightforward ... among the tears, if something entertaining struck her, she would say it, to amuse people'. Mme de Motteville thought the queen had changed for the better as a result of her trials. 'She did not have the fine and profound understanding that can be learned from reading; but her misfortunes had repaired that fault, and these trying experiences had given her real depth.' Henrietta Maria was no intellectual, but she was nonetheless a learner.

She also showed that characteristic of many strong people, turning her personal disadvantages into general principles. 'Since her beauty had only lasted the morning, and left before her midday, she used to say that women could not be beautiful after the age of twenty-two.' This was not something that Lucy Carlisle agreed with, to name but one.[1]

The queen's niece Anne Marie d'Orléans was another memoirist of the French court. Anne Marie, known as the Grande Mademoiselle, was Henrietta's brother Gaston's elder daughter. This formidable girl (seventeen when Henrietta Maria arrived in 1644) was destined for massive personal wealth. She was due to inherit her dead mother's vast possessions when Gaston died and was generally considered to be the richest woman in Europe.

The Grande Mademoiselle described how Henrietta Maria first kept the style of queen when she arrived in France but 'the household diminished bit by bit and not long afterwards nothing was left of her dignity but her normal entourage'. The Queen of England cut back because she was sending every penny she could to Charles I, although by 1648 it was hard to get anything through.[2]

*

Henrietta Maria also had the children to think of. When she sailed from Falmouth her two elder boys were fourteen and ten, living in Oxford with their father. Mary (twelve) was safe in The Hague with the Orange family, but three of the children were hostages to Parliament. Elizabeth (nine) and Henry (four) lived in London, at St James's Palace. The newborn Henrietta stayed at Exeter in the care of Lady Dalkeith until April 1646, when the city fell to Parliament and Lady Dalkeith took the little girl to Oatlands.[3]

In 1646 Henrietta Maria was joined by her eldest son, the Prince of Wales. After the Uxbridge talks failed, the king sent the younger Charles to the West Country as nominal head of the royalist forces there, supported by his own personal council, which included Edward Hyde, the future historian of the English Civil War. After his father delivered himself to the Scots at Newark, the prince sailed to the Scilly Isles, attended by his council.

Henrietta Maria did not like Hyde. She told him to be sure that the prince left the Scillies, which were not really fortified. 'I need not remind you of what importance to the king, and all his party, the safety of the prince's person is.' She was proven right when a parliamentary fleet appeared in search of the prince, but fortunately it was dispersed by a storm, so the prince and his councillors managed to escape.[4]

Charles I now wrote to his son, telling him to join his mother in Paris and to obey her in everything 'except in religion, concerning which I am confident she will not trouble you'. The prince's council did not want the prince to leave English territory, and thought it a mistake for Charles to come under his mother's influence, but the prince himself decided to go to Paris, setting off from Jersey on 25 June 1647. Henrietta Maria at once tried to find him a wife.[5]

*

The richest woman in Europe would do. Henrietta Maria took her niece in hand. Before each party, the queen would check Anne Marie over to make sure she was correctly dressed and pour her wisdom into the teenager's ear. Like her aunt, over whom she towered, Anne-Marie was a strong character and no fool. 'I saw in a moment,' she later wrote, 'that the Queen of England much wished me to believe he [the Prince of Wales] was in love with me.'

It was the beginning of a long campaign by Henrietta Maria to marry her son; indeed, Anne Marie's powerful royal persona might have suited the future Charles II. In addition, the Grande Mademoiselle found the prince rather attractive except for the fact that he had no kingdom and no money, and apparently no French. Prince Rupert helped the prince by translating his wooing conversations to Anne-Marie, who found the notion of a future with limited French extraordinary.[6]

After one extravagant party, the Grande Mademoiselle characteristically recorded her own grandeur.

> My dress was embroidered with diamonds, with tassels of crimson, black and white; I had on me all the crown jewels and those of the Queen of England, who still had some at that time. You could never see anything better or more magnificently adorned than I was that day, and there was no lack of people who told me, quite reasonably, that my height, my bearing, my pale skin and the brilliance of my blonde hair adorned me no less than all these treasures which shone on my person.

At this celebration of Anne Marie's total wonderfulness, she sat on a throne raised on a dais above the crowd, while her two first cousins, the King of France and the Prince of Wales, were happy at floor level. Everybody told the Grande Mademoiselle that she had never looked so relaxed as when she sat on this elevated throne. She agreed. 'The prince ... at my feet ... like my eyes, my heart looked down on him from a great height ... it was then my desire to marry the emperor.'⁷

*

In August 1646, Henrietta Stuart, aged just two, also arrived in Paris. At Oatlands Lady Dalkeith realised that she would soon be forced to hand the princess over to somebody chosen by Parliament, but the royal governess had no intention of being pushed around. Lady Dalkeith disguised herself as a hunch-backed beggar, took with her a *valet de chambre* as her husband, also dressed as a beggar, did her best to encourage Henrietta to behave as though she were their son Peter (or Pierre) – not very successfully, since, as every parent knows, two-year-olds like to do the opposite of what they are asked – and, carrying the child, walked from Oatlands to Dover, where they took the cross-channel packet to Calais like anyone else.

On arrival in France, the tall and usually elegant Lady Dalkeith cast off her rags and sent a message to Henrietta Maria, who at once sent carriages. When the party reached Paris, the queen was wild with joy. 'She embraced, she hugged, she kissed again and again that royal infant' and at once decided this child at least should be raised in the Catholic faith. The queen's gratitude to her sister-in-law Anne of Austria was also made gracefully evident. From this time, Princess Henrietta was known as Henriette Anne.⁸

*

When Oxford fell in 1646, James, Duke of York, was taken into the custody of Parliament. He joined Elizabeth and Henry at St James's, where the Earl of Northumberland was guardian to all three.

Two years later, in April 1648, the children were playing hide and seek inside the palace. James told his sister and brother that he knew a wonderful place to hide, where they would never find him. As they (and their attendants) averted their eyes, he went outside into the park, left through a door in the park wall, having prepared himself with the key, and joined Colonel Bampfield, who was waiting with a set of women's clothes made to fit. It was some time back at St James's Palace before the royal children's guardians realized how true it was that the Duke of York would, as he had said, never be found in the palace or the gardens.

Convincingly disguised as a girl, James sailed to Tilbury with Bampfield, where they transferred to a Dutch vessel which sailed to Middelburg. On 30 April 1648 James arrived at The Hague, where his sister Mary was delighted to welcome him. He liked to tell people that his outfit was so good that the sailors on the passage over thought he was a woman of easy virtue. He did not travel to Paris until early 1649. By this time, anyway, Henrietta Maria had the comfort of knowing that four of her children were beyond the reach of Parliament.[9]

*

In January 1649, Charles I was put on trial for treason, the argument being that he had used his inherited powers to pursue his own interests, not those of the country. The trial began on 20 January 1649 in Westminster Hall and concluded on 27 January, when he was declared guilty and sentenced to death. The king conducted his own defence magnificently, refusing to recognise the authority of the court, refusing to enter a plea. What he said was ignored. Witnesses were called and heard in the Painted Chamber, off Westminster Hall, but the king was not allowed to question them.

The king was right. The court that tried him was illegal. The House of Lords refused to support the trial so the Commons alone was represented. Parliament could act as a court, as in impeachment proceedings, but there was no precedent for the Commons alone acting as a court of law.

Nor was the Commons the body that had been elected. The Lower House was purged by the army. On 6 December 1648 Colonel Thomas Pride and his Regiment of Foot stood on the stairs leading to the House of Commons and refused admittance to any Member thought to be unreliable. Out of around 470 Members qualified to sit, about 110 were forcibly prevented from attending, and another 250 immediately stayed away. 'Pride's Purge' reduced the Long Parliament to a rump. Some of the estranged Members returned, but not those who were forcibly excluded. In all, 135 Commissioners were chosen from the Rump Parliament to sit in judgement on the king. Of these, only sixty-seven actually voted on his guilt.[10]

In this way Cromwell and his supporters forced the verdict through. On 30 January 1649, 'a very cold day', the king was beheaded in front of the Banqueting House of Whitehall Palace.[11]

Parliament had started its campaign against Charles I ten years before because the years of his personal rule threatened its rights and went against the tradition of the sovereign consulting Parliament. The Members were especially suspicious of the king's religious reforms, and thought the policies of Laud were a step away from returning the country to Roman Catholicism, which would damn both their souls and their property. The arguments of men such as John Pym and John Hampden were that the king was subverting the English constitution – these were also the charges against Henrietta Maria when her impeachment was first proposed – but by 1649, with the army in charge, the boot was on the other foot. The notion of a hereditary sovereign being guilty of treason was fraught with contradictions. Ignoring the will of the House of Lords was unheard of. The decimation of the Commons to achieve the vote of 'guilty' was a constitutional travesty. Whatever justice there was in Parliament's complaints against Charles I, the iron grip of Cromwell led to judicial murder.

36

A RELUCTANT MESSENGER

As her husband's trial approached, Henrietta Maria found herself in the middle of another civil war. The collapse of France both ruled out further French pressure on Cromwell, and obstructed what communication there was. At the worst possible time, Henrietta Maria became marooned.

The French civil war, called the Fronde, started in 1648 as a parliamentary protest against taxation. Barricades appeared in the streets of Paris, but they did not prevent Anne of Austria from leaving the city on 13 September. The queen regent was back in the Palais-Royal quite soon, because the royal government made concessions to the *parlementaires*, but this was not the conclusion of the parliamentary Fronde, it was only the start of a much longer period of disorder that spread to other parts of France. However, no French Pym emerged, the powers of the Parlement de Paris were much less than those of the English Parliament anyway, and there was never the religious undercurrent that was key in England and Scotland, so the French civil war turned into a very different type of conflict.

Just before the trial of Charles I, Anne of Austria decided to leave Paris a second time, in order to besiege and if necessary bombard her capital. This was possible in a way it had not been the previous September because French troops had come back from the war in Germany. The two greatest conflicts of the age – the Eighty Years War of the Dutch against Spain, and the Thirty Years War in Germany – had been concluded by the Peace of Westphalia, a series of treaties finalised in October 1648.[1]

In the small hours of 6 January 1649, on the feast of the Epiphany – the feast of the Three Kings – Anne of Austria and the French court left Paris for St Germain-en-Laye. It was done in total secrecy. No preparations were made at St Germain, and no announcement was made in Paris, in case the barricades returned.

Like others, the Grande Mademoiselle was woken in the dark to be told that the king and queen required her to join them in the carriages downstairs. The court escaped to St Germain-en-Laye, where nothing was ready. There were three camp beds in the Chateau Vieux, which Mazarin had arranged, for Louis XIV, Anne of Austria and himself. The flower of France spent the night on straw. The Orléans family took over the Château Neuf, where the Grande Mademoiselle – it being midwinter – slept in a room with no glass in the windows.[2]

The next day some beds were delivered, of which her father Gaston took his pick. He handed over the comfortable room he first slept in to his daughter. He did not bother to tell anyone else about his change of room, so the next morning the Grande Mademoiselle was woken by a considerable bustle in her new room, opened the curtains that closed in the bed, and was amazed to see a crowd of servants, completely unknown to her, preparing for her father's *levée*. They were more surprised than she was.

*

Françoise de Motteville had the opportunity to join the queen regent outside Paris but was too lazy to get out of bed in the middle of the night. She soon regretted this. When it became known that the royal court had abandoned Paris, hundreds of confused and frightened people rushed into the streets. In the end, after some increasingly dangerous brushes with rampaging hordes of Parisians, Mme de Motteville, with her sister and other ladies, found refuge with Henrietta Maria in the Louvre. Here she heard the citizens calling out, 'To arms, to arms!' during the night.[3]

Henrietta Maria's generosity cost little, but she had little to spend. Earlier in the year, not long after the departure, in June

1648, of the Prince of Wales for The Hague, where he planned to take charge of the English ships that had come over to his father's side, Mme de Motteville and a friend called on the queen, who was then on retreat at the Carmelite convent on the Faubourg St Jacques. Henrietta Maria showed her visitors a gold drinking cup and told them it was the only piece of gold she now possessed.

In the cold, dangerous January of 1649, Paul de Gondi visited Henrietta Maria in the Louvre, where he found her playing with her youngest daughter, who was still in bed. 'You see,' said the queen, 'I am keeping Henriette company. The poor child has not been able to get out of bed today because there is no fire in her room.' Her mother by now lived purely on a perfectly generous French pension but this, Gondi said, had not been paid for six months. He went to the Parlement de Paris to tell them how the daughter and granddaughter of Henri IV were living, and they voted Henrietta Maria a grant of 40,000 *livres tournois*.[4]

*

'To arms, to arms!' was nothing new to the Queen of England but it was a violent, frightening and impoverished time when Henrietta Maria learned that her husband was facing his worst crisis. Other than her youngest, the queen was without the support of her children, relying instead on Harry Jermyn, her most trusted lieutenant, and on her confessor Cyprien de Gamache.

She did what she could. In early January 1649 she wrote to Lord Fairfax, the parliamentary commander-in-chief, and to the French ambassador in London, the Comte de Grignan, to arrange a passport so that she could go to England just to be with the king. Nothing was done, but it was a remarkably brave attempt since she was thought to be a traitor in England. Her impeachment was never formally concluded, but the army's dominance at this time meant it was as good as done.[5]

The news came through uncertainly, with at least one false story about the king being rescued from the scaffold by his people. Henrietta Maria suffered a drawn-out agony, waiting for news, hoping for the impossible.[6]

On 19 February 1649 (in England 9 February), the queen wondered at the delayed return of a gentleman she had sent to St Germain-en-Laye for news from England. Harry Jermyn and the others in her court now knew for certain that Charles I had been executed; this was incalculable news for every one of them, but, worse, they did not know how to break it to their mistress.

Time passed. Just one person, the queen, in ignorance, was fretting about the messenger. Where had he got to? At last Jermyn said that the messenger was so faithful that he would not delay if the news he had were good. He managed to find the words. Henrietta suddenly understood that her husband was dead.

She went into a state of shock. She could not speak and could not move. She was 'like a statue'. Whatever her friends said, nothing penetrated. Time passed, night fell. The queen sat, immobile, staring, silent. Then the Duchesse de Vendôme, of whom she was extremely fond, came in tears, and kissed her hand and talked gently to her, and now Henrietta Maria was roused from the stupor into a long period of mourning.[7]

*

The next day Mme de Motteville was due to leave the Louvre and join the French court at St Germain, so she went to take her leave of the queen, who had saved her life in those awful first days of the strange siege of Paris, a permeable siege in which people went in and out of the city if they were provided with a pass. She knelt by the queen's bed while Henrietta Maria gave her a message for Anne of Austria. The queen said that Charles I had died because he had never been told the truth of the situation. She said that the people were a 'savage beast', and she advised Anne always to listen for the truth, saying that the worst thing that kings could ever do was to ignore the truth.[8]

In this way Henrietta Maria found consolation in the idea that her beloved husband had been deceived, which is not quite the verdict that historians have delivered on the tragic king, whose character was not really suited for the challenges he faced. However, it is possible the queen included self-deception in her understanding. At any rate, she shared Charles I's view of autocratic kingship and supported his struggle with matchless energy and total devotion to his cause. If he had been deceived, so had she.

PART SIX

RESOLUTION

Living and growing old are so much joined together, that even our imagination has difficulty in separating them.

François de Malherbe, letter to the Princesse de Conti, 29 July 1614

37

THE ROYAL OAK

On 9 March 1649, having been tried and found guilty of treason, the Duke of Hamilton, the Earl of Holland and Lord Capel were beheaded in Westminster Yard. Was it treason to fight for the King of England? Could a Scot – Hamilton – be guilty of treason against England? The rule of law in England seemed a shimmering mirage.

Henrietta Maria wrote to Hamilton's brother and heir, 'For consolation, it is not easy for me to offer you any ... We must turn ourselves to God and receive it of him, for this world cannot afford it.' Hamilton and Holland had been her friends, while Capel was a trusted member of her son's council. On the scaffold Capel told the priest George Morley that he had always been troubled by his decision, as a Member of the Commons, to vote for Strafford's execution in 1641, and now he was atoning for that sin with an identical death.

For the queen it was a time of deaths, one after another. They were not all royalist. The parliamentary envoy sent to the Dutch Republic was set upon and killed by a group of royalist Scots.[1]

*

The bleak new risen sun Cromwell followed a heavenly trajectory, reassured by success that God was on his side. He pursued the logic of the king's trial by closing and abolishing the House of

Lords on 19 March 1649, with the result that Parliament now consisted solely and entirely of a truncated House of Commons obedient to the army. Cromwell – 'personable but not handsome, nor did he look great nor bold' – is known for the destruction of the monarchy, but this was the first stage of his destruction of Parliament.[2]

At the end of April 1649, Henrietta Maria told her son, now Charles II, that he should go urgently to Ireland to lead the troops stationed there. At the beginning of the year, just before the execution of Charles I, Ormond and the Irish Confederacy agreed an alliance. A delicate balance for many reasons, it nonetheless held out the promise of a united Irish army for the young king. Charles II, however, was beaten to the charge by Cromwell, who, after being made Lord Lieutenant, travelled to Ireland with an army of twelve thousand to win the third Stuart kingdom for Parliament.[3]

From August 1649 to May 1650, Cromwell ran a vigorous Irish campaign whose main objective was to defeat royalist garrisons. An important secondary aim was naturally to return the country to obedience to England. In this both he and his men were inspired by fanatical anti-Catholicism. Cromwell's convictions were expressed when he wrote to Lord Wharton from his winter quarters, saying that his work in Ireland was like that of Phinehas, who ran his spear through an Israelite and a Midianite concubine, killing both as they were making love, thus healing the plague that was destroying the Israelites.[4]

That righteousness – that lack of pity – made its mark during Cromwell's sack of Drogheda (11 September 1649) and of Wexford (11 October 1649), in which taken together at least five thousand were killed, including Catholic clergy slaughtered in cold blood. The royalist governor of Drogheda, Sir Arthur Aston, was clubbed to death after he had surrendered. Cromwell's men stormed Wexford when the town was still negotiating surrender articles. Such actions, never forgotten by the Irish people, brutally returned Ireland to its status as an English colony and ruled out a royalist Irish renaissance.[5]

*

Elizabeth and Henry Stuart (respectively fourteen and nine at the beginning of 1650) were still living in England. Elizabeth was a prodigy who, unlike her mother (and father), could read and write Hebrew, Latin, Greek, Italian and French before she was eight. To the Stuart family, so keen on hunting, games, parties and battles, she was a luminous reminder of sixteenth-century learning.

Elizabeth and Henry saw their father quite often after he came south from Newcastle, especially once he was installed at Hampton Court. Elizabeth and Henry had the traumatic experience of meeting Charles I the day before he was executed. He held nothing back at this encounter, telling them his head would be cut off, and instructing Henry not to permit Parliament to put him on the throne in preference to either of his elder brothers. He said Parliament would only cut off the heads of the two elder boys, and then also that of Henry himself. Henry replied, 'I will be torn to pieces first.'[6]

Three months after her father's death, Elizabeth petitioned Parliament to be allowed to join her sister Mary in The Hague, a request rejected by a narrow majority in the House of Commons. Soon after, Henry and she were sent to live at Penshurst Place in Kent, in the care of the Countess of Leicester, who was instructed to treat them as the children of a noble family but with no royal honours.[7]

*

Meanwhile the Scots were angry that the English killed their king. Two days after the execution of his father, Charles II was proclaimed King of Scotland by the Edinburgh Parliament.

After Cromwell subjugated Ireland, Scotland was the only real option for the Stuarts. However, it was difficult to find terms of engagement because, as always, the Kirk faction in Scottish government insisted on their king being Presbyterian. Regardless, Henrietta Maria encouraged her son to maintain contact with 'our friends of the Scottish nation'.[8]

Henrietta Maria headed the 'Louvre group' of the English exiles. She supported almost any concessions to the government of Scotland short of signing the Covenant, but was opposed by advisers of Charles II such as Edward Hyde and Edward Nicholas. When she met her son and Nicholas in Beauvais in February and March 1650, there was a long battle from which the queen emerged 'red with fury'. In practical terms the problem was that

Charles II had given a commission to the Marquess of Montrose to lead troops against the Covenanter government, which he refused to withdraw. Pursuing that commission, Montrose was later captured.[9]

Charles II increasingly listened to advisers who feared his mother's opinions and character: Hyde, Nicholas, Ormond. The result was that during the 1650s the queen lost influence. This was not so different from her experience while Charles I was alive, since her husband habitually stuck to his own counsel, but Henrietta Maria's relationship with her husband had always been close and strong. She influenced his style, his determination and his direction, perhaps, more than individual decisions. She was also party to all family decisions such as the marriage of children. Her adult children were less interested in these inputs.

An early sign came when the young king, who had returned to France from The Hague, left his mother's court for Jersey in September 1649. With him he took his brother James, 'more to annoy his mother, with whom there is little love lost, than because prudence required it'.[10]

The widowed queen was always fighting to assert control of her children – except Henriette Anne, always the exception – both to help them in a world gone mad and to preserve her position. One has to remember how she twice knelt on the ground when her own mother arrived at St James's Palace in 1638, to understand the weight and force of parental authority in this period of history.

*

Despite royal quarrels, negotiations between the exiled court and the government of Scotland in the end led to an attempt to restore the Stuart monarchy in England.

Among the necessary concessions was acceptance of the death of Montrose on 21 May 1650 as punishment by the Scots for his long-drawn-out defiance of the Scottish government. Montrose went to the scaffold in a scarlet cloak 'moir beseiming a brydegrome, nor [than] a criminall going to the gallowis'. While Charles II did not sign away Montrose's life, as his father signed away Strafford's, and while the marquess must bear some responsibility for his own actions (he could have avoided capture if he had shown more caution), Montrose's death is another example of 'reason of state', all the more brutally absurd since the Scottish government was now ready to assist the king for whom Montrose fought.[11]

On 24 June 1650, Charles II landed at Garmouth, near Elgin. With him were a number of cavalier courtiers such as the Duke of Buckingham and Lord Wilmot, whose extravagant and, if they had the opportunity, immoral style was a horror to the Kirk party. The young king signed the Covenant and had to go further, signing, in August, a more-than-usually humiliating and pointless declaration which expressed his shame at his mother's idolatry and his father's many errors, and which disavowed the treaty in Ireland between Ormond and the Confederation (because the Confederation was Catholic). All such decisions were of course outside the queen's control.

The English Parliament took the Scottish threat seriously. They ordered the removal of Elizabeth and Henry from Penshurst to Carisbrooke in the Isle of Wight. The princess asked if she could stay at Penshurst on grounds of her health, but Parliament was afraid of having a Stuart princess available less than forty miles from London. The two were moved to Carisbrooke, where Elizabeth's health collapsed.

Sir Theodore Mayerne was asked by Parliament if she were really ill. She really was. On his last prescription for her, Mayerne wrote, 'She died on 8 September, about three o'clock in the afternoon, from a malignant fever then raging in the Isle of Wight, far from physicians and medicines.' He was a perceptive physician, noting that 'after the death of her father, she fell into great sorrow wherby all other ailments from which she suffered were increased'. Absorbing this horrible news – her daughter was little more than a child when she died – Henrietta Maria cast about hopelessly. She wrote to Christine, 'Although ... she may be happy to be out of the hands of these traitors ... and I should find reason to rejoice, I cannot be anything other than powerfully moved.' Henry was left alone with a handful of attendants, in a bleak castle off the English coast. The collateral damage was mounting.[12]

A second piece of family news was good, at least. On 4 November 1650 Mary gave birth to a son, the queen's first grandchild, another William of Orange, the first heir to Great Britain in the next generation. Yet the bad luck of the Stuarts could be seen even in this, since the baby's father, Mary's husband William, died of smallpox eight days before his son was born. Any hope of support from the Dutch state from now on vanished as the House of Orange confronted its domestic opponents in the States of Holland, who refused to grant the infant the rank of Stadholder. Henrietta Maria wrote to Christine, 'It seems God wants to make me see that I must detach myself entirely from the world, by taking away the people who make me dwell on it.' Republicanism was spreading.[13]

*

Charles II made uncertain progress in the north. After adventures including a failed coup and worse humiliation when the king fled and was retrieved by Scottish soldiers, the Kirk party, bar the extremists, realised that bullying their king was a mistake. They were right. It was no time for infighting. Cromwell had crossed the border in July 1650 with the intention of doing the same to Scotland as he had to Ireland. The Scottish government had to deal with a hostile invader.[14]

Cromwell taunted the indecisive Scots. In a letter of 3 August 1650, written from Musselborough, he made his famous appeal to the General Assembly of the Kirk, referring to their acceptance of Charles II – 'I beseech you, in the bowels of Christ, think it possible that you may be mistaken' – and went on to tell the Covenanters that 'there may be a Covenant made with Death and Hell', and advised them to read the text of Isaiah: 'We have made lies our refuge … '[15]

On 3 September, Cromwell engaged David Leslie's much larger army outside Dunbar, east of Edinburgh, the English troops numbering eleven thousand and the Scots twenty-two thousand. Leslie was deployed so that he threatened Cromwell's land route back to England, the Berwick Road, and it seemed impossible for Cromwell to win against these odds. Numerical superiority – at least parity – was usually essential for victory in battle. Having realigned his men in the dark before dawn, Cromwell attacked when there was barely any light, and delivered a surprise knockout blow to the Scottish right wing, then turned on their centre and drove them from the field. The confrontation that should have been his total defeat was his crushing victory. After the battle he was consumed with uncontrollable laughter.[16]

Exactly a year after Dunbar the second decisive battle of the Third English Civil War took place, and the final battle of the civil wars in Britain. It was some time before the crescendo because of Cromwell's poor health and the indecisiveness of the royalist Scots. Charles II was crowned King of Scotland at Scone on 1 January 1651, but when the campaigning season started later in the year Cromwell showed a sure grasp of strategy by advancing into the north of Scotland in August 1651. He did this to encourage the royalists to invade England. The royalists in Paris also wanted the king to advance on London. We do not know for sure whether Henrietta Maria supported a march into England, but the woman who was constantly telling her husband to be resolute can hardly have urged anything else on her son.[17]

Charles II took the bait. Against the advice of his general David Leslie, the king decided to advance towards London, thinking he would pick up support on the way. He led the Scottish army through Lancashire and the Welsh borders, which had provided his father with thousands of men, yet very few joined him because he was leading a foreign army under a foreign commander (Leslie), as parliamentary propaganda pointed out. On 22 August 1651, Charles II occupied Worcester with twelve thousand troops under his command, of which only two thousand were English. By contrast, Cromwell added to his army as he marched in pursuit. He had turned the tables. The odds were the opposite of those at Dunbar. Cromwell now led over thirty thousand men.[18]

*

The assault began on 3 September 1651. Charles II watched from the tower of the cathedral. He rushed down to rally his men when Cromwell captured the fort on the south east of Worcester, Fort Royal, and turned the guns on the city. The fight continued in the narrow streets as the parliamentarians poured in. Charles II tore off his heavy armour and joined battle in a shirt, urging his men to stand and fight. The weight of numbers told with the result that the king, sporting his garter star on his cloak, left Worcester at six in the evening with what remained of the main body of horse as escort.[19]

News of the battle reached Henrietta Maria in France soon afterwards. She wrote to the Mother Superior of the nunnery she had founded on the outskirts of Paris, 'I cannot go today to Chaillot ... on account of the bad news from England ... My uneasiness renders me unfit for anything, until I receive the news which arrives tonight.' That evening's despatches did nothing to clarify the whereabouts of Charles II.[20]

As she worried, Henrietta Maria had the company of James, and of Henriette Anne, but she had recently quarrelled with the former about his marriage plans, and the latter was seven. There would never be a good time to hear about the Battle of Worcester, but it was unusually bad timing for Henrietta Maria, since she had just attended (7 September) the ceremony at which the majority of Louis XIV was announced, which terminated the regency of Anne of Austria. The King of France was home and dry, while the King of Great Britain was missing.[21]

*

Charles II wanted to return to the fight after galloping away at Worcester, but a brief council of war at Barbons Bridge outside the city changed his mind. He decided to head for Scotland to regroup. Many royalist commanders had been killed, including the 2nd Duke of Hamilton (whose brother was executed in March 1649), but the Duke of Buckingham was with him, plus the earls of Derby and Lauderdale, and lords Talbot and Wilmot. In total, Charles II had about sixty followers on horseback.[22]

After the scoutmaster Richard Walker lost his bearings, Charles II and his diminished group of councillors decided to give up the attempt to return to Scotland. They also decided their large group attracted attention. Derby proposed that Charles II take refuge in Boscobel House, a secluded farmhouse belonging to the Catholic Giffard family, where Derby had himself stayed on the way to Worcester. Charles Giffard, one of the king's escort, suggested going first to his larger house White Ladies, built on the site of a Cistercian priory.

Here the king divested himself of his jewellery, including the garter George, handing different items to different courtiers for safe keeping, and after taking some desperately needed refreshment – 'sack and biscuit' – changed into a green suit and leather doublet, and left White Ladies by a back door with only one attendant and guide, Richard Penderel, a Giffard tenant. The king was going into hiding.

The rest of the party set off for a rendezvous with General Leslie, who was marching north by another route, but were attacked, and many taken prisoner, by a body of men under the parliamentarian Colonel Blundel. Not long after the cavaliers left White Ladies, other parliamentary soldiers arrived at the house looking for refugees. Charles II was right to disappear into the wilds of Shropshire. In this he was well advised by the Giffards and Penderels. They were well prepared to help, 'being accustomed to persecution and searches' because they were Catholic.[23]

At daybreak on 4 September 1651 the rain was pouring down, which meant that searches in the sodden outdoors were less likely – a help to the king, hidden in Spring Coppice, a wood near Boscobel House. Charles II watched as a troop of parliamentary horse rode past the wood, thinking they were men from the local militia rather than the New Model Army. He was brought food by the Yates and Penderel families, and at nine in the evening he and Richard Penderel set off for Madeley, planning to cross the River Severn and hide in Wales.[24]

At Madeley the king spent the night in a barn, while Richard Penderel discussed with his friend Mr Woolf – the barn's owner – the chances of a successful crossing of the Severn. They decided the bridges were too well guarded. The next day the king and Penderel returned to Boscobel, where another royalist Catholic, Colonel William Careless, was now in hiding. Richard's sister-in-law fed Charles II and dried his shoes and stockings.

Although Boscobel was remote, the chances were that soldiers would come back. Careless therefore suggested that he and Charles II hide in the woods once more. They climbed a large oak tree in an open field and stayed there all day, fortified by bread, cheese and beer supplied by the Penderels. Some of the time the king slept, his head in Careless's lap. They watched soldiers thrash through the nearby wood, the obvious hiding place.[25]

In the evening they returned to Boscobel House, where Charles II allowed Richard Penderel's brother to cut his hair short, and then he and Richard set off for Moseley, where Wilmot was staying in a house belonging to the Whitgeaves, also Catholics, who had an attendant priest, Fr Huddleston.

The king's day in the branches of the Boscobel oak was not his last adventure, nor was he wearing the last of his disguises, but it was the beginning of the escape of Charles II. Disguised as the servant of Mrs Lane, travelling with a party of gentry, the king headed for the coast, hoping to find a ship at Bristol, then on the Sussex coast. In the latter he was finally successful, setting off with Wilmot from the fishing village Brighthelmstone (now Brighton) on 15 October 1651, almost six weeks after the Battle of Worcester, and landing at Fécamp on the Norman coast.

*

The king and Wilmot travelled incognito to Rouen, where they stayed at the house of a Mr Scot, who sent a message to Henrietta Maria in Paris. It was not until 29 October that Charles II set off to see his mother, his brother James and his sister Henriette Anne. Henrietta Maria had suffered an agony of nearly two months while she waited to hear whether her son was alive.

The queen took exuberant delight in her son's presence and in his amazing cool in the course of these adventures. His safety had been secured by the Catholic families of Shropshire, which gave his mother a deep satisfaction. In his disguise as a servant he unsurprisingly made mistakes, but carried off the nerve-wracking act without a word of complaint, and apparently without fear. He was recognised more than once, but never betrayed, so there was loyalty to the king in England.

When he found the opposite he enjoyed himself. On the road to Bristol Charles II found himself in conversation with a smith, whom he asked for news of any refugees from Worcester. The smith said he had not heard whether that 'rogue Charles Stuart' had been taken, and Charles II replied, 'If that rogue were taken, he deserved to be hanged more than all the rest.'[26]

Safe in France, Charles II came down from the high. The different moods of mother and son were noted in a November despatch from Paris, which recorded that the queen 'is constantly wonderful merry, and seemeth to be overjoyed to see the king safe near her, but he is very sad, and sombre for the most part ... he is very silent always, whether he be with his mother, or in any other company'. The king's experience of Scotland and England was a baptism of fire from which he emerged fully adult, fully king. He was not happy in his mother's company and was not the only person to think that the queen was 'not easily pleased'.[27]

38

THE CONSOLATIONS OF RELIGION

Among the more depressing acts of Cromwell's regime was the abolition of Christmas on 24 December 1652. Soon after, on 20 April 1653, Cromwell rid himself of Parliament by personally dissolving the Rump Parliament, striding out of the empty House of Commons holding the parliamentary mace, the symbol of power. He was not the king, nor yet was he even Lord Protector. Even if he was the king, the dissolution went against the Act passed in 1641, by which only Parliament could dissolve itself. Just like Charles I, he brought a troop of soldiers with him to make sure the Members obeyed. Just like Charles I, he found the self-aggrandising behaviour of the Parliament impossible. So much for the civil war.[1]

Henrietta Maria had longed for the end of Parliament – 'certainly I wish a peace ... but I would the disbanding of the perpetual parliament first' – and now it was achieved by her greatest enemy, and still more irritatingly the New Model Army made possible the union of England and Scotland in a single realm, something all the Stuarts wanted.[2]

Cromwell became Lord Protector of the Commonwealth of England, Scotland and Ireland on 15 December 1653, after the dissolution of the 'nominated assembly' or Barebones Parliament, which briefly and unsatisfactorily replaced the Rump. As its name makes clear, this failed 'Parliament' was unelected.[3] The Barebones Parliament was named after one of its members, Baptist Praisegod Barbon, whose name seemed absurd to its critics.

*

In France, the Fronde turned into a rebellion of the Princes of the Blood, mainly the Prince de Condé (but also Gaston d'Orléans), against the royal government. On 8 May 1652, Henrietta Maria wrote to Christine in Savoy, 'Nobody dares go outside the gates of Paris without risking their life, whether from soldiers, robbers or peasants, who are ruined, so they hide in the woods and kill the passers-by.' She told her sister she was short of food, and did not know where she would be safe. Her psychological vulnerability once more emerged with characteristic honesty: 'It is true that after my troubles I should not be afraid, death offering nothing frightening, but the manner of death is something to fear, not coming when one would like it.' Fatalism followed: 'God wants to humiliate kings and princes. He began with us in England. I pray that France is not going to follow.'[4]

In July, Paris was so unsafe that she left the Louvre at night to take refuge at St Germain with the French court, something she had not considered in 1649. At Anne of Austria's court everyone was nervous. When Henrietta Maria offered advice to her sister-in-law, Anne asked her if she wanted to be Queen of France as well as England.[5]

The princely Fronde reached its climax in Paris in summer 1653, when the Grande Mademoiselle, having persuaded the Parisians to open the city's gates to admit Condé's army, turned the Bastille cannons on the pursuing royal troops, prompting Mazarin to remark that she was 'killing her husband', meaning Louis XIV. Having failed to become either Queen of Spain or Empress, Anne Marie now wanted to marry her cousin, eleven years her junior. Louis XIV was not killed by Anne Marie's cannons, but her hopes of making him her husband naturally were. In fact, Louis XIV, soon back in Paris, thought it wise to banish the Grande Mademoiselle to internal exile.[6]

As the civil disturbances died down, the Prince de Condé traitorously transferred his allegiance to the King of Spain, with whom France was still at war, so the Fronde melted into the ongoing war between France and its traditional enemy. These events, and most of all this war with Spain, were the priority of Mazarin. By comparison, the problems of the Queen of England were unimportant.

Henrietta Maria's hopes were knocked further when Mazarin approached Cromwell's Commonwealth in early 1654 to sound out an alliance. Mazarin had not turned enemy to the queen and her family; his concern was Spain, which was looking for the friendship of Cromwell against France. He asked Cromwell whether he would pay Henrietta Maria the revenues from her dower, due on the death of her husband. Cromwell ruthlessly answered that she had never been crowned queen so nothing was owed.[7]

Mazarin continued Henrietta Maria's pension – she was a Daughter of France – but the talks meant that Charles II had to leave France in order to set his court up elsewhere. In July 1654 he went first to Spa, then to Cologne. An alliance was agreed between France and the Commonwealth, which precluded French support for the return of the Stuarts.[8]

*

Henrietta Maria turned forty-five in 1654. For her miseries, which included poor health, she found consolation in religion. The queen founded a new convent on the outskirts of Paris at Chaillot, in a large house that had belonged to François de Bassompierre situated on rising ground on the north bank of the Seine. She bought Chaillot on 14 July 1651 with money donated by her friends. Here the queen installed eleven nuns of the Order of the Visitation, founded by St François de Sales, one of the leaders of the French Counter-Reformation. With the nuns came support staff, including an apothecary, Brother Nicholas, who labelled his drugs with sketches of the herbs which went into them.[9]

Salesian Catholicism had its share of mysticism but was new in its emphasis on the spiritual life of the laity, of ordinary people – religion was not the specialty of those in holy orders, it was for everyone (almost a Protestant concept!) – and in proposing that charity was a more important path to God than penance. Henrietta Maria's brand of Catholicism was modern, generous and practical. She was not a natural reader but she repeatedly read religious texts, notably Thomas á Kempis's *Imitation of Christ*, again a text of the new Catholicism.[10]

The interior of the building at Chaillot was originally magnificent, too much so for the nuns, who refused to live in the grand rooms and installed themselves in the attic until the ornamentation was removed. They were probably influenced by the fact that before they moved in it had been a brothel.

The queen had a set of rooms overlooking the river always at her disposal. While at Chaillot she submitted herself to the rule of the convent, including the authority of the Mother Superior, which was perhaps not exercised with great force but was real authority, like that of the queen's personal confessor. She was often there, sometimes staying several months, during which time, like a nun, she spoke to visitors through a grille.[11]

*

During and after the Battle of Worcester, Henry, Duke of Gloucester, aged eleven, was at Carisbrooke Castle. The Commonwealth then largely lost its fear of the Stuarts, and did not want the expense of maintaining a royal prince. Henry was released from house arrest in December 1652.

In early 1653 he travelled to the Dutch Netherlands, where his elder sister Mary happily took him in. Henrietta Maria quickly insisted on Henry's joining her in Paris, where he arrived in April. For the first time Henry really made his mother's acquaintance, and that of his eldest brother, Charles, whom he last saw when he was left behind at St James's Palace, aged eighteen months. Henry was an intelligent, nice-looking boy who attracted crowds of visitors to his mother's court.[12]

The departure of Charles II for Flanders in 1654 left the young prince entirely under the authority of Henrietta Maria. Sometimes James, Duke of York, came to Paris, but he was now in full-time employment serving in the French army under his hero the Vicomte de Turenne. Henrietta Maria wrote to Christine, 'The little one stays here, I want to make something good for him, if I can.' In July 1654, just after his departure, Charles II wrote to Henry to make everything clear, with instructions to obey his mother in all things, 'religion only excepted' – the same instructions his father gave him eight years before. Both parts of this message were weighty.

It was important that Henry understood his duty of obedience to the queen, but it was important to protect royal Protestantism.[13]

Henrietta Maria briskly hauled out the siege artillery. By mid-October 1654 Henry was sent to Pontoise, fifteen miles outside Paris, under the care of Wat Montagu – Fr Wat, the Abbé de St Martin. He was told that his Catholic education would now begin. When she took Henry in hand in this way, Henrietta Maria thought she was acting within her rights as queen, mother and of course as a Catholic, and she thought it was the best for Henry. The inevitable anger of Charles II would hopefully come too late.

In her defence, there were other factors. The prince suffered from the way he was brought up, cut off from his family, surrounded by spies. Spoiled by new attention and respect, Henry was a bit disturbed – perhaps even, by the strict standards of his mother's court, out of control. The Protestant royalist Lord Hatton, who was living in Paris, said that Henry's 'carriage to all persons is unsupportable' and worried that the boy would 'contract so great rudeness (besides other vices) as may be very troublesome'. Henrietta Maria told Charles II that Henry was shirking his studies. The queen wanted to instil discipline.[14]

She also wanted a future for Henry, not just in the world of eternity but in the fallible world of the seventeenth century too, where a cardinal's hat – or a rich Catholic wife – might be essential. In addition, like France, the Protestant powers – the Danes, the Dutch and the Swedes – had made terms with the Commonwealth. If Henry converted, it would be a sign to Spain, the Pope and the Emperor – the only powers that had not recognised the Commonwealth – that the Stuarts had a spark of life in them.

The queen's plans leaked. Hatton, living in Paris, wrote to Sir Edward Nicholas, secretary of Charles II, telling him that carpenters were busy constructing quarters for his brother at the Jesuit college at Clermont. In England it was reported that Henry had already gone to the college and was rewarded by a fat pension. Charles II was therefore alerted soon enough. He was sure that a Catholic conversion would savage his cause in England, with the result that Edward Hyde told Mary of Orange, 'I have never in my life seen the king in so great trouble of minde.'[15]

The trouble was not just the conversion project; it was also the fact that his authority as king was being defied by his mother, and perhaps – was Henry compliant? – by his brother. Mary wrote to Hyde that the attempt to convert Henry was 'this great misfortune'. In Paris, Henrietta Maria was devious. She blocked the posts to and from her son's court so that he would remain in the dark about Henry, and to give time for the conversion.[16]

On 20 November Lord Ormond arrived in Paris, ordered by Charles II either to persuade Henrietta Maria to desist or remove Henry from her influence. Henry's own wishes became clear when he asked both his brothers for help. Because the queen refused to play ball, Ormond went to Pontoise without her permission, and after some difficult meetings with Henrietta Maria was obliged to escort her son to Lord Hatton's house in Paris. From there they left France in mid December 1654.

Henrietta Maria told Charles she had not promised to leave Henry Protestant, only that she would not force his conversion. If Henry wanted to convert, she could hardly stand in his way. With some justification, the king thought that his mother's actions were 'as much acts of force as can reasonably be supposed to be offered'.

In a characteristic combination of memory lapse and certainty, Henrietta Maria then told Charles that his father could not have prevented her from encouraging the conversion of Henry had he been alive. It made matters worse that she was not acting alone. Anne of Austria told Henry he should obey his mother and convert, exactly the sort of foreign interference dreaded by the king's councillors and always deeply resented in England.

Henrietta Maria lost face. She told Henry 'she would no more own him as her son' and 'forbid him any more to set his foot into her lodgings'. She told Ormond that she 'would take no more care of him [Henry]'. Ormond had to pawn his garter star to raise funds to transport the prince to Cologne, because the queen ordered her servants to refuse the prince food – and to strip his bed.[17]

39

MARY'S VISIT

The Princess of Orange arrived in Paris in February 1656, to spend time with the mother she had not seen for fourteen years. It was another reunion. Her brother Charles tried to stop the visit because he was working up an alliance with Spain against the Commonwealth – a friend of France was an enemy of Spain – and because of the trial of strength with his mother. Mary wrote to Charles in November to calm him down, saying 'how reasonable a thing' it was for her to see her mother. Henrietta Maria knew she was up against her son and did not stop 'commanding me [Mary] to make all the haste I can'.[1]

Mary believed that members of their various courts had stirred up trouble within the Stuart family. She told her brother, 'Do not think this journey has any thing in it of a desire to see France, or Paris, but merely to see the Queen and sastisfie her in those things which she has been ill informed concerning myself.' She had already told Charles of the 'hot heads which has [sic] studied nothing but how to make the Queene angre with you and me'.[2]

At this time the widowed princess was in the habit of travelling outside the Dutch Republic in order to see her brothers, who were forbidden to visit her on Dutch territory. She was a person of interest, being royal, beautiful, single and rich. In Paris, the people who were curious about Henry became obsessed with Mary. They flocked to the Queen of England's court to see her glamorous twenty-four-year-old daughter, dressed in black to conform with her mother's rule of perpetual mourning but covered in fabulous pearls and diamonds.[3]

During the visit, Henrietta Maria's life was transformed. The French tended to keep away from her rooms in the Palais-Royal because there was nothing to gain from an impoverished court, but the dazzling Mary of Orange was another matter. Mary alone was worth the view and there was gossip about a second husband: the King of Sweden, the Duke of Savoy, the Duke of Brunswick? The Duke of Buckingham had already tried. Perhaps there would be a French husband. Perhaps, despite being Protestant, the beautiful Mary was eying the King of France.

On 18 February 1656 Henrietta Maria wrote to Charles II, 'I think she is very weary of visitors from morning till evening; she has enough for me too. I am almost dead with them.' Having told Charles it was a duty trip, Mary now wrote to say what fun she was having. She was laden with presents, including a petticoat of cloth of silver with leather embroidery, and she was repeatedly in the company of Louis XIV, who visited the Palais-Royal in masquerade – she arrived in time for carnival – and gave parties for her at the Louvre. Mary enjoyed herself so much that she stayed until the following autumn.[4]

On a visit with her mother to the Grande Mademoiselle, still living away from the court, Mary effusively embraced her haughty cousin, whom she had put in the shade. Sitting later with her aunt, Anne Marie was pleased to hear the queen tell her, 'My daughter is not like me. She makes a show of magnificence. She has her jewels, money, loves spending. I tell her every day one has to manage things, one has to be a manager, that I was like her – and better – and now she sees the state I am in.'

Henrietta Maria also told Anne Marie that if she (Anne Marie) had only married Charles II, then she (Henrietta Maria) would get on a lot better with her son. The Grande Mademoiselle, in a rare effusion of tact, replied that if the king could not get on with his mother, with whom could he possibly get on? Another tactic was to reassure Anne Marie that a marriage with Charles II would return her to favour in the French court (probably true).[5]

It could not be denied that the queen and her eldest son were on poor terms. Henrietta Maria does not appear to have found the strength to rise above the Henry quarrel, so it was left to Harry Jermyn to pour oil on troubled waters. He told the king not to judge his mother's feelings by her words and style, which both had a 'sharpness that in her heart she is not guilty of', and reassured him that Henrietta Maria felt towards him (Charles II) 'all the tenderness and kindness which can be imagined'.[6]

There was a political reason for distance between Henrietta Maria and her son. The king secured the alliance he wanted with Spain, under which he hoped to command six thousand soldiers provided by Philip IV. This deal in itself reduced the influence of Henrietta Maria, since France was still at war with Spain. Could Spain spare six thousand solders for the Stuarts? Nobody was going to tell Henrietta Maria.

*

The queen took her eldest daughter out of the nursery when she was ten, sacrificing the child for the interests of the father. There was nothing odd about this. Royal children were born to be used. But there is no reason to think it was an easy thing for mother or daughter.

Mary repaid this rejection with affection and political projects, exactly what Henrietta Maria needed. One of the problems of the Princess Royal's life was that she regarded her mother-in-law Amalia as her social inferior, which was true by the standards of the time[7] but wrong, and probably unnecessary, to belabour. This inevitably led to family problems and an appeal to her mother.

Before he died in 1650, Mary's husband William left a letter which said that in the case of his death, only Mary's orders should be followed – not, by implication, those of Amalia. There were important matters of business to settle after his death, such as the guardianship of their infant son and the stewardship of the fortune of the House of Orange. Since the Prince of Orange was so close to being a monarch, these matters required the attention of the States of Holland, not just the family. The prince's letter was suppressed by Baron Dohna, a supporter of Amalia, with the result that Mary was shut out from control of the money, since Amalia and others feared she would give too much to the Stuart cause. Mary at least shared the official guardianship of her son William with Amalia and the Elector of Brandenburg. She also found the letter, which made family relations worse but did not change the settlement of the estate, which the States of Holland had already agreed.[8]

Mary asked Henrietta Maria for help. Her obsession was the regency of the principality of Orange itself, in the south of France, which she felt was hers by right. With the connivance of Anne of Austria, who ordered neighbouring French garrisons to stand by, Henrietta Maria sent a group of armed men to surprise the fortress at Orange, and to capture or kill the governor (an Amalia loyalist).

The plot was betrayed. People thought Henrietta Maria's intention was to sell the principality to the highest bidder in order to raise money for the Stuart cause in England (alone she could not do this). However, it helped her recover her energies at a bad time, and Mary's later visit to Paris was energising. The quarrels over Orange continued and ultimately led to the loss of the territory to France. In 1656 Mary asked Louis XIV for help, which he later provided, but French help never increased the power of the House of Orange.

*

Before Mary returned to The Hague, Henrietta Maria met another famous exiled queen, Christina of Sweden, who was visiting France because she too was part of a conspiracy, in her case a more ambitious one against the Kingdom of Naples. Henrietta Maria, with her daughters, headed the welcoming group in the Place Royale, when Christina, ignoring the elaborate rolling platform carefully constructed to carry her in state, entered Paris on horseback on 8 September 1656, dressed in a scarlet skirt and bodice and a hat with black plumes over her blonde wig.

The twenty-nine-year-old Christina, only child of the warrior king Gustavus Adolphys, was a famous oddity. Having announced she would never marry, she abdicated the crown of Sweden on 6 June 1654 in favour of her cousin, converted to Catholicism and took up residence in Rome. She was a brilliant scholar and connoisseur, speaking eight languages, including perfect French.

The Duc de Guise, who met her in Lyon, wrote a pen portrait. 'She wears a man's wig ... Her bodice is laced crosswise at the back; it is made almost like a man's vest ... The skirt is very badly fastened and not straight. She always wears a lot of powder and lots of face cream and she hardly ever wears gloves. She wears men's shoes and she sounds and moves like a man as well ... she knows more than the whole of our Académie at the Sorbonne.' Mme de Motteville met Christina later, and took to her after a pause at the 'clothes and her odd hairstyle' but added she was 'sunburnt, and she looked like a sort of Egyptian street girl'. Although they were very dirty, she thought the queen's hands were nicely shaped.[9]

It is sad there is no record of the conversations between the two queens. Although Henrietta Maria did not have either the learning or eccentricity of Christina, there was a good deal of common ground. Both were exiles, both Catholics, both were daughters of famous soldier kings who died violently. Both were small.[10] There were two visits while Christina was in Paris, one by Henrietta Maria to Christina at the Louvre and one by Christina to Henrietta Maria at the Palais-Royal, at which the Swedish queen was observed to stay for longer than expected and to be more attentive and interested than anywhere else. Once again, the charm of Henrietta Maria was evident.

The Naples conspiracy, of which Henrietta Maria knew nothing, would have placed Christina on the throne of the Kingdom of Naples, in place of the Spanish viceroy, leaving it, when she died, to the Duc d'Anjou, the brother of Louis XIV. It came to nothing.[11]

*

With the help of Anne of Austria, Henrietta Maria in 1657 bought the Château de Colombes, seven miles north-west of Paris, as her country home from then on. The acquisition of Colombes marks the time when Henrietta Maria decided to spend the rest of her life in France.

Although she was perennially short of money, court life in France was filled with entertainments like those she once organised herself: ballets, plays, picnics, summer bathing parties in the Seine. She occupied the highest rank in society. She had the consolation of religion in Chaillot, and spectacular Catholic celebrations such as the Corpus Christi procession in early summer, when the streets of Paris were hung with tapestries, altars were erected outside and the houses were adorned with holy images.[12]

Her sons were living independently, scorning her authority, but she had Henriette Anne to settle. This girl, the most loved, the only Catholic child, was raised as a French princess. 'I would wish that the beauty of her body was as great as that of her soul, because she really is a good girl ... the desire I have for her to be beautiful makes me think, perhaps, that she is not.'[13]

Not that Henrietta Maria turned against the English. 'Her Majesty had a great affection for England ... Her discourse was much with the great men and ladies of France in praises of the people and of the country; of their courage, generosity, good nature; and would excuse all their miscarriages in relation to unfortunate effects of the late war as if it were a convulsion of some desperate and infatuated persons.'[14]

The queen's appetite for life came back with Mary's visit, thanks to her daughter's warmth, and to the crowds she attracted. By 1660 Henrietta Maria's court at the Palais-Royal was more popular than the French royal court at the Louvre, 'the good humour and wit of our queen mother, and the beauty of the princess her daughter giving greater invitation than the more particular humour of the French queen, being a Spaniard'. A friend bore witness to Henrietta Maria's sharp intelligence, her quickness, but also her lack of malice: 'Her conversation was free and entertaining ... even though she was innocent in intention, someone in the group was often a bit wounded [by what she said].'[15]

She did not hope for change in Britain during her lifetime. The fun-hating Commonwealth had international recognition and seemed to have a stable constitution on the Dutch model, with a Lord Protector as head of state, a bit like the Stadholder, but really with far greater powers, in fact like an autocratic king. Cromwell's confidence was shown in his expansion of the navy. He was happy to order a likeness of himself on the figurehead of a new warship, featuring six figures in national clothing: a Scot, an Irishman, an Englishman, a Dutchman, a Spaniard and a Frenchman. The Lord Protector reared above on a stallion, trampling them underfoot.[16]

40

RESTORATION AND LOSS

Cromwell won the Battle of Dunbar on 3 September 1650, and the Battle of Worcester on 3 September 1651. In 1658 the Lord Protector was worn down by the painful death from cancer of his favourite daughter, Elizabeth Claypoole (6 August), and in his depressed state a recurrent malarial fever made him sick, which led to a chest infection, then pneumonia. He slipped into feverish dreams, alternating with periods of lucidity, during one of which he named his eldest son, Richard, as his successor. He died less than a month after his daughter, by a weird coincidence on 3 September 1658.[1]

When she heard the news, the firebrand Henrietta Maria wrote surprising words to Mme de Motteville: 'I thought you would hear with joy the death of that wretch; yet ... I will confess to you that I have not felt myself any great rejoicing.' There was no triumphalism.[2]

The new Lord Protector, Richard Cromwell, was admired for his dignity, his gentleness of manner and economy of words, but these were not the qualities to hold the Protectorate together. A new parliament was called, and met for the first time on 27 January 1659. It did not last. On 22 April it was dissolved because the army was opposed to discussion of army reform. After pressure from the generals, the Rump Parliament was recalled, being based on army support. Richard Cromwell resigned as Lord Protector on 25 May, but the new Rump only lasted until 13 October, when the Commons was again emptied by military command.

The army now ruled the Commonwealth under generals Lambert, Desborough and Fleetwood, the latter being known as the 'weeping Anabaptist'.[3]

*

Without Parliament money could not be raised to pay the soldiers, but this was a purely English problem. The commander of the English army in Scotland, George Monck, had recently received a grant, so his men were happy and also well equipped. A highly experienced professional soldier who had fought for Charles I and then, when royalism seemed defeated, for Parliament, Monck disliked the emerging religious extremism. On 20 October 1659, having started a purge of the radical officers in the Scottish garrisons, Monck sent a message of defiance to the army council in England.

On 8 December 1659, he advanced to Coldstream on the English border to await events. Lord Fairfax, once Commander-in-Chief of the New Model Army, occupied York in support of Parliament against the English generals, while the English army at Newcastle, which was meant to block Monck, disintegrated because of lack of pay and because the military government was losing credibility. In the south of England there were mutinies and protests. The Rump returned. In very cold weather – 'the frost was great and the snow greater' – Monck led his army into England and south to London.[4]

He was now the champion of the reconstituted Parliament, but like everyone else he found that Parliament was an unreliable friend. In February 1660 it made an attempt to assert its authority by depriving him of the rank of Commander-in-Chief. Backed by troops, he held the whip hand and refused to accept dismissal. The general defied the Rump, but what did he want in its place? Charles II saw his opportunity. The king sent agents and letters to Monck, who realised that he could benefit personally from the return of the Stuarts. The popular mood was turning to royalism; Monck could turn with it.

After negotiating, quite amicably, with the sitting Members, Monck decided to readmit to Parliament the Members removed in Pride's Purge at the end of 1648, those who were opposed to the trial of Charles I. He did this on the agreement that Parliament would at once dissolve itself and vote for new elections. He favoured an end to military rule on condition that the slate was wiped clean. For once the Commons stuck to their bargain and voted for dissolution and new elections.

On 25 April the Convention Parliament met and recognised a House of Lords, although one that did not at first include peers that had come of age since the Lords was abolished. There was a royalist majority regardless that went with popular feeling. To people across the country, the Commonwealth seemed a dismal experiment to be instantly terminated. Monck showed exceptional judgement throughout, insisting that the key to the settlement was the will of the Commons.[5]

The Commons and the Lords then voted, on 1 May 1660, for the return of the Stuart monarchy with no conditions attached. Samuel Pepys recorded the atmosphere: 'Great joy yesterday at London, and at night more bonfires than ever, and ringing of bells, and drinking of the King's health upon their knees in the streets, which methinks is a little too much.'[6]

On 23 May 1660 Charles II sailed from Schevelingen for Dover, where he was met by General Monck and Mrs Monck. He called the general 'father'. On his thirtieth birthday, 29 May 1660, the king entered London with his brothers. He rode through the city between long files of foot soldiers, surrounded by Londoners gone mad with joy. Many of these people were the same who violently demonstrated against his father in the early 1640s, the apprentices grown up.

The king went to Whitehall Palace. It was in a poor state of repair, so he used his presence chamber as a chapel, giving thanks to God for the miraculous sequence of events that brought him home. Writing to her son, Henrietta Maria also made the point – 'we must, amidst all this, praise God; all this is from His hand'; 'the hand of God is perceptibly traced therein'. For three days and nights bonfires were lit in the streets of London, and effigies of Cromwell burned.[7]

*

One drama followed another. After twenty-four years of war, France and Spain made peace by signing the Treaty of the Pyrenees (in 1659), whose terms included the marriage of Louis XIV and the infanta Maria Teresa of Spain. The wedding took place on the French Atlantic coast at St Jean de Luz on 9 June 1660 (after a proxy wedding in Spain). This was soon after the restoration of Charles II, so Henrietta Maria stayed in Paris waiting for news from England, but when the young King of France and his ash-blonde and very pious wife made their official entry into Paris (26 August 1660), she was watching the procession at the side of Anne of Austria, from the Hôtel de Beauvais.

The Stuarts then prepared to gather in Whitehall Palace. What would happen when Henry met his mother, who had thrown him out six years before? Like his brother James, Henry went into Spanish service (Spain was allied with Charles II). On 14 June 1658, James and Henry fought in the Battle of the Dunes outside Dunkirk. The encounter finished with a French victory over Spain, which led to the Peace of the Pyrenees. It provides the one slight piece of evidence we have that Henrietta Maria had forgiven Henry. On 21 June, Jermyn wrote to Charles II at Paris to ask for news of the dukes of York and Gloucester.[8]

When Charles II landed at Dover, hundreds of people cried out, 'God save the king!' again and again, but Henry was heard to be shouting, 'God bless General Monck!' After the royal party was settled in London, Henry attended the House of Lords as Duke of Gloucester, and took part in the debates. This promising young man fell ill with smallpox at the beginning of September. After the doctors gave a confident prognosis of recovery, he died on 13 September 1660, aged twenty. It cannot have been easy news for his mother.[9]

*

By Henrietta Maria's standards, the situation of James, Duke of York, was little better. While the Stuarts were in the wilderness James had fallen in love with Anne Hyde, the strong-minded daughter of Charles II's Lord Chancellor Edward Hyde. James and Anne met in Paris, when Anne was in attendance on Mary during that prolonged 1656 visit. Anne found she was pregnant in spring 1660, just as her lover's prospects were about to be transformed – in short, at the worst possible time.

James asked his brother the king for permission to marry her, and was refused. James was now heir to a perfectly viable throne, so his wife and his children were raised – or lowered – to the status of pawns in the European chess game. Of course there would be more suitable wives for the Duke of York than a daughter of the middling gentry, and, as Charles II already knew from personal experience, there was nothing wrong with an illegitimate child. However, the king changed his mind, with the result that on 3 September 1660 – two years exactly after the death of Cromwell – James and Anne were married in secret.[10]

On 22 October, Anne gave birth to a son. As the labour pains increased, she was repeatedly asked who the father of the child was. She stuck to the truth, that the father was the Duke of York, but her situation was complicated by the refusal of James at this critical moment to acknowledge the marriage. At the same time, Charles Berkeley and Harry Jermyn told Charles II that Anne was involved with them too (it was not true). The parents tactfully named the infant Charles.

Here was the second legitimate grandchild of Henrietta Maria, but the queen detested Anne's father Edward Hyde, and refused to accept what was anyway an impossible marriage. The flavour of her relationship with Hyde can be caught in her earlier remark that 'the chancellor was so far from giving her fair words and flattering her, that she did verily believe, if he thought her to be a whore, he would tell her of it', testimony which Hyde considered a compliment.[11]

Anne naturally kept the pregnancy a secret from her father until the king's view on the situation was clear, but Hyde discovered the truth when Charles II (informed by his brother) instructed lords Ormond and Southampton to bring him up to date. He flew into a panic which vaporised every drop of paternal love, and demanded that his daughter be put on trial. The ludicrous reaction was ignored by the king, who understandably decided that his chancellor was suffering from a spell of insanity, but it shows the terrible embarrassment of the situation for all involved. Part of Hyde's hysteria was fear of Henrietta Maria.

On 28 October, the queen wrote to Christine, 'A girl who abandons herself to a prince will easily give herself to another man. I leave tomorrow for England to marry the king my son and try to unmarry the other.' It was hardly a fair comment – it was possibly the opposite of the truth – but, harried by such thoughts, at the beginning of November 1660, Henrietta Maria travelled to London, bringing with her Henriette Anne, and her nephew Prince Edward of the Rhine, the son of Elizabeth of Bohemia. It was widely believed that, before she heard about Anne, she had not intended to travel to England at all.[12]

However, the queen also had important financial agreements to conclude. She was owed money from her dower lands, which had not been paid for many years. Much of her property now belonged to others, and the land was wrecked by war, needing investment before it could become productive again. Instead she was offered a pension of £30,000 a year, which Charles II bumped up with another £30,000 a year from his own income. Second, and just as important, she needed to secure a dowry for Henriette Anne, who was due to marry her cousin, Philippe d'Orléans, brother of Louis XIV (known as Monsieur). Their cousin the Comte de Soissons was the ambassador extraordinary sent to London to negotiate the marriage formally. In short, the return of the queen was not a gracious progress to see her beloved English – it was an attack on Anne Hyde, and a business trip.[13]

*

Samuel Pepys found the Thames was crowded with boats to watch the queen arrive at Whitehall, but he counted only three bonfires in the streets of London to celebrate her return. When he saw her dine in Whitehall with her two daughters – Pepys thought Henriette Anne 'very pretty' but was alarmed by her frizzy French hairdo – he saw 'a very little plain old woman, and nothing more in her presence in any respect nor garb than any ordinary woman'. She made a better impression on those who met her properly: '[She] charms all who see her … she has constantly received visitors since she came.'[14]

The queen intended to return to Paris after she had released James from captivity, but the king had already allowed the marriage, so at Whitehall the status of Anne as Duchess of York was being recognised. Cardinal Mazarin stepped in, writing to 'suggest' that Henrietta Maria accept the *fait accompli* – and her son's authority – since the alternative was to look ridiculous. She (and Mazarin) knew only too well that the dowry of Henriette

Anne had to be decided, and it would be decided by Charles II and his chief minister – Edward Hyde.[15]

Henrietta Maria was not good at humble pie, but she was a brilliant court performer. She accepted these forces of reality and on New Year's Day 1661 received Anne publicly, in front of a large crowd of courtiers desperate for the next instalment of the royal soap opera. She kissed Anne, as did Henriette Anne, then permitted Anne (and James) to sit in her presence, and also agreed to be godmother to the baby. Shortly after this she met Hyde and told him she expected him to return the favour she showed Anne with goodwill and friendship, which meant the dowry (which he agreed to).[16]

To her astonishment, Henrietta Maria found herself with a daughter-in-law whom she greatly liked. Anne Hyde spoke wonderful French, and made a stately and capable Duchess of York who dominated her husband. To begin with the couple embarrassed the court by kissing and holding hands in public, but soon it was clear that, like his brother Charles – and like their grandfather Henri IV – James could not keep away from other women. Nonetheless, Anne was the dominant partner and, while baby Charles did not survive, she was often pregnant, and gave birth to two future queens of England. Nonetheless, Henrietta Maria had failed to 'unmarry' James and she also failed to marry Charles II. She seems to have had in mind Hortense Mancini, one of the nieces of Mazarin, who would bring a gigantic cash dowry.[17]

*

The York marriage was not the worst excitement of 1660. When Henrietta Maria arrived in London, the ravishing twenty-nine-year-old Mary of Orange was already in residence at Whitehall, having left her Dutch home in September with relief, and having deflected her mother's attempt to make her come to Paris first.[18]

At the end of November, Mary complained of feeling unwell. Doctors diagnosed measles or smallpox and started the destructive treatment of bleeding, which weakened her. On Christmas Eve she dictated her will. She was asked what her wishes were regarding her son, and replied that she trusted her brother and mother with him.

Although she had left William (now ten) behind with the Dutch, and had earlier abandoned him for nine months, when she was enjoying herself in Paris, she apparently also said, 'My greatest pain is to depart from him.' Mary was bled once more, her eyes dimmed, and she died that evening. The doctors probably killed her. Her mother, who had personally chosen the doctors to look after Mary, was hit very hard by this second death, and told her son that she too would die if she stayed in England.[19]

In pouring rain, over sodden roadways and swollen rivers, Henrietta Maria set out to Portsmouth, accompanied by the king but not by the Duke of York, who was also recovering from illness. In her luggage the queen took the jewels that Mary had brought with her from Holland, keeping them safe from avaricious Dutch hands. With Henriette Anne, she set off from Portsmouth on 2 January 1661 to sail for Le Havre. 'Mam's bad luck at sea', already a family legend, struck again. In thick fog, the queen's ship ran into a sandbank.[20]

They were afloat with the tide, but returned to Portsmouth since it was now Henriette Anne who was unwell. She developed measles – it could have been smallpox – so the royal party stayed in Portsmouth until she was out of danger, and then sailed for Le Havre without mishap. In this way Henrietta Maria failed to attend the coronation of Charles II, which took place on 23 April 1661, just as she had missed that of his father.[21]

*

The queen had lost her brother Gaston, in February 1660. There was another important death, that of Cardinal Mazarin, on 9 March 1661. Mazarin, it turned out, had given Henrietta Maria more support than people knew. Among the papers of his estate was the record (signed by the queen) of money owed by Henrietta Maria. Mazarin had gone some way to financing her life in exile by lending her 661,566 *livres tournois*.[22] His death was just one more sign of time passing. He was seven years older than Henrietta Maria, while Gaston was only eighteen months older. How much longer did she have?

Henriette Anne was married to Monsieur on 31 March 1661 at the Palais-Royal, the ceremony being private because it was Lent and because of family mourning for Henry and Mary. The Bourbons also mourned Mazarin, their saviour during the Fronde. Louis XIV loved his godfather Mazarin, yet all mentors have a shelf life. Now the young King of France was liberated, and started fifty-four years of personal rule, determined, like Charles I, to reign untrammelled.

Henrietta Maria remembered the difficulties of her first years as a married woman. She knew that marriages did better when other people kept out of them, so she retired to Colombes. There was every reason to hope for Henriette Anne's happiness in France. There could be no higher connection in the royal world than the Bourbon family, Monsieur was unfailingly polite to his mother-in-law and clearly felt real esteem, and the same was true of Louis XIV. The truth was that Henrietta Maria had a more straightforward relationship with her French relations than with her English children.

41

HENRIETTA MARIA'S IDENTITY

In 1661, Henrietta Maria celebrated her fifty-second birthday. She looked like a nun, dressed in black – unchanging as fashions changed – only she wore a large string of pearls over her lace collar, and her hair, in the words of an earlier biographer, was 'eternally and defiantly black'.[1] Family and religion were her preoccupations. She was almost removed from politics, although there was one further strictly political service to come, which she would perform as an intermediary between France and England. In which country did she feel most at home? After everything, where did her heart lie?

After her marriage in 1625, the queen lived in England for nearly twenty years, with her English husband and children. Since 1644, she had been in France for another seventeen years. Her rediscovered French identity was reinforced, after the dizzying excitement of May 1660, by a trip to London that was traumatic, in fact tragic. Two of her children died and a third nearly followed.

What could be expected from this country that savaged her husband and her children? In Whitehall lay memories that took Henrietta Maria back to the depths. When she found herself near the place where Charles I had been executed, she collapsed in tears. At Somerset House, Inigo Jones's chapel was still standing but the interior was ruined by the Puritan vandals who had used it as a meeting place for their prayer meetings. The altars and confessionals were gone, the treasures destroyed. The house where the Capuchins had lived was pulled down and replaced by another, with someone else living in it. No wonder she wanted to be back in France at the earliest possible opportunity.[2]

England, however, called.

*

After the marriage of Henriette Anne, who now became 'Madame', Henrietta Maria stayed in France a further eighteen months. Madame was soon pregnant, and gave birth to a daughter, Marie Louise, on 26 March 1662. It was reported that when she heard it was a girl, the mother cried out that the baby should be thrown in the Seine. For the time being, Madame's success lay elsewhere.[3]

The pious, pretty girl taught by the nuns of Chaillot blossomed into a leader of fashion and, alarmingly, very nearly into the lover of her brother-in-law, Louis XIV. The court of France, and the King of France, were intoxicated with the devastating natural charm of Henriette Anne, suddenly unleashed. Thin, suffering from scoliosis – her shoulders were at slightly different heights – and not even blonde, so strictly she did not qualify as a court beauty, the elegant Henriette Anne radiated warmth, intelligence and glamour. Queen Marie Thérèse lacked the confidence to take part in court life in the way the French liked, and was quickly pregnant, and happy to be removed from the centre of activity. Through a summer of parties and picnics, Madame took over, always at Louis XIV's side.

Madame's husband did not appreciate her. Monsieur was a hedonist given to cross-dressing and male lovers, spoiled by massive wealth, not permitted any responsibility by his brother, burned up with jealousy of his wife's success. He diligently maintained sexual relations with Madame, so she was often pregnant, but it was a bad match which went downhill, even though Louis XIV's scandalous attraction for his sister-in-law was diverted towards Louise de la Vallière (one of Madame's ladies).

Poor Madame's terrible marriage was a baffling reversal of Henrietta Maria's French hopes. In July 1662, the queen mother most uncharacteristically ran away from a situation she could not handle and sailed for England, although it was not only the Orléans disappointment that caused her to move. She now had a large income paid by England, and was expected to give back by residing and holding court in England for at least part of the year. On 28 July she was at Woolwich, and in August she arrived in London.

*

As usual, Henrietta Maria had her own agenda. Having formed an alliance with Spain when he was an exile, Charles II chose a princess from Spain's enemy Portugal as his wife in return for an immense cash dowry, the possession of Tangier and Bombay, and trading concessions in Brazil and the East Indies. The Catholic Catherine of Braganza married Charles II on 21 May 1662. Henrietta Maria told Christine that she had to meet the woman who replaced her as queen. The prayers for the royal family were now redrafted to urge the congregations to 'pray for our gracious Queen Catherine, and Mary, the queen mother'.[4]

Mary, the queen mother, when she met Catherine of Braganza, loved her: 'The best creature in the world, from whom I have so much affection, and I have the joy to see the king love her extremely ... she is a saint.'[5]

Henrietta Maria stayed in London. She set up an English household with Harry Jermyn as her lord chamberlain, Wat Montagu as her grand almoner, Kenelm Digby as her chancellor, and John Winter as her secretary. Her ladies were the Dowager Duchess of Buckingham, the Countess of Denbigh and the Countess of Newport. She had four coaches, each drawn by six horses. She had an escort of twenty-four guardsmen, dressed in black velvet with gold embroidered badges, under the command of the portly Jermyn. She had musicians, she had buckhounds.[6]

Somerset House and Placentia, at Greenwich, were now her residences. She spent a good deal of money to make sure Somerset House reflected her status, adding an Italian garden, a gallery based on the designs of Inigo Jones and a suite of state rooms overlooking the river. She ordered a refurbishment of the whole building including her personal apartments, and ordered new paintings. When it was ready, young courtiers went to Somerset House to pay their respects to the tiny queen mother, whose memories had unique glamour, whose personal story was so extraordinary, whose royal professionalism was mesmeric.

Her home was a paradigm of elegance, filled with works of art and touches of magic, as on the stone stairs leading to the garden, where an echo sounded long enough to combine in harmony three notes sung separately.[7] Her court was the most fashionable, the most entertaining in England, outshining Whitehall, where the timid young queen barely presided.

She paid visits to members of the nobility and gentry, such as John Evelyn, who had a famous garden at Sayes Court at Deptford. Here she delighted her host by staying late, and entertaining him with stories about the various dogs she had owned and loved. The queen mother was 'never gayer or more happy' and she was a craze.[8]

The Capuchins came back to Somerset House. Catholics crowded her restored chapel, while few went to Catherine of Braganza's chapel at St James's Palace. Henrietta Maria re-established the peculiarly Catholic Confraternity of the Rosary in London, dedicated to the unbroken recitation of prayer.[9]

She did not see Jeffrey Hudson again, but found a replacement in a 'Chinese' boy brought to her from the docks. This gentle teenager was picked up somewhere in the Far East by a merchantman, and brought to Somerset House when someone recalled Henrietta Maria's affection for human curiosities. By the time he reached London, the boy spoke English. He was taken into the queen mother's household, and turned over to Fr Cyprien to be instructed in Catholicism, whose tenets he readily adopted, only puzzled by the absolutely critical doctrines of the Trinity, the Incarnation and the Eucharist. At his baptism – he was named Peter, after the Duke of Richmond's Catholic brother – Henrietta Maria was godmother.[10]

With religion went charity, consistent with the teaching of St François de Sales. The queen mother was especially concerned about people in debtors' prisons for small sums owed, and continually sent money to help those in this position to start their lives again. Henrietta Maria gave money to those in need, focused on the Catholic community but not restricted to it.[11]

The accumulation of piety did not close Henrietta Maria's mind. On 7 September 1662, Pepys visited Somerset House and found the extended royal family: Henrietta Maria sitting with Catherine of Braganza, plus the king's mistress Lady Castlemaine and the king's fifteen-year-old bastard son (by Lucy Walter), James Crofts – soon to be made Duke of Monmouth – who was taken with Lady Castlemaine. Charles II arrived, followed by the Yorks. When the guests left, one royal coach contained the king, the queen, Lady Castlemaine and James Crofts. Although Henrietta Maria headed a court of high moral tone in the 1630s, and had a spotless marriage, she was unfazed by the foibles of kings, as she always had been.

*

A spotless marriage? The story resurfaced of her relationship with Harry Jermyn, the man whom Parliament suggested was her lover in 1641, the year of the Army Plot.

In 1662 Jermyn was Henrietta Maria's most trusted courtier, as he had been for nearly forty years. Recognising Jermyn's services to his mother – for the moment forgetting the turf battles which stained the years of exile – Charles II made Jermyn Earl of St Albans in 1659, and ambassador to France in 1661. Court gossip made Jermyn second husband of Henrietta Maria, and father of her secret final child (a daughter).[12]

Henrietta Maria was a devoted wife who would not have taken a lover during her husband's lifetime. After Charles I died, everything the queen ever said about the marriage of royal persons made Jermyn an almost impossible husband for reasons of caste. Perhaps not *entirely* impossible, however, when one considers that she was prepared to marry her son Charles to Hortense Mancini (but Hortense had special advantages: money without end and the sponsorship of a great cardinal). Was Jermyn, then, her lover during her widowhood?

Jermyn was often called the queen's favourite, but the term does not automatically denote a sexual relationship – Olivares was the favourite of Philip IV – and anyway throughout her adult life Henrietta Maria went to Mass and Communion, which would have been a mortal sin if she had a lover who was not her husband. Jermyn is better characterised by the poet Andrew Marvell, who called him 'full of soup and gold'.[13] It is unnecessary to marry Jermyn to Henrietta Maria to explain the fact that he married nobody else.

The truth can be seen in Henrietta Maria's remark to Mme de

Motteville when she said that kings and queens were like priests: always entrusted with the secrets of others, which they must keep to themselves. Her intimacy with the men and women of her inner court was not romantic or sexual, it was, at its most intense, sacramental. The legacy of Jermyn is not found in a secret line of descendants of Henrietta Maria, but in St James's Square in the middle of London, which he developed and built, and of course the neighbouring Jermyn Street.[14]

*

On 27 December 1663, Christine, Duchess of Savoy, died. Henrietta Maria had also lost Elizabeth of Bohemia, who died in London on 13 February 1662; Elizabeth was not a woman with whom she had a close understanding, but she was a companion in spirit, another exiled queen, another mother of many children. Another Stuart loyalist.

These losses do not appear to have dented the queen mother's spirits unduly, but since the birth of Henriette Anne, Henrietta Maria's health had been poor. The banks of the Thames were a bad place to spend the winter. Fog and damp invaded Somerset House, whose renaissance elegance did not include insulation. The queen mother dwelt on her health more than before and in 1665 decided that the doctors of France were more reliable than English physicians, although the way she expressed it was that the climate of France was more clement, and a visit to Bourbon had always helped.

Her plans to leave London were accelerated by a plague outbreak that would become the worst of the century. On 29 June 1665, Henrietta Maria left England for France. She was sick at the time herself, 'being in a consumption'.[15] She took two of the Capuchins with her, leaving eight to continue divine services at Somerset House Chapel and to visit Catholics in London (two of these died in the plague).

Another reason for going to France was the always fragile Henriette Anne, who, having given birth to a son in 1664, was again pregnant. Madame miscarried, but her mother was now with her. The two of them went to Colombes and stayed until the end of August. In England it was believed that Henrietta Maria's journey to France was for a visit to Bourbon, and she would return in a year's time, but she never came back. The queen wanted to die in France, although that, at the time, was not quite how she would have put it.[16]

Despite the affection she had for England, and despite the entertainment, Henrietta Maria felt more secure in the country of her birth. In addition, her English responsibilities were over. Her children were either dead or married, and the King of England was not much interested in her opinions. She ended as she began, a Frenchwoman.

*

Even so, this final retirement across the Channel heralded the queen mother's last political act. On 4 March 1665 Charles II declared war on the Dutch Republic, a decision based on competition in trade and colonies but influenced by the opinions of his brother James that it was a war he would easily win.

There were English victories, such as the Battle of Lowestoft (13 June 1665) and the St James's Day Battle (4 and 5 August 1666), but no decisive action took place in the first two years. A complication arose in January 1666 when, because of treaty obligations, Louis XIV entered the Anglo-Dutch War on the Dutch side, so from this date England and France were at war. The hostilities included a fashion attack. Louis XIV dressed his footmen in the new 'vest' (a type of waistcoat) to ridicule Charles II, who pioneered it in England by wearing it himself.[17]

Awkwardly, Henrietta Maria stayed in France. She told her nephew Louis XIV she could not pray for a French victory, which did no harm to his affection for her. Everyone could see that the King of France loved his aunt 'like a son'. The queen mother had settled into her pre-restoration pattern of summer at Colombes, with a visit to Bourbon to take the waters, and Paris during the winter, now at the recently built (and therefore comfortable) Hôtel de la Bazinière, loaned by Louis XIV – all interspersed with time at Chaillot. After the outbreak of the Great Fire of London (2–5 September 1666) triggered another round of English anti-Catholicism, it was harder for the queen mother to return to London, but the truth was that she no longer wanted to.[18]

She could not keep out of the political arena. A year after the Anglo-Dutch War began, Henrietta Maria offered to mediate to secure a peace, an initiative at once refused by her son. Charles II instead asked his mother to return to England. At a time of war, it was embarrassing that the English queen mother lived on English revenue in an enemy country. Having his mother take a profile in peace negotiations would highlight the situation.[19]

Henrietta Maria had no intention of returning to London. The pointless war did not change her reasons for living in France, and in fact her French residence did provide a service to her son. In September 1666, Louis XIV visited Henrietta Maria at Colombes, and soon after that Jermyn was sent to London to start talks with the government of Charles II. What emerged was a top-secret plan between England and France to collaborate against the Dutch.[20]

The Dutch admiral Michiel de Ruyter put a stop to this in June 1667 with his daring Raid on the Medway, when Dutch ships sailed into the Thames Estuary to attack the English fleet laid up in the Chatham dockyards. A number of English ships were destroyed, London was threatened and Ruyter towed the English flagship – the *Royal Charles* – back to Holland as a prize. Coming on the heels of the 1665 plague and the 1666 fire, the devastating raid was the knockout blow to force a peace (which duly followed).

During this time, Henrietta Maria's quiet retreat at Colombes was a *poste restante* for her son and nephew. The letters between the royal 'brothers' were addressed to Henrietta Maria (who re-addressed them), and in this way avoided the diplomatic channels, watched by spies. What could be more normal than letters from the King of England to his mother, or from the King of France to his aunt? In this way Henrietta Maria played a key part in re-establishing friendly relations between France and England.[21]

*

English austerity resulted from the Anglo-Dutch War. In this period, war always cost far more than planned (or hoped) and often led to financial crisis. For her assistance with the French, his mother was rewarded by Charles II with a 25 per cent cut in her income in the winter of 1668/9, as part of the cutbacks. The queen mother's repeated energetic and eloquent protests drew no very clear response from her son, although no evidence survives that her quality of life was hit by this bad news. By her admittedly high standards, she was already living simply.

At Colombes, the queen was surrounded by treasure. She had more than fifty oil paintings, mainly family portraits or religious subjects. They included works by Tintoretto, Titian, Coreggio, Perugino, Palma Vecchio, Andrea del Sarto, Giulio Romano and Bassano. Of these, the sixteenth-century paintings were thought to show a specially refined taste. The collection included a Madonna by her niece Louise Hollandine of the Rhine, who was a pupil of Honthorst, and just one picture of Charles I, the miniature found in the Indian box.

The furniture was expensively covered, the 'black bed' – black for mourning – with velvet, embroidered with gold and silver. There was a 'greate chair' to match, with two footstools, also black velvet with silver fringes. There were Persian carpets, Indian screens and six sets of tapestries, including a set which told the 'History of Vulcan and Venus', and another which told the 'History of Hero and Leander'. Henrietta Maria is usually considered to have had no interest in mythological subjects, but the tapestries suggest otherwise. Everywhere there were clocks, looking glasses, sets of porcelain and silver – including one silver set which consisted of five sconces, two pairs of andirons and a looking glass – and a large number of richly moulded cabinets, worked with silver, tortoiseshell, lapis lazuli, mother of pearl, amber, agate and crystal. There were piles of linen, especially items suitable for someone leading the life of an invalid – dressing gowns and night garments.[22]

Henrietta Maria increasingly spent time with Mme de Motteville, now her close friend, who retired to Chaillot after the death of Anne of Austria in 1666. The two widows agreed on almost everything, including a fear of death. Henrietta Maria's worry was whether she would have time to prepare. At some time in 1669 she told Mme de Motteville that she planned to join her at Chaillot, live there full-time, forget the doctors and think of spiritual things. Towards the end of July she remarked that she felt her death was imminent.[23]

Within the family the queen mother's concern was Henriette Anne, whom she often visited at the magnificent Château de St Cloud on the banks of the Seine. Madame's new scourge was the Chevalier de Lorraine, an especially selfish and vindictive man, the lover of Monsieur, in fact the great love of Monsieur's life. Madame lost her toddler son in December 1666 but became pregnant once more and on 27 August 1669 gave birth to Anne Marie. Henrietta Maria's life was filled with small children. At this time she was housing her four-year-old granddaughter Anne, the second daughter of the Duke and Duchess of York, who was visiting France for the same reason as her grandmother, medical attention (for an eye complaint).

*

Henrietta Maria had a consultation with four doctors at Colombes on 8 September 1669, her own in addition to the physicians who tended to Louis XIV, Monsieur and Madame: Duquesne, Vallot, Esprit and Yvelin respectively.

She was not a classic invalid. In England the queen mother still had the reputation of being a good dancer.[24] She presented a cheerful face to all comers, and thought people who complained about health displayed 'great weakness or little resolution'. In fact Henrietta Maria saw the medical delegation because Henriette Anne in particular asked her to do so.

Nonetheless, it is evident that the queen mother was in poor health, that her strength was reduced. By now she really was drawing back from life. Her niece, the always vigorous Grande Mademoiselle, said that Henrietta Maria was almost always ill.[25]

The doctors listened to her description of her complaints. They agreed that the treatments prescribed by Duquesne were correct, and that her symptoms did not suggest anything life-threatening. Vallot suggested that more sleep would help, and recommended a dose of three grains of laudanum as a sedative. The queen mother replied that Sir Theodore de Mayerne had forbidden her opiates; she did not want the laudanum. Vallot said he was confident that the composition of the laudanum was risk-free. Henrietta Maria accepted his professional opinion, although he was hardly in a position to know her as Mayerne did, or Duquesne did. Of the other doctors, only Yvelin commented that he did not know the composition of the 'grains' but added, with political correctness, that he had every confidence in Vallot.

The next day, the queen mother had a long conversation with her confessor Fr Cyprien to prepare her for taking Communion. In the evening she had a large meal and was in high spirits, with the result that she could not sleep. She called Duquesne and asked for the laudanum to be administered. She took it mixed with the yolk of an egg. The doctor stayed at her side, watching as she fell into a deep sleep. He became worried by her very slow breathing and pulse, and tried to wake her, but could not. He called for help. The queen mother was in a drugged coma. The dosage was too high. Misled by her poise, her authority, her vigour, Vallot had totally overestimated the queen mother's physical strength. At about three o'clock in the morning of 10 September 1669, Henrietta Maria died.[26]

42

THE BETRAYED QUEEN

Henrietta Maria was buried at St Denis on 21 November 1669. There was another memorial service at Notre Dame on 25 December. Both ceremonies were paid for by Louis XIV. Her heart was sent in a silver box to Chaillot, as she had asked. There was a scrap about her estate, when Monsieur made an effort to claim everything in his wife's name, but the final settlement was entirely in favour of Charles II.[1]

Jacques Bossuet, Bishop of Condon, preached a sermon at a service at Chaillot on 16 November, requested and probably paid for by Madame. He described a great queen and, more than this, a woman who came to see that earthly glory held, at its centre, a void. Bossuet was correct. The older woman looked to withdraw from the world entirely at Chaillot. The young queen was widely thought to be a party girl but by 1635 – when she turned twenty-six – she was already looking for a British cardinal.

The truth is that, in her time, Henrietta Maria was unique. Like other men and women of her caste she was wrapped in luxury, but the English implosion put her into an extraordinary position where everything was at risk. Without hesitation, she joined the fight. She should be a legendary figure; a woman who repeatedly risked death for her family, a survivor of two civil wars, a star in the final decade of her life.

*

Married at fifteen, arriving in England without a word of English and struggling with her reticent, insecure husband, the French princess had a rocky start, although one that many girls of her status would know. However, Henrietta Maria alone carried the expectations of the Catholic Counter-Reformation into a Protestant stronghold at the same time.

By the early 1640s, the queen was so much feared by her husband's critics that they decided to impeach her. In 1643 she was very nearly drowned in her first attempt to come back to England, and on her second she was attacked, at Bridlington, by a parliamentary cannonade aiming to kill.

In 1644 she left wartime Oxford so that her pregnancy would not be a problem for her husband. Having given birth in Exeter to her last child, she abandoned the baby to the nurses to make a run for France. Perhaps it is easy to underestimate the toughness of this decision. Sailing out of Falmouth, she ran into more parliamentary cannon. The queen fled, because she was afraid of the consequences if she were arrested by Parliament – not for herself but for Charles I.

Henrietta Maria forgot her strict Catholicism when she instructed the captain to set fire to his store of gunpowder if they were captured, so that she – and everyone else on board – would die in the explosion, rather than yield to Parliament. At the time it appears she did not regard this instruction as either suicidal or murderous.

Surrounded by the dangers of the Fronde in Paris, the queen lost, in succession, her husband – to judicial murder on the Whitehall scaffold in 1649 – and her second daughter, Elizabeth Stuart, in 1650. The death of young people was not unusual then, but the circumstances were hard. Henrietta Maria had already lost three children: premature Charles in 1629, Katherine in 1639, Anne in 1640.

In the strange year of 1660, the queen rejoiced when her son Charles II was restored to the throne in May but then lost two more children when Henry died in September and Mary in

December. She soon found that the marriage she had arranged for Henriette Anne, which had seemed the perfect match – and not just to Henrietta Maria – would cause nothing but misery for her youngest daughter. After blows like these, it seems extraordinary that she would herself die as the result of an opium overdose administered on the orders of Louis XIV's doctor.

*

From 1644, Henrietta Maria suffered from continuous bad health. This did not prevent her from working hard from the start of the crisis and throughout her French years to support first Charles I, then her son Charles II. Shortly before the Stuart restoration her court in the Palais-Royal outshone the main French royal court, just as Somerset House put Whitehall in the shade when she lived in England from 1663 to 1665. Similarly, the remote philosophy of her 1630s masques and plays conceals the advantages of a high moral tone at this time in history, and her attempt to introduce civilised values after the tacky hedonism of James I.

Behind her energy lay a depressive streak, noted by the papal envoy Gregorio Panzani, and by the doctor Theodore Mayerne. Maybe it came from the shocks of childhood. She knew her father only as an absence; she lost her sister Elizabeth to Spain when very young and her mother to exile (for a time – but an impressionable time). As an adult she suppressed this melancholy ruthlessly, making a display of charm and fire.

Her family and the court were the focus of Henrietta Maria's politics, but that does not make her apolitical. At a time when other royal consorts were timid and retiring (the wife of Louis XIV, the wife of Charles II), Henrietta Maria stepped forward. She helped her husband re-establish his court after the death of Buckingham in 1628, she conspired (clumsily) against her enemies in France and England in the early 1630s, then matured as a constructive court politician.

The moral support she gave her husband as civil war approached and during the conflict was powerful, even disconcerting. She negotiated directly with her husband's opponents before Strafford's trial, and supported the Army Plot to some extent. She found money and arms for Charles I, and led an army from York to Oxford in 1643 to add to his forces. She was lampooned as the

Catholic power behind the throne, although Charles I invariably followed his own decisions. She was heroic in her attempt to join her husband in England shortly before his trial and death.

Henrietta Maria was one of the reasons the English Civil War broke out, but she was not one of its causes. The parliamentary and popular fear of Catholicism and crypto-Catholicism met in the unhappy coincidence of the queen and her enemy William Laud. If there had been no Catholic queen of this mettle, it would have been much harder to whip up a rebellious fury in the Commons, and among the Londoners. Yet the reasons for opposing the personal rule of Charles I did not originate with the Catholic queen. Court Catholicism was reasonably strong in the late 1630s but in itself was no threat to the Church of England, the House of Commons or the London apprentices.

Henrietta Maria did not understand Parliament, and could not see that the solution to the difficulties of Charles I and Parliament could only be domestic. Her endless plans to find troops outside England and use them to restore her husband or son – to impose a solution from outside – were shown to be hollow by the way the restoration actually took place in 1660, thanks to General Monck and thanks especially to public opinion in England, which influenced him. The failure of Charles II at Worcester in 1651 was down to numbers, because his leadership of a foreign (Scottish) army into England made the locals reluctant to join his troops. Here was the foreign army that backed the king and failed.

To the great nineteenth-century historian S. R. Gardiner, Henrietta Maria lacked substance and capacity: 'All she wanted was to live the life of a gay butterfly passing lightly from flower to flower.' To her most recent (and very thorough – and affectionate) biographer Alison Plowden, she was an 'ardent, warm-hearted, devoted, fiercely protective little creature'.[2]

Such remarks hardly do Henrietta Maria justice. In British history she is doomed for her gender, perhaps, but also for the fact that she appears on the losing side.

In fact, Henrietta Maria's side won. The Stuart monarchy returned, and monarchy remains. The English people preferred the principles she promoted to the gloom and hardness of Cromwell and the army. Two of her children became kings of England, and three of her grandchildren inherited the throne. She is the ancestress of the

Scottish Duke of Buccleuch, the English dukes of Grafton, Richmond and St Albans, and the Spanish Duke of Alba. Her grandee descendants reflect a vanished world but also stand for continuity.

*

If her religious mission was the promotion of Catholicism in England, it failed. If it was the protection of English Catholics, it largely succeeded during the years of peace.

Catholicism continued to be a bugbear in Britain through the seventeenth century, not least as a result of the later conversion of Henrietta Maria's son James. Diversity as something normal emerged later, through Enlightenment thinking, although Henrietta Maria's personal tolerance, and her principles – loyalty, justice, generosity – suggest that Enlightenment thinking might not have been so foreign to her as has been assumed. The queen was always devotedly religious but she was always modern as well.

The evidence that we have suggests Henrietta Maria's sophistication extended to her faith: she was not spiritually simplistic. In 1642 she wrote to her husband from the Continent to express her love, saying she was his 'after death, if it be possible'.[3] The fear of death that she discussed with Mme de Motteville suggests a similar uncertainty, one often found in people of a religious temperament. The fact that her husband was not a Catholic raised a hundred questions about orthodoxy. Did Henrietta Maria really believe that Charles I did not go to heaven when he died? What did she think of her dead Protestant children?

Religion for the queen was not reasoned certainty. To Henrietta Maria, Catholicism was both a civilisation and a meditation.

*

Henrietta Maria's cultural influence was enormous. The canvasses of van Dyck are one of the building blocks of the English tradition of portraiture, connecting English art to the Continental tradition. Her protégé Inigo Jones introduced classical principles to English architecture. Porticoes, columns, arches, even the classical orders and sometimes even classical proportion, are with us still. In his masque productions Inigo introduced the elements of stage design – the proscenium arch, side flats and back shutters – which led to the developed English theatre. Henrietta Maria also foreshadowed the craze for French culture, which obsessed fashionable society from the late seventeenth century well into the nineteenth and has not entirely gone. Her patronage was inspired, and made possible, by her husband, as well as by her own background, which included the fabulous Medici tradition, but she cannot be considered a follower. She was avant-garde and took her own initiatives.

Henrietta Maria has her admirers, but she continues to be nearly invisible in the main accounts of the Stuart period. It is a betrayal of a life lived in this way that her contribution merits so little thought and almost no respect. When she wrote to her sister Christine in September 1654, she said, 'These "reasons of state" are terrible things and I swear that I do not understand them.'[4] By repudiating the coldness of politics, Henrietta Maria has left a remarkable legacy, and it is for everyone.

DESCENDANTS OF HENRIETTA MARIA

The main branches are as follows.

Children of Charles II

James Scott, Duke of Monmouth and Buccleuch (by Lucy Walter), and subsequent dukes of Buccleuch
Henry FitzRoy, Duke of Grafton (by Barbara Castlemaine) and subsequent dukes of Grafton
Charles Beauclerk, Duke of St Albans (by Nell Gwynne) and subsequent dukes of St Albans
Charles Lennox, Duke of Richmond (by Louise de Kérouaille) and subsequent dukes of Richmond

Children of Mary, Princess Royal and Princess of Orange

William III of Orange and of England, Scotland and Ireland (by William II of Orange)

Children of James II

Mary II, Queen of England, Scotland and Ireland (by Anne Hyde)
Anne, Queen of Great Britain (by Anne Hyde)

James Francis Edward (by Mary of Modena), father of 'Bonnie Prince Charlie'

Louisa Mary (by Mary of Modena)

Henrietta Fitzjames Stuart (by Arabella Churchill), Lady Waldegrave (and by second marriage Countess of Newcastle), leading to the earls Waldegrave

James Ftizjames Stuart (by Arabella Churchill), Duke of Berwick, Duc de Fitzjames, Duque de Liria y Xerica and subsequent (French) ducs de Fitzjames and (Spanish) duques de Liria y Xerica, leading to the Duque de Alba

Henry Fitzjames Stuart (by Arabella Churchill)

Children of Henriette Anne, Duchesse d'Orléans

Marie Louise, Queen of Spain (by Philippe d'Orléans)

Anne Marie, Duchess of Savoy and Queen of Sardinia (by Philippe d'Orléans), leading to the kings of Italy and to the later Bourbon kings of France (through Louis XV)

NOTES

1 A Legacy

1. Brotton *The Sale of the Late King's Goods* p. 347.
2. Griffey *Inventory* p. 162.

2 Just Another Girl

1. Babelon *Henri IV* p. 856.
2. The grand duke's wife was Christina of Lorraine. Maria's mother was the Joanna (Habsburg) of Austria. The others were cousins and in-laws.
3. *Descrizione delle felicissime nozze di Madama Maria Medici* (Florence 1600).
4. Carmona *Marie de Médicis* p. 32.
5. L'Estoile *Journal pour le règne de Henri IV* vol. 1 p. 629.
6. Dubost *Marie de Médicis* p. 94.
7. Malherbe *Ode à la Reine Marie de Médicis*.
8. For the king's wait in the rain see Sully *Mémoires* vol. 3 p. 88. For his letter, Henri IV *lettre missives* p. 296 quoted in Yves Cazaux *Henri IV – les horizons du règne* (1986). Ferdinando is quoted in Chevalier *Louis XIII* p. 18.
9. Dubost *Marie de Médicis* p. 101.
10. Héroard *Journal* 1989 edition arranged by Madelein Foisil, vol. I p. 1693. This entry confirms the date of birth. For the court reaction see L'Estoile *Journal pour le règne de Henri IV* vol. 2 p. 557.

3 A Delayed Coronation

1. There were two palaces at St Germain-en-Laye. A second, more modern building, the Château Neuf, was built nearby soon after the works were completed on the Château Vieux.
2. For the nursery see Batiffol *Vie Intime* vol. 1 pp. 260 and 289.
3. Green *Letters of Queen Henrietta Maria* pp. 2–3. On the scoliosis see Moore *The History of the Study of Medicine in the British Isles* p. 176.
4. Told for instance in Carmona *Marie de Médicis* p. 87.
5. Babelon *Henri IV* p. 175–6 quotes the contemporary memoirist Pierre de Brantôme about Queen Margot. On her later appearance see Batiffol *Vie Intime* vol. 1 pp. 298–300. Margot's mother was Catherine de Médicis, a distant cousin of Marie.
6. Héroard vol. II 1602–7.
7. Green *Letters* p. 4.
8. Héroard vol. I, 85.
9. L'Estoile *Journal pout le règne de Henri IV* vol. 3 p. 73.
10. Petitfils p. 63; Richelieu Mémoires p. 18.
11. Sully Mémoires vol. 5 pp. 379–403 for the queen's irritation. Henri IV did not allow the coronation before because it was expensive.

4 The Hand of God

1. For the coronation see Dubost *Marie de Médicis* pp. 276–282.
2. On Charlotte, Bassompierre, *Mémoires* p. 212. On the wedding Babelon *Henri IV* p. 952.
3. It was later.
4. The first volume of *Don Quixote* was published in Madrid in 1605.
5. On the king's pursuit, and Condé's escape see Babelon *Henri IV* pp. 959–962. For his despair see Bassompierre *Mémoires* p. 256.
6. Wilson *Thirty Years War* pp. 229–238.
7. For marriage negotiations, Babelon p. 964. Henry Stuart was not yet Prince of Wales. On St Antoine see *The Lost Princes – the Life and Death of Henry Stuart* accompanying the exhibition at the National Portrait Gallery, London (2012). See the chapter 'Prince Henry and his World' by Malcom Smuts p. 23.
8. Sully Mémoires vol. 5 p. 381.
9. Various accounts, see especially Fonteny-Mareuil *Mémoires* pp. 15–16.

5 The Loss of Elizabeth de Bourbon

1. Batiffol *Vie Intime* vol. 1 pp. 248–250 and Petitfils *Louis XIII* pp. 66–7. The French intervention in Germany continued but the troops deliberately arrived just in time for the surrender of the Archduke Leopold, so France was not a decisive factor.
2. In a *lit de justice* the king made a ruling or assertion to the Parlement de Paris which carried absolute authority.
3. L'Estoile *Journal pour le Règne de Henri IV*; Petitfils Louis XIII pp. 75–76.
4. *The Life and Death of Henrietta Maria de Bourbon (HMB)* p. 3 and Dupuy *Henriette de France* p. 20.
5. Petitfils *Louis XIII* pp. 155–156.
6. Dubost *Marie de Médicis* p. 468. Baptism took place soon after the birth of royal children, but the ceremonial Christening was much later.
7. Chevalier *Louis XIII* p. 100–102.

6 Bridge of Sighs

1. Leonora was originally called Dori but assumed the more noble 'Galigai'. See Dubost *Marie de Médicis* p. 127 on Leonora's responsibilities. Batiffol *Vie Intime* vol. 2 p. 19 on her appearance.
2. For Leonora's disrespectful manner see Fontenay-Mareuil quoted in Petitfils *Louis XIII* pp. 159–160.
3. Nevers and Mayenne, as members of the Gonzaga and Guise families, were almost royal. The Estates General agreed the Spanish marriages.
4. Petitfils *Louis XIII* p. 191 quotes Bartolini the Tusan ambassador, as reported in Françoise Kermina 'Marie de Médicis'.
5. *HMB* p. 4.
6. Chevalier *Louis XIII* pp. 86–88.
7. Nicolas Pasquier *Lettres Paris* 1623 pp. 556ff quoted in Petitfils *Louis XIII* p. 210; and Pontchartrain *Mémoires* p. 306 and p. 300.
8. Petitfils *Louis XIII* p. 216.
9. Petitfils *Louis XIII* p. 229–230 and Pontchartrain *Mémoires* p. 387.
10. The critical intermediary between Louis XIII and his mother was Luçon/Richelieu.
11. On the little girl's caution, see *HMB* p. 5.

7 The King of Scotland

1. Dupuy *Henriette Marie* p. 35.
2. The German Electors were the princes who had a vote when the emperor was chosen. There were seven, of whom three were archbishops. The two Palatinates were separate blocks of territory, one on the Rhine with Heldelberg as capital, one bordering on Bavaria with Amberg as capital. For Mary Tudor's marriage see de Lisle *Tudor* p. 290–1.
3. Henry Stuart died in 1612, just before his sister's wedding.
4. Wilson *Thirty Years War* pp. 269–307.
5. Huguenot rights were guaranteed by Henri IV's Edict of Nantes of 1598.
6. For Madame Henriette's campaign against her sister-in-law, see de Motteville *Mémoires* I pp. 185 and 222.
7. 'Dinner' was a midday meal.
8. Carlton *Charles I* p. 39.
9. Lockyer *Buckingham* p. 140.
10. For the narrative see Lockyer *Buckingham* pp. 125–165. Whether Buckingham persuaded the prince to go to Madrid, or whether Charles was the instigator, is not clear, but it was probably the prince's determination that counted.
11. Motteville *Mémoires* I pp. 283–4. Scotland was a poor kingdom of immemorial antiquity while Spain was a rich kingdom, but only unified in the fifteenth century. Peninsular Spain consisted of several autonomous units, of which Castile and Aragon were the largest.
12. Chamberlain *Letters* p. 482 for the arrival of English courtiers.
13. Carlton *Charles I* p. 43.
14. de Mottevillle *Mémoires* I, p. 219.

8 The Feminine Touch

1. York House was one of Buckingham's London homes; the other was Wallingford House.
2. Chamberlain *Letters* pp. 515–6.
3. Chamberlain *Letters* p. 542, for weather p. 544.
4. Recusants generally meant Catholics, although literally it meant people who refused to attend Church of England services. See Lockyer *Buckingham* p. 190 for the petition of the Commons against recusants.
5. The king's accusation shows the constant preoccupation with the world of classical antiquity. In the second century BC the Roman

statesman Cato the elder repeatedly urged the destruction of Rome's enemy Carthage with the formula '*Carthago delenda est*' – 'Carthage must be destroyed'.
6. Lockyer *Buckingham* p. 196.
7. On Louis XIII's remarks Petitfils *Louis XIII* p. 311 quoting Bassompierre *Mémoires*.
8. Bone *Henrietta Maria* p. 21.
9. For Fr Gray's report, see Cogswell *The Blessed Revolution* p. 123, for the sporting presents see Chamberlain *Letters* p. 539.
10. *Cabala vol.* 2 p. 290.
11. On Kensington, de la Porte *Mémoires* pp. 295–6.
12. *Cabala* vol. 2 pp. 286–7 and 290.
13. *Cabala* p. 288.
14. For Soissons see *HMB* p. 8, for Olivares see *Cabala* p. 292.
15. Lockyer *Buckingham* pp. 190–1.
16. For the signatures see Chamberlain *Letters* pp. 590–1, for the Pope see Lockyer *Buckingham* p. 213.
17. *Somers Tracts* pp. 264–8.
18. Lockyer *Buckingham* pp. 233–4.

9 The Wedding

1. de la Porte *Mémoires* pp. 291–6, Petitfils *Louis XIII* pp. 373–4.
2. Skrine *Manuscripts* p. 5 on papers, CSVP 16 May 1625 on the faith of Chevreuse. The Henri/Marguerite wedding was Protestant/Catholic.
3. For the wedding, CSVP 16 May 1625; and *A True Discours of all the royal Passages, Tryumphs and Ceremonies observed at the contract and mariage of the High and Mighty Charles, King of Great Britain, and the most excelents of ladies, the Lady Henrietta Maria of Burbon...* (1625 – drawing on the official record).
4. Michel *Rubens* p. 44.
5. Ellis *Letters* Series I vol. III p. 194.
6. For the celebrations see Richelieu *Mémoires* pp. 328–9.
7. For the 'consummation' CSVP 9 May 1625. Houssaye *Bérulle* p. 3 for Senlis, and Oman *Henrietta Maria* p. 25 for the Carmelites.
8. Skrine *Manuscripts* p. 11.
9. Ellis *Letters* series I vol. III pp. 188–9 for the clothes; de la Porte *Mémoires* pp. 295–6 and Petitfils *Louis XIII* p. 374 for the sensation of Buckingham.
10. Lockyer *Buckingham* p. 20 quotes d'Ewes; de Motteville *Mémoires* p. 14.

11. de Baillon *Henriette-Marie* p. 53; Houssaye *Bérulle* p. 14.
12. de Baillon *Henriette-Marie* p. 54 on Amiens; Britland *Drama* p. 8 on the pageants.
13. Petitfils *Louis XIII* pp. 377–9.
14. On numbers see Cogswell *Crown, Parliament and War 1623–1625* p. 508.
15. Petitfils *Louis XIII* p. 380.
16. For the delay see de la Porte *Mémoires* p. 297. For the date of crossing I have used the account by the Venetian ambassador Zuane Pesaro, see CSVP 27 June 1625. See *Cabala* p. 302 and Plowden *Henrietta Maria* p. 24 for the comments.

10 Queen Mary

1. Hutchinson *Memoirs* p. 126 for the fatality, and see de Lisle *Tudor* pp. 293–4 for Mary Tudor as burner of Protestants. Queen Henry is recorded in Chamberlain Letters p. 617.
2. For the ruling on mourning CSPV 9 May 1625. The preparation of Dover Castle is recorded in CSPV 27 June 1625. The complaints of Tillières are in his own memoir p. 89.
3. On coronation planning CSPV 27 June 1625, Chamberlain *Letters* p. 614.
4. English or Old Style date.
5. In his *Mèmoires*, Tillières is filled with complaints against the English court. See p. 90 on the arrival of Charles.
6. For Kensington's comment see Cabala p. 287. On the high heels the story is found in Birch *Court and Times* I p. 30, also p. 31 for the conversation alone.
7. For the queen's lack of reading de Motteville *Mémoires vol.* I p. 224. For courtly education see Edward Herbert *Life* pp. 31–2.
8. See variously *Cabala* vol. 2 pp. 290 and 302.
9. For tears HMB p. 12, for kisses Birch *Court and Times* vol. 1 pp. 30 and 31, for the bad impression made by Charles I Tillières *Mémoires* p. 90. The queen's appeal to Charles I is recorded by the king himself in Petrie *Letters*, pp. 42–3.
10. Plowden *Henrietta Maria* p. 26 records the queen's eating her fill. See Whitaker *Royal Passion* pp. 55–6 for a discussion of the seating incident, also in Petrie *Letters* p. 43 among others. See Chamberlain letters p. 622 for comments on the queen's late arrival in England.
11. Richelieu *Mémoires* p. 291.
12. Tillières records the unease of Henriette Maria in his *Mémoires* p. 91.

See Birch *Court and Times* vol. I p. 31 for bolting the doors. For the queen feeling unwell Skrine *Manuscripts* p. 21.

13. Russell, *Parliament and English Politics* p. 213 for the plague. Skrine *Manuscripts* pp. 13 and 22 for the coronation plans.

14. Ellis *Letters* Series I vol. 3 pp. 199 and 196–7 for the welcome.

15. Skrine *Manuscripts* p. 22 on weather. On the trousseau see Griffey *Inventory* p. 164 and Hibbard in Griffey *Piety* p. 117.

16. Richelieu *Mémoires* p. 352 and Hibbard in Griffey *Piety* p. 117.

17. For fear of plague see CSPV 27 June 1625. Chamberlain *Letters* p. 624 and Skrine *Manuscripts* p. 23 for the absences of Henrietta Maria. Ellis *Letters* Series I vol. 3 p. 201.

11 Pious Hopes

1. On the queen's irritation see Ellis *Letters* Series I vol. 3 p. 206. Skrine *Manuscripts* p. 23 on her anti-social behaviour. Chamberlain *Letters* p. 625 on the French ladies.

2. Russell *Parliaments* p. 205.

3. For the plague CSPV 18 July 1625.

4. *HMB* pp. 16–17 on Mamie and the king. Tillières *Mémoires* p. 92 on the second seating argument.

5. Green *Letters* pp. 7–9. As wife of King Ahasuerus of Persia, Esther protected her people, the Jews, from persecution in the Old Testament Book of Esther. Clothilde, the Catholic wife of the Arian Clovis, first King of the Franks in the fifth century AD, converted her husband to Catholicism. Adilberga, or Bertha, was the Christian wife of the pagan Ethelbert, King of Kent, in the sixth century AD, who similarly converted her husband to Christianity.

6. Houssaye *Bérulle* pp. 4–5 and 7–9.

7. For the suspension of the penal laws Russell *Parliaments* p. 209.

8. ODNB *Richard Mountague*, John S. Macauley.

9. Lingard *History* p. 329.

10. See Russell *Parliaments and Politics* 1621–29 p. 407. Arminianism was a branch of Protestant doctrine based on the ideas of Jacobus Arminius, a theologian of the Dutch Reformed Church. It was moderate by comparison with strict Calvinism, and notably modified the doctrine of Predestination (which proposed that individual salvation/damnation was predestined, and could not be won by individual choice).

11. Petrie *Letters* p. 44.

12. Baillon p. 73, Tillières *Mémoires* p. 101, Skrine p. 38.

13. Evelyn *Diary* I October 1651 p. 267.

14. Lockyer *Buckingham* p. 251.
15. Hibbard in Griffey *Piety* p. 129.
16. ODNB *Henrietta Maria*, Caroline Hibbard.
17. Petrie *Letters* p. 44, also *HMB* p. 16.
18. de Motteville (1904 edition) p. 19; Clarendon History vol. I p. 48.
19. Louis XIII's opinion noted in Malcolm Smute in Griffey *Piety* p. 16. Charles I told Buckingham that his (Buckingham's) advice to be kind to Henrietta Maria was not paying dividends – see Petrie *Letters* p. 41 (letter dated 20 November 1625). For the 'many neglects' by the queen see p. 43.
20. CSPV 31 July 1625.
21. Lockyer *Buckingham* pp. 293–4 on the October letter, p. 262 on the return to the recusancy laws. Skrine *Manuscripts* p. 37 on the forty Frenchmen.
22. Lockyer *Buckingham* p. 262.
23. Lord Cromwell to Conway, Lockyer *Buckingham* p. 228.
24. CSVP 14 February 1626.
25. Buckingham intended to lead the fleet himself but fell ill. For Eliot's speech see Lockyer *Buckingham* p. 309.

12 Frisking and Dancing

1. CSVP 13 February 1625.
2. For the queen's attempt at a Catholic coronation see Chamberlain *Letters* p. 627, Skrine *Manuscripts* p. 43 Tillières *Mémoires* p. 117 on Mende's trip to France.
3. Fuller *Church History* vol. 6 p. 32.
4. The plate on which the communion wafer would be placed.
5. Fuller *Church History* vol. 6 p. 28.
6. See the account in *The Manner of the Coronation of King Charles I of England* by Christopher Wordsworth, London 1892, drawing on Ellis *Historical Letters*.
7. Tillières *Mémoires* p. 188, Lockyer *Buckingham* p. 334.

13 Departure of the French

1. Fuller *Church-History*, vol. 6, p. 34 on Pembroke. The York House Conferences tried to follow the pattern of the Dutch Synod of Dort in 1618–19, which pronounced definitively against Arminianism.
2. Cust *Charles I* p. 51.

3. Lockyer *Buckingham* p. 300. The Valtellina was a valley in north Italy which gave access from Milan to the Danube watershed to the north east, and to south Switzerland, and hence to the Habsburg France-Comté to the north-west.
4. Richelieu *Mémoires* vol. 3 p. 110.
5. Lockyer *Buckingham* pp. 321–323. Parliamentary impeachment usually cast the Commons as the accuser, and the Lords as the judge.
6. Lockyer *Buckingham* p. 319; ODNB *Thomas Howard, fourteenth Earl of Arundel* R. Malcolm Smuts.
7. Skrine *Manuscripts* p. 57.
8. Lockyer *Buckingham* pp. 338–9.
9. Ellis *Letters* Series I part 3 pp. 238–44. Tillières *Mémoires* pp. 145–7. *HMB* pp. 14–15. Petrie *Letters* p. 45.
10. For the remaining French see Hibbard in Asch and Birke (ed.) *Princes, Patronage and the Nobility* pp. 393–417, p. 405. On the bedchamber appointments, the first three were sister, wife and niece of Buckingham, the fourth the wife of the powerful Earl of Carlisle, and the mistress of Buckingham. Wolfson in *Female Bedchamber* pp. 316–7. Russell *Parliaments* p. 19 for Lucy Carlisle as mistress of Buckingham.

14 Bassompierre

1. Bassompierre left his own story of the embassy, from which this narrative mainly comes.
2. Wat Montagu, the second son of the Earl of Manchester, had been involved in the marriage negotiations.
3. Chamberlain *Letters* p. 625.
4. For the contentment of Henrietta Maria see Skrine p. 85.
5. Britland *Drama* p. 57.
6. In his text Bassompierre claimed to release sixty priests but this appears to have been a considerable exaggeration.
7. Skrine *Manuscripts* pp. 99 and 103.

15 The Duke's Destiny

1. Christian IV was defeated at the Battle of Lutter 27 August 1626, so the troops had to go to Denmark instead.
2. Lockyer *Buckingham* p. 351.
3. Cust *Charles I* p. 68; Lockyer *Buckingham* pp. 378–404.

4. Lockyer *Buckingham* p. 459.
5. Lockyer *Buckingham* pp. 458–9.
6. Clarendon *History* vol. I p. 37.
7. Britland *Drama* p. 63 for the ring, Skrine *Manuscripts* p. 161 for Wellingborough.
8. Cogswell *Crown, Parliament and War* p. 77, Michel *Rubens* p. 125, *HMB* p. 18.
9. Wolfson *Female Bedchamber* p. 319.
10. Finet *Ceremonies* p. 75.

16 Heirs to the Throne

1. CSPV 5 April 1630.
2. *HMB* p. 18 on the birth.
3. Birch *Court and Times of Charles I* vol. I p. 356.
4. For Jeffrey see Page *Lord Minimus*. On falling out of the window p. 60.
5. Caroline Hibbard in Griffey *Piety* pp. 131–2.
6. Birch *Court and Times* vol. 2 p. 77.
7. Birch *Court and Times* vol. 2 pp. 302–3.
8. Birch *Court and Times* vol. 2 pp. 63, 67, 68 and 301–3.
9. Bone *Henrietta Maria* p. 76; CSVP 14 June 1630. Sedan chairs were used a great deal by rich people in France, after being popularised by Queen Margot. Dupuy *Henriette Marie* p. 97.
10. Green *Letters* pp. 14–15; *HMB* p. 18; Fraser *The Weaker Vessel* p. 140; ODNB *Jane Ker, Countess of Roxburghe* Helen Payne.
11. Charles I complimented his Scottish subjects by choosing two Scottish peers as proxy godfathers. Weston was now treasurer and chief minister.
12. Finet, *Ceremonies* pp. 89–90.
13. Green *Letters* pp. 17 and 18.
14. Green *Letters* pp. 16–19.
15. *HMB* p. 23.
16. Whitaker *Royal Passion* p. 117.
17. ODNB, *James Hamilton, First Duke of Hamilton* John J. Scally. Birch *Court and Times* vol. I p. 419.
18. Whitaker *Royal Passion* p. 100. Skrine *Manuscripts* p. 169. ODNB *Thomas Howard, Fourteenth Earl of Arundel* Malcolm R. Smuts.
19. Finet *Ceremonies* pp. 28 and 30.
20. Smuts *Puritan Followers* p. 34.

17 The Excitements of Marie de Médicis

1. Dubost *Marie de Médicis* pp. 773–4.
2. Petitfils *Louis XIII* p. 512.
3. Dubost *Marie de Médicis* p. 777ff.
4. The king and cardinal probably agreed on solidarity before the scene in the Luxembourg, but Richelieu could not be sure of his ground until Louis XIII explicitly showed his favour.
5. Finet *Ceremonies* pp. 114–115.
6. CSVP 19 September 1631.
7. Dubost *Marie de Médicis* p. 808.
8. Smuts in Griffey *Piety* pp. 23–4; Cousin *Chevreuse* p. 406.
9. CSVP 21 June 1630; Bone *Henrietta Maria* pp. 78–83.
10. Smuts in Griffey *Piety* p. 24; CSPV 4 March 1633.

18 A Perfect World

1. Whitaker *Royal Passion* p. 119.
2. On the Prince of Wales's sickness CSVP 7 and 28 September 1635. On the medicine Green *Letters* pp. 28–9; Plowden p. 146 on the date. On Elizabeth Finet *Ceremonies* p. 249. On the best mother Whitaker *Royal Passion* p. 120.
3. Finet *Ceremonies* pp. 153–5.
4. Whittaker *Royal Passion* pp. 118–19.
5. Aubrey *Lives* p. 145 on Wilton. Hamilton *Henrietta Maria* p. 121 on Bolsover.
6. Page *Lord Minimus* pp. 97–8.
7. Green *Letters* p. 32.
8. CSPD 1633–4 p. 50, Bone *Henrietta Maria* pp. 85–6.
9. Katherine Gorges to her brother-in-law Sir Hugh Smyth quoted in Britland *Drama* p. 30.
10. Britland *Drama* p. 45.
11. Britland *Drama* p. 41. Neoplatonism proposed a perfect world separate from the everyday world, and promoted a notion of chaste love – whether entirely chaste, or chaste in the sense of restricting sex to marriage.
12. Britland *Drama* p. 60; Page Lord Minimus pp. 51–3.
13. Britland *Drama* p. 64.
14. Page *Lord Minimus* p. 87; Britland *Drama* p. 97.
15. *Love's Triumph* lines 218–21 quoted in Britland *Drama* p. 68.
16. Britland *Drama* pp. 75ff.

17. Britland *Drama* p. 100, see also Historic Royal Palaces website.
18. Britland *Drama* p. 113 refers to Sophie Tomlinson's conference paper of April 1998. The critic's verdict in Harbage *Cavalier Drama* p. 14 quoted in Britland *Drama* p. 113. On the queen's English, *Birch Court and Times* vol. 2 p. 176.
19. Birch *Court and Times* vol. 2 p. 216.
20. The Star Chamber court was composed of Privy Councillors and common law judges. It was first established to ensure fair trials of nobles and other grandees, whom ordinary courts would be reluctant to find guilty. By the reign of Charles I, the Star Chamber also looked into cases of the ill-defined offence of sedition, in other words it had become politicised by the royal government.
21. ODNB *William Prynne* William Lamont. On the text see the *Cambridge History of English and American Literature* in 18 volumes (1907–1921) vol. VI pp. 40–46. Prynne's prison sentence was cancelled.
22. Birch *Court and Times* vol. 2 p. 205. For Sir Ralph see Verney *Memoirs* II p. 12.
23. See Britland *Drama* p. 132.
24. Britland *Drama* p. 136.
25. Cust *Charles I* p. 188 quoting *Warwick Memoirs* pp. 73–4.

19 Holyroodhouse

1. Burton *Jacobeans at Home* p. 204.
2. For the preparations CSPD 1631–33 p. 551, CSPV 4 March and 8 April 1633, Bute *Coronation* p. 71. The account of the coronation comes from the latter's detailed account.
3. Charles I was born in Dunfermline on 19 November 1600.
4. Lee *Road to Revolution* p. 127. Today's Holyroodhouse is largely due to Charles II who expanded the building from its early sixteenth-century base.
5. They would be joined by Bishop Guthrie of Moray, who had come in the procession as Lord High Almoner.
6. Cust *Charles I* p. 219.
7. CSPV 1633 5 August 1633; Whitaker *Royal Passion* p. 172.
8. CSPV 25 March 1633. Cust *Charles I* p. 219. Lee *Road to Revolution* pp. 129–30, 135–6.
9. Lee *Road to Revolution* pp. 131–4, 157–8. Balmerino was let down by John Dunmure made a copy, and showed it to Peter Hay of Naughton, who took it to the Archbishop of St Andrews. (ODNB

John Elphinstone, Second Lord Balmerino John Coffey). Charles I handled Scotland badly from the start. See Cust *Charles I* pp. 212–6 on the Act of Revocation which made landowners think him a threat.

20 The Sound of Silence

1. Plowden *Henrietta Maria* p. 100.
2. ODNB *George Conn* R. Malcolm Smuts.
3. Bone *Henrietta Maria* pp. 89–90 including the quote from Panzani's memoirs.
4. The term 'Puritan' emerged at the end of the sixteenth century. By the time of Charles I Puritans preferred to call themselves 'Godly'.
5. Papalencyclicals.net *Regnans in Excelsis* articles 3, 4, 5.
6. Bone p. 92 quoting Panzani *Memoirs*.
7. ODNB *Richard Weston, First Earl of Portland*, Brian Quintrell.
8. R. Malcolm Smuts *Puritan Followers* p. 35 quoting Amerigo Salvetti, and quoting Sennetterre dispatch.
9. ODNB *William Juxon*, Brian Quintrell.
10. Whitaker *Royal Passion* pp. 137, 140–1; CSPV 24 October 1637.
11. Bone *Henrietta Maria* p. 91 quoting Panzani *Memoirs*.
12. *Burlington Magazine* vol. 90 no 539 (February 1948) pp. 50–51; Inigo Jones – *Puritanissimo Fiero* R. Wittkower.
13. Green *Letters* pp. 30–4 quoting reports of Conn and Panzani; for the king's remark CSPV 18 September 1636.
14. The description of the first Mass is by Fr Cyprien de Gamache in Birch *Court and Times* vol. 2 pp. 311–313.
15. CSVP 12 September 1636.
16. Birch *Court and Times* 2 p. 250.
17. Green *Letters* p. 32 quoting Panzani despatches.

21 Gold Damask and the Blood of Martyrs

1. See Clarendon *History* vol. I p. 94ff on the happy state of England.
2. Michel *Rubens* pp. 127–8.
3. Brown *van Dyck* pp. 164–5.
4. Veevers *Drama* p. 111; Harris and Higgott *Inigo Jones* pp. 190, 193, 196, 208, 236.
5. See Brotton *Sale* pp. 165–6 which explains that Henrietta Maria made the commission. The bust was destroyed in the fire that engulfed Whitehall Palace at the end of the seventeenth century.

6. In the *Book of Genesis* 27:36 Rebekah, wife of Isaac, says, 'I am weary of my life because of the daughters of Heth.' Heth was the ancestor of the Hittite.
7. ODNB *Alexander Leighton*, Frances Condick.
8. Gregg *Free-born John: the Biography of John Lilburne* pp. 47; ODNB *John Bastwick* Frances Condwick.
9. Prynne *A new discovery of the prelates tyranny* 62–4 quoted in ODNB.
10. Smuts *Puritan Followers* p. 26.
11. Smuts in Griffey *Piety* p. 25.
12. See ODNB *John Hampden* Conrad Russell. Ship money was originally raised from coastal counties only but the scope was widened.
13. CSVP 16 January 1637.
14. For food prices see ODNB *John Hampden* Conrad Russell.

22 Queen Mother Weather

1. Cousin *Chevreuse et Hautefort* pp. 7 and 55.
2. Mme de Motteville, quoted in Cousin *Chevreuse et Hautefort* p. 125.
3. Poisson *Chevreuse* p. 136.
4. CSVP 1 September 1637.
5. Marcillac kept the jewels safe and later returned them. He later inherited his father's dukedom and is now better known as François de la Rochefoucauld, author of the *Maximes*.
6. Poisson *Chevreuse* p. 154.
7. CSVP 12 December 1637 for Marie's arrival in Madrid, 18 February 1638 for the impression she made there. 28 May 1638 for her speaking Spanish (translating between a Spanish envoy and Henrietta Maria.
8. Finet *Ceremonies* pp. 13 and 245–6. On the weather, Wedgewood *The King's Peace* quoting Strafford MSS X 192; CSVP 7 May 1638. For Marie's use of the *tabouret* CSVP 27 July 1638.
9. Laud *Works* vol. 7 pp. 452–3 and 425. CSVP 14 May 1638.
10. CSVP 4 September 1637.
11. Laud *Works* vol. IV p. 114. Laud *Works* vol. VI pp. 379–80.
12. CSPV 5 February 1638.
13. *Marie de Médicis entrant dans Amsterdam.*
14. Laud *Works* vol. III, p. 230.
15. Puget de la Serre *Histoire de l'entrée de la Reine Mère dans la Grande Bretagne.*
16. CSPV 19 November 1638; Finet pp. 254–5.
17. CSPV 1638 12 February.

18. Brown *van Dyck* pp. 176–7.
19. CSVP 1638 19 February. Veevers *Images* pp. 143–5. Britland *Drama* pp. 170–1, 173.
20. ODNB *Walter Montagu* Thompson Cooper, Revd Edward Charles Metzger; *Henry Jermyn* Anthony R. J. S. Adolph; for Lady Newport see CSPV 13 November 1637.
21. Laud *Works* vol. VI pp. 379–80.
22. Whitaker *Royal Passion* pp. 149–50; CSPV 28 May 1638.
23. Strafford Letters vol. 2 pp. 57, 128, 165.
24. CSPD 1637–38 p. 14. Birch *Court and Time* vol. 2 pp. 314 and 343.
25. CSPV 15 October 1638.
26. Memoirs of Col Hutchinson p. 120.

23 Romisch Superstition

1. Lee *Road to Revolution* p. 203.
2. For the historicity see ODNB *Jenny Geddes* David Stevenson; John Row *History of the Kirk* pp. 408–9.
3. ODNB *David Lindsay* David Stevenson; Row p. 409.
4. Lee p. 209; ODNB *Alexander Henderson* John Coffey.
5. ODNB *John Stewart, First Earl of Traquair* J. R. M. Sizer.
6. ODNB *Archibald Johnston* John Coffey; Minority of James VI, uphold true religion, oppose Catholicism, Johnson *Diary* 1.267.
7. CSPV 9 April 1638, 16 July 1638.
8. Wedgewood *King's Peace* p. 238. ODNB *James Hamilton, First Duke of Hamilton* John J. Scally.
9. CSPV 11 February 1639.
10. CSPD 1639 p. 622. Clarendon *History* p. Wedgewood *King's Peace* p. 264.
11. Wedgewood *King's Peace* p. 270; ODNB *Henry Rich, First Earl of Holland* R. Malcolm Smuts. Clarendon *History* I, p. 156; Wedgewood *King's Peace* p. 271.
12. Wedgewood *King's Peace* p. 275 – someone under sentence of excommunication was not permitted to take Holy Communion.
13. Wedgewood *King's Peace* pp. 273, 277.

24 *Salmacida Spolia*

1. Wedgewood *King's Peace* p. 265; Hibbard *Popish Plot* pp. 102–3.
2. Whitaker *Royal Passion* p. 162; Plowden *Henrietta Maria* p. 134.

3. Wedgwood *King's Peace* pp. 277–9.
4. Wedgwood *King's Peace* pp. 299–300.
5. ODNB *John Finch, Baron Finch of Fordwich* Louis A Knafla.
6. Wedgewood, *Thomas Wentworth* p. 267, quoted in Whitaker *Royal Passion* p. 165. Strafford also was made Viceroy of Ireland, so that he could govern Ireland from London.
7. CSVP 9 March 1640.
8. Britland *Drama* p. 177. The original statement of the hermaphroditic nature of humanity is in Plato's *Symposium*.
9. Quoted in Plowden *Henrietta Maria* p. 139.
10. Britland *Drama* p. 184.

25 God Confound the Queen

1. Braddick, *God's Fury* pp. 89–91.
2. Wedgwood *King's Peace* p. 364. The image is an engraving by John Glover from a portrait by Edward Bower.
3. ODNB *Francis Rous* Colin Burrow; *John Pym* Conrad Russell.
4. For the arrival of the Marques Vellada see CSPV 6 April 1640. One of the references to the intrigues of Marie de Médicis is CSPV 15 July 1639.
5. Wedgewood *King's Peace* p. 332.
6. CSPD 1640 p. 152–3.
7. CSPV 11 and 25 May 1640; CSPD 1640 p. 155.
8. Wedgewood *King's Peace* p. 331. Clarendon *History* vol. I p. 188.
9. Whitaker *Royal Passion* p. 172.
10. CSPD 1640 p. 174.
11. CSPV 25 May 1640. Plowden *Henrietta Maria* p. 141.
12. Wedgewood *King's Peace* pp. 338–9.
13. CSPV 1 and 15 June 1640.
14. ODNB *Henry, Prince, Duke of Gloucester* Stuart Handley; CSVP 27 July 1640.
15. Whitaker *Royal Passion* p. 174.
16. CSVP 7 September 1640; S. R. Gardner *History* vol. IX p. 197.
17. ODNB *John Pym* Conrad Russell.
18. CSPD 1640–41 p. 652, 46, 53; Wedgewood pp. 350–1; CSPD 1640–41 p. 23; ODNB *Calybute Downing* Barbara Donagan; Wedgwood p. 354.
19. Clarendon *History* vol. I p. 202.
20. Clarendon *History* vol. I p. 205.
21. Strafford's patent as captain general of the Irish army empowered

him to suppress sedition in Ireland, England or Wales (ODNB). He
was also the acting commander of the king's army in the north of
England because the official commander, Northumberland, was ill,
or pretending to be ill.

22. ODNB *Thomas Wentworth, Earl of Strafford* Conrad Russell.

26 The House of Orange

1. His 'silence' was variously explained as tact, cunning, or loquacity (a joke).
2. The Catalan revolt of May 1640 put Philip IV in a position similar to that of Charles I in relation to Scotland. It was followed in December 1640 by a rebellion in Portugal. The 'Palatinate' was now the Rhine, or Lower Palatinate. The Upper Palatinate which bordered Bohemia and Bavaria had been granted to Maximilian of Bavaria, along with the title and function of Elector.
3. Philip IV had benefitted from the opportunism of Charles I who, for a price, assisted him in transporting men to Flanders, something that the Dutch wanted to stop. For Marie, see Batiffol *Duchesse de Chevreuse* pp. 194–5.
4. CSPV 30 November 1640.
5. d'Ewes *Journal ... Beginning of the Long Parliament* pp. 20 and 25 11 November.
6. Wedgewood *King's Peace* p. 390.
7. CSPV 21 December 1640' Wedgewood p. 376.
8. Laud *Works* III notes to p. 296; Wedgewood *King's Peace* p. 381.
9. For the loan Whitaker *Royal Passion* p. 185 – it never materialised, Barberini repeatedly arguing Charles I must convert before the Vatican could help him. CSPV 11 January 1641.
10. CSPV 14 December 1640, 14 January 1641. CSPV 25 January 1641.
11. CSPV 28 December 1640.
12. Prinsterer *Archives* III p. 430, Finet *Ceremonies* p. 298.
13. CSPV 22 January 1641.
14. Finet *Ceremonies* pp. 301–2.
15. Prinsterer *Archives* III 434, 437. Finet *Ceremonies* pp. 108–9.
16. Prinsterer Archives III pp. 431 and 435.
17. CSPD 1641 p. 560. The Stadholder did not offer military help for Charles I.
18. Finet pp. 310 and 312.
19. Prinsterer *Archives* III pp. 455 and 461; Finet *Ceremonies* pp. 310–12.
20. Prinsterer *Archives* III pp. 387 and 462.

21. Finet *Ceremonies* p. 112 and 304; CSPV 16 May 1641; Wedgwood *King's Peace* p. 397. Charles Louis was released by the French and returned to London in March 1641.
22. Prinsterer *Archives* III pp. 455–6.

27 Henrietta Maria in the Limelight

1. d'Ewes *Journal ... Beginning of the Long Parliament* p. 291.
2. Braddick, *God's Fury* p. 120.
3. CSPV 8 February 1641; d'Ewes *Journal ... Beginning of the Long Parliament* p. 285; Wedgewood *King's Peace* p. 393; Whitaker *Royal Passion* pp. 187–9. If the queen's role In the Goodman affair was known at court – the Venetian ambassador knew it – it was certainly known elsewhere.
4. ODNB, *Francis Russell, Fourth Earl of Bedford* Conrad Russell.
5. Wedgwood *King's Peace* p. 407.
6. CSPD 1641 p. 560; Wedgewood *King's Peace* p. 420.
7. She did not.
8. d'Ewes *Journal ... Beginning of the Long Parliament* pp. 323–4.
9. Hibbard *Popish Plot* p. 178.
10. CSPV 1 March 1641. ODNB *Russell, Francis, Fourth Earl of Bedford* Conrad Russell.
11. CSPV 19 February, 1 March 1641.
12. de Motteville *Mémoires* I p. 195; Sharpe *Personal Rule* pp. 947–8, Clarendon *History* I pp. 280–1.

28 That Fathomless Abyss

1. Wedgwood *Strafford* pp. 292–3.
2. *HMB* p. 32. Whitaker *Royal Passion* pp. 192–3. Prinsterer *Archives* III p. 430. On the bishops, see Wedgewood *King's Peace* p. 405. Bishop Williams of Lincoln created a loophole which took the bishops out of the line of fire – he said men of their cloth need not meddle in the life and death decision on Strafford, and might withdraw from the trial on moral grounds.
3. Wedgwood *King's Peace* pp. 404–6.
4. The 'precise' (godly) Harry Vane the younger, son of the Secretary of State, had found his father's notes, taken a copy and showed it to Pym, who wrote out his own copy in order to protect the young man from charges of disloyalty.

5. CSPD 1641 pp. 539–40.
6. Wedgwood *King's Peace* p. 415.
7. CSPD 1641 p. 567 – also Rushworth *Collections* IV p. 239. It would be the king's signature that made it into a legally binding Act, as for any other parliamentary Bill.
8. CSPV 3 May 1641. The Straffordians retaliated by nailing up lists of his enemies, those who had voted in favour, labelled 'Anabaptists, Jews and Brownists of the House of Commons'. CSPD 1641 p. 560; CSPV 1641 16 May; Wedgwood *King's Peace* p. 425.
9. CJ 3 May 1641; CSPD 1641 p. 569.
10. CSPD 1641 p. 571; CSVP 1641 17 May; Wedgwood *King's Peace* pp. 407–9, 422–5.
11. CSVP 17 May 1641; Wedgwood *King's Peace* p. 423.
12. CSPV 1641 24 May.
13. Prinsterer *Archives* III p. 460 and p. 463.
14. CSPV 31 May 1641; CSPV 24 May 1641.
15. For the king and Strafford's death see Clarendon *History* vol. I pp. 338–341.
16. ODNB, *Russell, Francis, Fourth Earl of Bedford* Conrad Russell.
17. Wedgwood *Wentworth* quoting Rushworth III I pp. 267–9; *Brief and Perfect Relation* pp. 96–7.

29 Pouring Rain

1. Beza succeeded Calvin both as Moderator of the Company of Pastors, the group that headed the congregations of Geneva, and as theologian; ODNB *Sir Theodore Turquet de Mayerne* Hugh Trevor-Roper.
2. *Verney Papers* p. 107.
3. Moore *History* p. 176.
4. Wedgwood *King's Peace* p. 435; CSVP 17 June 1641.
5. Ferrero *Lettres* p. 58.
6. CSPV 21 June 1641.
7. Verney papers p. 109.
8. Ferrero *Lettres* p. 57.
9. Wedgewood *King's Peace* pp. 444–5.
10. Wedgwood *King's Peace* p. 448.
11. CSPV 23 August 1641.
12. CSPV 23 August 1641.
13. Ferrero *Lettres* p. 58.
14. de Motteville *Mémoires* I, pp. 203–4.
15. CSPV 10 January 1642; CSVP 15 November 1641.

16. CJ 1 November 1641.
17. Wedgwood *King's Peace* p. 470.
18. CSVP 15 November 1641.
19. Prinsterer *Archives* p. 501; Whitaker *Royal Passion* pp. 213–14.
20. The king's time in Scotland was in fact contentious. In the so-called Incident, Charles I was implicated in an abortive plot to kidnap the marquesses of Hamilton and Argyll and the Earl of Lanark.
21. See CSPD p. 243 on floods in early January, CSPV 10 January 1642 on the weather improving; Whitaker *Royal Passion* p. 215.
22. CSPV 10 January 1642; Prinsterer *Archives* III p. 498; Whitaker *Royal Passion* p. 217.
23. See for instance ODNB *John Williams, Archbishop of York* Brian Quintrell.
24. CSVP 17 January 1642 records the queen would be indicted on charges of 'conspiring against the public liberty and of secret intelligence in the rebellion in Ireland; also Green *Letters* pp. 71–72.

30 The Walls and Sinews of the Parliament

1. HC and HL journals 3 January 1642. Mandeville sat in the Lords as Lord Kimbolton, but used the senior title Mandeville, the courtesy title of the eldest son of the Earl of Manchester; CSPD 1642 pp. 237 and 242.
2. HL journal 3 January 1642.
3. Whitaker *Royal Passion* p. 219.
4. Green *Letters* p. 72.
5. CSPD 1642 p. 236.
6. HL journal 3 January 1642.
7. CJ 4 January 1642.
8. CSPV 1642 17 January, d'Ewes *Journal... From the first recess...* p. 381.
9. d'Ewes *Journal ... From the First Recess* p. 381; Prinsterer III p. 499.
10. d'Ewes *Journal ... From the First Recess* p. 384.
11. d'Ewes *Journal ... From the First Recess* pp. 381–2; CSPD 1642 p. 242.
12. CJ 12 January 1641.
13. CSPD 1642 p. 246.
14. Gardiner *History of England* vol. IX pp. 132–141; de Motteville vol. I pp. 205–6.
15. For Lucy's friends and Henrietta Maria's knowledge of them see Evelyn *Diary and Correspondence* IV p. 75 quoted in Whitaker

p. 222. For the poet's admiration see John Suckling *Upon my lady Carlisle's walking in Hampton Court Gardens.*

16. Prinsterer Archives vol. III p. 460.
17. d'Ewes *Journal ... From the First Recess* pp. 383–4. French policy at this time was to keep England weak, so the ambassador was briefed to make and keep parliamentary as well as royal friendships.
18. CSPD 1642 p. 242, see also Warwick *Memoirs* p. 225 for the warning given by 'Lilly the Astrologer'.
19. Prinsterer *Archives* III p. 502.
20. Prinsterer *Archives* III p. 501.
21. Whitaker *Royal Passion* p. 225; HL journal 20 January 1642.
22. Ferrero *Lettres* p. 60; CSPD February 1642 p. 276; CSPV 17 January 1642; Prinsterer III p. 501 reference of Kings I, 12, 16. The text was the answer made by the people of Israel to King Rehoboam, when he said to them, 'My father chastised you with whips, but I will chastise you with scorpions.'.
23. Prinsterer *Archives* IV p. 1.
24. Prinsterer IV pp. 5 and 13.
25. CSVP 28 February 1642.
26. CJ 27 January 1642.
27. CSPV 21 February 1642.
28. ODNB *Sir Edward Nicholas* S. A. Baron; Whitaker *Royal Passion* p. 235; Green *Letters* pp. 118–9; CSPD p. 286 for ships.
29. Fr Philip was released from custody at the end of 1641. Birch *Court and Times* II p. 349.
30. CSPV 7 March 1642; de Motteville *Mémoires* I 208.

31 Getting Help

1. Sophia of Hanover *Memoirs* p. 42.
2. Birch *Court and Times* II p. 349.
3. Prinsterer *Archives* III p. 490; CSVP 3 March 1642.
4. *News from Holland* ....
5. de Motteville I 209; Ellis letters series 2 III 295.
6. Prinsterer *Archives* IV p. 48; Green Letters p. 63.
7. Green pp. 64 and 84; Prinsterer *Archives* IV p. 44.
8. Prinsterer *Archives* IV pp. 29–30, 38, 40, 56.
9. Prinsterer *Archives* IV p. 71; CSPV 17 March 1642.
10. See for instance Hamilton *Henrietta Maria* p. 197 on Elizabeth of Bohemia's wish that the queen would be an 'angel of peace'; Green *Letters* p. 62; CSVP 12 May 1642.

11. Green *Letters* p. 77; CSPV 5 September 1642.
12. Bone *Henrietta Maria* p. 149; Green *Letters* pp. 191 and 193.
13. *The Queen Majesties Message* ....
14. de Motteville *Mémoires* I 209 says Henrietta Maria raised enough to arm 40,000 men, which is clearly an exaggeration. ODNB *Charles I* Mark Kishlansky and John Morrill on the king's troops.
15. Braddick, *God's Fury* p. 250.
16. *Somers Tracts* p. 311ff.
17. Green *Letters* pp. 54, 55, 61, 63, 68, 70.
18. Green *Letters* pp. 61, 128.
19. Green *Letters* p. 109.
20. Green *Letters* pp. 63, 91, 86–9, 147. The plan was for Sir John Pennington to be lieutenant to Admiral James.
21. Green *Letters* pp. 122, 147, 153.
22. Green *Letters* pp. 117 and 147.
23. CSVP 11 February 1643. The queen also lost a ship on her passage to Brill a year before CSVP 17 March 1642.
24. CSVP 11 February 1643; Green *Letters* pp. 161–2; de Motteville I p. 210.
25. Ferrero *Lettres* pp. 62–3; Green *Letters* 166–8.
26. de Motteville *Mémoires* I, 211. The queen showed no rancour against her Dutch escort, understanding the difficulties of neutrality.

32 The Impeachment of Henrietta Maria

1. Ireland became divided between royal garrisons, under the Marquess of Ormond, and the Irish Confederacy, which was the rebel government.
2. BCW Project online – timeline 1643.
3. CSVP 10 April 1643, ODNB *Sir John Hotham* David Scot.
4. CSVP 3 April 1643; Green *Letters* pp. 181, 197.
5. Green *Letters* pp. 189, 194, 205; Bone *Henrietta Maria* p. 163.
6. Green *Letters* p. 185; Bone *Henrietta Maria* p. 163.
7. Green *Letters* p. 177; Birch *Court and Times* 2 p. 352; Wedgwood *King's War* p. 196.
8. Bone *Henrietta Maria* pp. 161–2; *Somers Tracts* p. 319; CJ 23 May 1643.
9. CSPV 1 May 1643; Green *Letters* p. 216.
10. Green *Letters* p. 215.
11. *HMB* p. 36; de Motteville *Mémoires* I p. 211.
12. The queen had a real job, which was to command the baggage train, if they ran into enemy troops; Green *Letters* p. 222.

13. On dates Dugdale *Diary* pp. 52 and 53.
14. Cust *Charles I* p. 417.
15. English Puritanism divided between the Presbyterians and the 'independents' (different sects), whereas Scottish Protestantism was uniformly Presbyterian, and opposed variety. The agreement with the Scots papered over these cracks for a relatively short time.
16. For the Brooke Plot see Gardiner *Civil War* vol. I p. 316.
17. Wedgwood *King's War* p. 271.
18. Ferrero *Lettres* p. 62; Dugdale *Diary* p. 65.
19. Cust *Charles I* p. 417.
20. Green *Letters* p. 243; de Motteville *Mémoires* I pp. 184, 212.
21. Dugdale *Diary* p. 69; Green *Letters* p. 248.
22. CSPD 1644 pp. 314–5.
23. ODNB *Henrietta-Anne, Duchess of Orléans* John Miller.
24. CSPD 1644 p. 318; Warwick *Memoirs* p. 307; Strickland *Lives* vol. VIII p. 113.
25. See Green *Letters* p. 249, the reference to the 'company' sent back to Charles I from Falmouth.
26. Green *Letters* pp. 249–250.
27. Green *Letters* p. 294 quoting the Bishop of Angoulême.
28. Prinsterer *Archives* p. 106, de Motteville *Mémoires* pp. 212–3, Green *Letters* p. 250–1 There are different accounts of the Falmouth voyage, I have mainly used the Dutch records as those have the least interest in exaggeration.

33 Unrepentant

1. Motteville *Mémoires* I, p. 215. I have placed Mayerne in France with Henrietta Maria because the timing of the Motteville narrative seems to fit, and because it is natural that he accompanied his patient until she was safe.
2. Green *Letters* p. 252.
3. *Thomason Tracts, Perfect Occurrences* 9 August 1644.
4. Green *Letters* pp. 244–5; Oman *Henrietta Maria* p. 163.
5. ODNB *William Crofts, Baron Crofts* Stephen Porter; Page, *Lord Minimus* p. 173.
6. Green *Letters* p. 260; Page, *Lord Minimus* p. 178–9, 180ff.
7. de Motteville *Mémoires* I p. 222.
8. de Motteville *Mémoires* I pp. 185 and 222.
9. Green, *Letters* p. 326.
10. Green *Letters* pp. 270, 273, 277, 289.

11. Cust *Charles I* p. 389.
12. bcw-project.org.
13. The Battle of Lostwithiel was several encounters culminating in the decisive confrontation on 21 August 1644.
14. There were certain key exceptions to the Self-Denying Ordinance, such as Cromwell, who continued as an MP as well as a general.
15. Cust Charles I quoting 'the King's Cabinet Opened' pp. 14 and 24; Warwick *Memoirs* p. 187.
16. For the watchword see *Rushworth Collections* vol. VI, 'Battel at Naseby June 14 th'.
17. Cust *Charles I* p. 400; Braddick, *God's Fury* p. 376.
18. Cust *Charles I* p. 405; Bone *Henrietta Maria* p. 187; Braddick, *God's Fury* p. 381.

34 Man of Blood

1. Bone *Henrietta Maria* pp. 188–9.
2. Bone *Henrietta Maria* pp. 187–194; for the hectoring see ODNB *Kenelm Digby* Michael Foster, quoting Aubry *Brief Lives*; ODNB *Edward Somerset, Second Marquess of Worcester* Stephen K. Roberts.
3. Braddick *God's Fury* p. 472.
4. Stevenson, *Revolution* pp. 58–9.
5. Petrie *Letters* pp. 166 and 174.
6. Braddick *God's Fury* p. 474, Wedgwood *King's War* p. 611.
7. Scrofula is a tubercular infection of lymph nodes, typically in the neck, producing swellings in the affected area. Usually found when the immune system is weak. The kings of England and France were thought to be able to cure scrofula by touching the patient.
8. Braddick *God's Fury* p. 494 quoting Gentles *New Model Army*.
9. Braddick *God's Fury* pp. 465–506.
10. Ashburnham *Narrative* p. 102; Berkeley *Memoirs* p. cxxxii–iii.
11. ODNB *Oliver Cromwell* John Morrill.
12. Braddick *God's Fury* pp. 545–50.

35 30 January 1649

1. de Motteville *Mémoires* I pp. 222–3 and 224.
2. De Montpensier *Mémoires* I, p. 26.
3. After Edgehill the two young Stuarts were for a time moved into a

house in the city, where they could be more closely watched; CSPV 7 November 1642.

4. Green *Letters* pp. 314–5; ODNB *Edward Hyde, First Earl of Clarendon* Paul Seaward.

5. Petrie *Letters* p. 180.

6. De Montpensier *Mémoires* part I pp. 32, 35.

7. De Montpensier *Mémoires* part I, p. 35.

8. Birch *Court and Times* 2 pp. 409–10.

9. Mary was now Princess of Orange, her father-in-law Frederick Henry having died in March 1647. There are various accounts of James's escape e.g. ODNB *James II and VII* W. A. Speck; Birch *Court and Times* 2 pp. 395–7; de Motteville *Mémoires* II p. 54.

10. Blair Worden *The Rump Parliament* p. 23. Worden estimates that the longer-term reduction in the sitting Members was something like 270 in total.

11. For the temperature, Warwick *Memoirs* p. 383.

36 A Reluctant Messenger

1. At last the problem of the Palatinate was solved. A diminished Palatinate, and his electoral dignity, was now returned to Charles Louis, Charles I's nephew.

2. For the narrative see De Montpensier *Mémoires* part I, pp. 49–51.

3. The narrative is in de Motteville *Mémoires* II, 282–301.

4. Paul de Gondi is known to history as Cardinal de Retz. Gondi was a leader of the Fronde, but very changeable in his allegiances.

5. Green *Letters* pp. 348–9.

6. de Motteville *Mémoires* II p. 351.

7. Birch *Court and Times* 2 pp. 381–2.

8. Motteville *Mémoires* II p. 353.

37 The Royal Oak

1. Green *Letters* p. 361; ODNB *Arthur Capel* Ronald Hutton; Ferrero *Lettres* p. 72.

2. Worden *Rump Parliament* p. 24; Reresby *Memoirs* p. 39.

3. Green *Letters* pp. 361–2. Rinuccini left Ireland about the same time.

4. *Numbers* 25 1–9; ODNB *Oliver Cromwell* John Morrill.

5. ODNB *Oliver Cromwell* John Morrill.

6. Elizabeth recorded the conversation herself – see Carlton p. 356.

7. ODNB *Princess Elizabeth* Gordon Goodwin, Revd Sean Kelsey.
8. Green *Letters* p. 364.
9. Nicholas, *Mr Secretary Nicholas* p. 246.
10. CSVP 28 September 1649.
11. Nicoll *A Diary of Public Transactions and other Occurrences p. 13.*
12. Trevor-Roper, *Europe's Physician* pp. 363–4; Ferrero *Lettres* pp. 89–90.
13. Ferrero *Lettres* p. 93.
14. ODNB *Charles II* Paul Seaward.
15. See *Isaiah* 28:15; *Speeches and Letters of Oliver Cromwell* letter 120 (olivercromwell.org).
16. ODNB *Oliver Cromwell* John Morrill.
17. CSPD 1651 p. 311.
18. I have taken the numbers from Blount and the ODNB on Charles II – there are higher estimates, but the king was certainly heavily outnumbered. Blount *Boscobel* p. 18.
19. Blount *Boscobel* pp. 25–6; for the George see Blount p. 33.
20. Green *Letters* pp. 372–3.
21. ODNB *James II and VII* W. A. Speck on quarrel; Dupuy *Henriette Marie* p. 259. At this time Henrietta Maria moved from the Louvre, which was now the king's home in Paris, to the Palais-Royal.
22. bcw-project.org; Blount *Boscobel* pp. 28–9.
23. Blount *Boscobel* p. 29. The Earl of Derby, a consistent and bellicose royalist throughout the civil wars, was then tried by court-martial and on 15 October was beheaded in Bolton as a traitor.
24. Blount *Boscobel* p. 120.
25. Blount *Boscobel* pp. 51, 136–7.
26. Blount *Boscobel* pp. 140–1.
27. Green *Letters* p. 373; Nicholas *Mr Secretary Nicholas* p. 265.

38 The Consolations of Religion

1. No biblical confirmation of the date of Christmas.
2. Green *Letters* p. 177.
3. Cromwell worked with two more parliaments, and tried to restore the Upper House in a new guise, but he dissolved them both in exactly the same way as Charles I had. See ODNB *Oliver Cromwell* John Morrill.
4. Letter to Christine quoted Dupuy *Henriette Marie* p. 253; Ferrero *Lettres* p. 90.
5. Dupuy quoting Mme de Motteville, *Henriette Marie* pp. 263–4.
6. Barker *Brother to the Sun King* p. 38.

7. de Motteville *Mémoires* IV p. 95.
8. Greenspan *Public Scandal* pp. 399–400.
9. Evelyn *Diary* p. 260.
10. Bossuet *Oraisons* p. 66. *The Imitation of Christ* was a fifteenth-century work proposing a personal and internal spirituality, and a rejection of the material world.
11. Bone *Henrietta Maria* p. 238.
12. Greenspan *Public Scandal* p. 399; Nicholas *Papers* II 5–6; Ferrero *Lettres* pp. 104–5.
13. Ferrero *Lettres* pp. 109–110.
14. Greenspan *Public Scandal* p. 407.
15. Greenspan *Public Scandal* pp. 400–1.
16. Greenspan *Public Scandal* p. 401.
17. Greenspan *Public Scandal* pp. 404, 406–8.

39 Mary's Visit

1. Lambeth MS 645 letters 18 and 22.
2. Lambeth MS 645 letters 22 and 27.
3. The May 1654 peace treaty after First Anglo-Dutch War stipulated that the enemies of the Commonwealth could not be entertained in the republic.
4. Green *Letters* p. 384; Lambeth MS 645 letter 31.
5. De Montpensier *Memoirs* 3 pp. 196 and 211; ODNB *Mary, Princess Royal, Princess of Orange* Marika Keblusek.
6. Lambeth MS 646 letter 35.
7. Amalia was a daughter of the Count of Solms-Brauenfels, nothing better than noble.
8. If decisions about the child were not agreed, Mary had one vote, while Amalia and the Elector shared a vote.
9. Buckley *Christina* pp. 283–4, 306.
10. Buckley *Christina* p. 283.
11. Dupuy *Henriette Marie* pp. 278–82.
12. On Corpus Christi in Paris, see Evelyn *Diary* p. 263.
13. Ferrero *Lettres* p. 108.
14. Reresby *Memoirs* p. 43.
15. Reresby *Memoirs* p. 45; de Motteville *Mémoire d'Henriette d'Angleterre* p. 28.
16. In 1657 Cromwell was offered the title of king but turned it down. On Colombes see Hamilton p. 244, Oman pp. 253–4. For the boat, Evelyn *Diary* 9 April 1655 p. 304.

40 Restoration and Loss

1. ODNB *Oliver Cromwell* John Morrill.
2. Green *Letters* pp. 388–9.
3. Bryant *Charles II* p. 70.
4. Bryant *Charles II* pp. 70–1.
5. The Convention Parliament was so called because it was summoned without the command of a sovereign.
6. Pepys *Diary* 2 May 1660; ODNB *Richard Cromwell* Peter Gaunt; ODNB *George Monck* Ronald Hutton.
7. Warwick *Memoirs* p. 473; Green *Letters* p. 399; CSPV 10 June 1660.
8. Lambeth MS 646 letter 39.
9. de Witt *Lathom* p. 249 on the doctor's prognosis.
10. He had an eleven-year-old son currently known as James Crofts by Lucy Walter. James would later be duke of Monmouth and Buccleuch.
11. Ashburnham *Memoirs* Appendix pp. xciv–xcv.
12. Ferrero *Lettres* p. 124 ; *HMB* p. 55; de Witt *Lathom* p. 254; Ferrero *Lettres* p. 121.
13. *HMB* pp. 61–65; *Ferrero Lettres* p. 122.
14. Pepys *Diary* 2 and 22 November 1660; de Witt *Lathom* p. 256.
15. Pepys *Diary* 27 November 1660; CSVP 24 December 1660.
16. CSVP 14 January 1641; de Witt *Lathom* pp. 260–1.
17. De Montpensier *Mémoires* 3 p. 502; ODNB *Anne Hyde* John Miller; de Motteville *Mémoires* IV, p. 227.
18. Green *Letters* pp. 402–3.
19. de Witt *Lathom* p. 258; CSVP 7 January 1661.
20. de Witt *Lathom* p. 262; Oman *Henrietta Maria* p. 30.
21. CSVP 28 January 1661.
22. Bertiére, *Mazarin* p. 582.

41 Henrietta Maria's Identity

1. Oman p. 307.
2. Plowden *Henrietta Maria* p. 241. Birch *Court and Times* 2 p. 429.
3. Hamilton *Henrietta Maria* p. 253.
4. Charles II had two wedding ceremonies, one private and Catholic, the other Protestant. Oman *Henrietta Maria* pp. 311–2.
5. Ferrero *Lettres* pp. 126 and 128.
6. *HMB* p. 65.
7. Oman *Henrietta Maria* pp. 306 and 320; Griffey *Inventory* p. 162; Pepys *Diary* 21 January 1665. Inigo Jones died in 1652.

8. Pepys *Diary* 30 and 31 December 1662. On the Evelyn visit, Plowden *Henrietta Maria* p. 250. On the happiness of Henrietta Maria, de Witt *Lathom* p. 291.
9. Pepys *Diary* 24 February 1664; Birch *Court and Times* 2 pp. 432–3.
10. Birch *Court and Times* 2 437–9.
11. Oman *Henrietta Maria* p. 308; Bossuet *Oraisons* p. 44.
12. Pepys *Diary* 31 December 1662.
13. Marvell, *Last Instructions to a Painter.*
14. Bossuet, *Oraisons* p. 39 drawn from de Motteville *Life*; ODNB *Henry Jermyn* R. J. S. Adolph.
15. Pepys *Diary* 29 July 1665.
16. See Plowden *Henrietta Maria* p. 251; Birch *Court and Times* 2 pp. 454–6; Pepys *Diary* 29 June 1665.
17. Pepys *Diary* 22 November 1666.
18. On Louis XIV's affection for Henrietta Maria, CSVP 6 April 1666.
19. CSVP 6 April 1666.
20. CSVP 6 September 1666.
21. Plowden *Henrietta Maria* pp. 252–3.
22. Griffey *Inventory* pp. 163–4, 167–8, 174.
23. Birch *Court and Times* 2 p. 467; Griffey *Inventory* p. 159.
24. Pepys *Diary* 2 April 1669.
25. Birch *Court and Times* 2 p. 465; de Motteville *Mémoire d'Henriette d'Angleterre* p. 28. On Anne Marie see Bone p. 251 note 74.
26. Griffey *Inventory* p. 159; Greene *Letters* pp. 416–7 for letter of Lord St Albans to Charles II. For narrative see Plowden *Henrietta Maria* pp. 256–7.

42 The Betrayed Queen

1. Plowden *Henrietta Maria* p. 258. On dates of the services Griffey *Inventory* p. 160.
2. Gardiner *History of England* vol. IX p. 228; Plowden *Henrietta Maria* p. 259.
3. Green *Letters* p. 109.
4. Ferrero *Lettres* p. 107.

BIBLIOGRAPHY

Contemporary sources

Ashburnham, John, *A narrative of his attendance on King Charles from Oxford to the Scotch army and from Hampton-Court to the Isle of Wight* (London: 1830)

Aubrey, John, *Brief Lives* (Secker and Warburg, 1958)

Bassompierre, François de, Marquis d' Harouel, *'Journal de ma vie'* in Michaud, J. F. and Poujoulat, J. J. F., *Nouvelle collection des mémoires pour servir à l'histoire de France, etc.* sér. 2 tom. 6 (1836)

Bassompierre, François de, Marquis d'Harouel (trans.), *Memoirs of the Embassy of the Marshal de Bassompierre to the Court of England in 1626* (John Murray, 1819)

Berkeley, Sir John, 'Memoirs' in Ashburnham, *Narrative* vol. II (London: 1830)

Birch, Thomas, *The Court and Time of Charles I* (Henry Colburn, 1848)

Bossuet, *Oraisons Funèbres* (Paris: 1874)

Bourgeois Boursier, Louise, *Récit véritable de la naissance de Messeigneurs et Dames les enfans de France* (Droz, 2000)

Bruce, John (ed.), *Notes of Proceedings in the Long Parliament* (printed for the Camden Society by John Bowyer Nichols and Son, 1845)

Buonarroti, Michelangelo, *Descrizione delle Felicissime Nozze della Christianissima Maestà id Madama Maria Medici Regina de Francia e di Navarra* (Giorgio Marescotti, 1600)

Cabala, sive Scrinia Sacra Mysteries of State and Government in letters of Illustrious Persons (G. Bedel and T. Collins, 1654)

Chamberlain, John, *Letters* vol. II (American Philosophical Society, 1939)

Bibliography

Clarendon, Earl of, *History of the Rebellion and Civil Wars begun in the year 1641 in England* (Clarendon Press, 1958)

Cromwell, Oliver, *Letters and Speeches* (olivercromwell.org)

d'Ewes, Simonds (ed. Wallace Notestein), *The Journal of Sir Simmonds d'Ewes from the beginning of the Long Parliament to the opening of the trial of the Earl of Strafford* (YUP, 1923)

d'Ewes, Simonds (ed. William Havelock Coates), *The Journal of Sir Simmonds d'Ewes from the First Recess of the Long Parliament to the Withdrawal of Charles I from London* (YUP, 1942)

de la Porte, Pierre, *Memoires de M. Pierre de la Porte, premier valet de chambre de Louis XIV: Contenant plusieurs particularités des règnes de Louis XIII et de Louis XIV*, in Petitot, C. B., *Collection complète des mémoires relatifs à l'histoire de France, etc.* ser. 2 tom. 59 (1827)

de Montpensier, Mlle, *Mémoires* (Paris: 1838)

de Motteville, Françoise (ed. Riaux), *Mémoires sur Anne d'Autriche et sa cour* (Charpentier, 1855)

de Motteville, Françoise, *On the life of Henrietta Maria* (Camden Miscellany, vol. 8, 1883)

de Sales, Francis, *Introduction to the Devout Life* (Dover Publications, 2014)

Dugdale, William, *The Life, Diary and Correspondence of Sir William Dugdale, Knight* (London: 1827)

Duval, François, Marquis de Fontenay Mareuil, '*Mémoires*' in Michaud, J. F. and Poujoulat, J. J. F., *Nouvelle collection des mémoires pour servir à l'histoire de France, etc.* sér. 2 tom. 6 (1836)

Ellis, Henry, *Original letters illustrative of English History* series I vol. III (1825)

Evelyn, John, *Diary* (M. Walter Dunne, 1901)

Finet, John (ed. Albert J. Loomie), *Ceremonies of Charles I – the note books of John Finet 1628–1641* (Fordham University Press, 1987)

Fuller, Thomas (ed. John Freeman), *The Worthies of England* (George Allen and Unwin, 1952)

Fuller, Thomas, *Church History of Britain from the birth of Jesus Christ to the year M.DC.XLVIII* (Oxford: 1845)

Groen van Prinsterer, *Archives ou correspondance Inédite de la maison d'Orange-Nassau* (Keminck et fils, 1857)

Hanover, Sophia of, *Memoirs* (1630–1680) (Iter, 2013)

Herbert of Cherbury, Lord (Edward Herbert), *The life of Edward, first Lord Herbert of Cherbury, written by himself* (OUP, 1976)

Héroard, Jean, *Journal* (Fayard, 1989)

l'Estoile, Pierre de, *Journal de l'Estoile pour le règne de Henri III, 1574–1589* (Paris: 1943) l'Estoile, Pierre de, *Journal de l'Estoile pour le règne de Henri IV (et le début du règne de Louis XIII, 1610–1611)* (Paris: 1948–60)

Lambeth Palace, *Library Manuscripts MS 645 and MS 646*

Laud, William, *Works* (Oxford: 1847–60)

Maria, Henrietta (ed. Mary Anne E. Green), *Letters of Queen Henrietta Maria, Including her private correspondence with Charles I* (1856)

Maria, Henrietta, *Lettres de Henrietta Marie de France, Reine d'Angleterre à sa soeur Christine, Duchesse de Savoie* (Bocca Frères, 1881)

Nicholas, Edward, *The Nicholas Papers: correspondence of Sir Edward Nicholas Secretary of State: Vol. IV, 1657–1660* (edited for the Royal Historical Society by Sir George F. Warner, 1920)

Pepys, Samuel, *Diaries* (pepysdiary.com)

Petrie, Charles (ed.), *The Letters, Speeches and Proclamations of King Charles I* (Cassel, 1935)

Phelypeaux, P., Seigneur de Pontchartrain, 'Mémoires concernant les affaires de France sous la Régence de Marie de Médicis ... depuis 1610 jusqu'en 1620, avec un Journal des Conferences de Loudon' in Michaud, J. F. and Poujoulat, J. F. F., *Nouvelle collection des mémoires, etc.* 2e série. tom. 5 (1836)

Puget de la Serre, Jean, *Histoire de l'Entrée de la Reyne Mere du Roy Tres-Chrestien Mary de'Medici, Queen Consort of Henry IV, dans la Grande Bretaigne, etc* (1775)

Reresby, Sir John (ed. Cartwirght), *Memoirs* (Longmans, Green & Co., 1875)

Richelieu, Armand du Plessis, Cardinal de, 'Mémoires du Cardinal de Richelieu sur le regne de Louis XIII depuis 1610 jusqu'à 1638: Testament de Richelieu' in Michaud, J. F. and Poujoulat, J. J. F., *Nouvelle collection des mémoires, etc.* 2e série. tom. 7–9 (1836)

Row, John, *History of the Kirk in Scotland from the year 1558 to August 1637* (Edinburgh Woodrow Society, 1842)

Rushworth, John (ed.), *Historical Collection of Private Passages of State etc.* (British History Online)

Somers, John, *A Third Collection of Scarce and Valuable Tracts, in the most Interesting and Entertaining Subjects: But chiefly such as relate to the History and Constitution of these Kingdoms* (London: F. Cogan, 1751)

Strafford, Earl of, *Letters and Despatches* (London: William Bowyer, 1789)

Sully, Duc de, *Mémoires* (Paris: Etienne Ledoux, 1822)

The Manuscripts of Henry Duncan Skrine, Esq., Salvetti Correspondence (London: 1887)

Tillières, Comte Leveneur de, *Mémoires Inédits* (Poulet-Malassis, 1862)

Verney, Frances, *Memoirs* (Longmans, Green and Co., 1892)
Warwick, Sir Philip, *Memoirs of Reign of Charles I* (**J. Ballantyne,** 1813)

Official papers

State Papers Domestic (British History Online – british-history.ac.uk)
State Papers Venice (British History Online – british-history.ac.uk)
House of Commons, Journal (British History Online – british-history. ac.uk)
House of Lords, Journal (British History Online – british-history.ac.uk)

Pamphlets

A True Discourse of all the royal Passages, Tryumphs and Ceremonies observed at the Contract and Mariage of the high and Mighty Charles King of Great Britain, and the most excellent of Ladies, the Lady Henrietta Maria of Burbon, sister to the most Christian King of France etc (printed by John Haviland for Hannah Barrett, 1625)
Le Triomphe glorieux et l'ordre des ceremonies obseruees au mariage du Roy de la Grand' Bretagne, & de Madame sœur du Roy. Par le sieur D. B. (Paris: I. Martin, 1625)
Marie de Médicis entrant dans Amsterdam: ou Histoire de la Reception faicte à la Reyne Mère du Roy très-Chrestien par les Bourgmaistres et Bourgeoisie de la Ville d'Amsterdam (Amsterdam: 1638)
News from Holland of the Entertainment of the Queen's most excellent Majesty, the young Princesses Marie etc (London: 1642)
The Life and Death of Henrietta Maria de Bourbon, Queen to that Blessed King and Martyr Charles I, Mother to His Late Glorious Majesty of Happy Memory King Charles II and to our Present Most Gracious Sovereign James II, King of England, Scotland, France and Ireland (Dorman Newman, 1685)
The Queen's Majesties Message and Letter from the Hague in Holland directed to the King's most excellent Majesty (I. Underhill, October 1642)

Secondary Sources

Asch, Ronald G. and Birke, Adolf M. (eds), *Princes, Patronage and the Nobility – the Court at the Beginning of the Modern Age c. 1450–1650* (London: OUP, 1991)

Babelon, Jean-Pierre, *Henri IV* (Fayard, 1982)

de Baillon, Charles, *Henriette Marie de France, Reine d'Angleterre* (Didier, 1877)

Batiffol, Louis, *Vie intime d'une Reine de France* (Calmann-Lévy, 1931)

Batiffol, Louis, *La Duchesse de Chevreuse* (Hachette, 1913)

BCW Project (bcw-project.org)

Bertière, Simone, *Mazarin – le Maître du Jeu* (Paris, 2007)

Blount, Thomas, *Boscobel, or the history of the miraculous preservation of King Charles II after the Battle of Worcester September the third* (Tylston and Edwards, 1894)

Bone, *Henrietta Maria: Queen of the Cavaliers* (Peter Owen, 1973)

Braddick, Michael, *God's Fury, England's Fire – a New History of the English Civil Wars* (Allen Lane, 2008)

Britland, Karen, *Drama at the Courts of Queen Henrietta Maria* (CUP, 2006)

Brotton, Jerry, *The Sale of the Late King's Goods – Charles I and his Art Collection* (Macmillan, 2006)

Brown, Christopher, *Van Dyck* (Phaidon, 1982)

Bryant, Arthur, *Charles II* (Longmans, Green, 1932)

Buckley, Veronica, *Christina, Queen of Sweden* (Fourth Estate, 2004)

Bute, Marquess of, *Scottish Coronations* (Alexander Gardner, 1902)

Carlton, Charles, *Charles I – the Personal Monarch* (Ark Paperbacks, 1984)

Carmona, Michel, *Marie de Médicis* (Fayard, 1981)

Castelot, André, *Marie de' Médicis – les désordres de la passion* (Perrin, 1995)

Cazaux, Yves Cazaux, *Henri IV – les horizons du règne* (Albin Michel, 1986)

Chevalier, Pierre, *Louis XIII, roi cornélien* (Fayard, 1979)

Cogswell, Thomas, *The Blessed Revolution* (CUP, 1989)

Cooper, Elizabeth, *Life of Strafford* (London: Tinsley Brothers, 1874)

Cousin, Victor, *Madame de Chevreuse et Madame de Hautefort* (Didier et Cie, 1856)

Cust, Richard, *Charles I – a political life* (Pearson Education, 2005)

Damas, Jacques (trans. William Mitchell), *Carriages* (Weidenfeld and Nicolson, 1968)

Desclozeaux, Adrien, *Gabrielle d'Estrées* (Paris, 1889)

Dubost, Jean-François, *Marie de' Médicis, la reine devoilée* (Payot, 2009)

Dupuy, Micheline, *Henriette de France, Reine d'Angleterre* (Perrin, 1994)

Fraser, Antonia, *The Weaker Vessel* (Phoenix Paperbacks, 1984)

Gardiner, S. R., *History of England from the Accession of James I to the Outbdreak of the Civil War 1603–1642* (Longmans, Green, 1884)

Gardiner, S. R., *History of the Great Civil War 1642–49* (Longmans, Green, 1886)

Greenspan, Nicole, 'Public Scandal, Political Controversy, and Familial Conflict in the Stuart Courts in Exile: The Struggle to Convert the Duke of Gloucester in 1654', *Albion: A Quarterly Journal Concerned with British Studies*, 35 (3) (Autumn 2003)

Gregg, Pauline, *Charles I* (Dent, 1981)

Gregg, Pauline, *Free-born John – a Biography of John Lilburne* (George Harrap, 1961)

Griffey, Erin (ed.), *Henrietta Maria – Piety, Politics, Patronage* (Ashgate, 2008)

Griffey, Erin, 'Henrietta Maria's Inventory at Colombes', *Journal of the History of Collections*, 12 (24) (2012)

Hamilton, Elizabeth, *Henrietta Maria* (Hamish Hamilton, 1976)

Harris, John and Higgott, Gordon, *Inigo Jones – complete Architectural drawings* (Zwemmer, 1989)

Hibbard, Caroline M., *Charles I and the Popish Plot* (University of North Carolina Press, 1983)

Hibbert, Christopher, *The Rise and Fall of the House of Medici* (Penguin, 1981)

Houssaye, l'Abbé M., *Le Cardinal de Bérulle* (E. Plon, 1875)

Jaffé, Michael (trans. Germano Mulazzani), *Rubens: Catalogo Completo* (Rizzoli, 1989)

Kelly, Francis M. and Schwabe, Randolph, *Historic Costume – A Chronicle of Fashion in Western Europe 1490–1790* (Batsford, 1925)

Kenyon, John, *The Civil Wars of England* (Weidenfeld and Nicolson, 1988)

Lee, Maurice, *The Road to Revolution – Scotland under Charles I 1625–1637* (University of Illinois Press, 1983)

Lingard, John, *A History of England from the first invasion by the Romans* vol. IX (London: 1826)

de Lisle, Leanda, *Tudor – the Family Story* (Chatto and Windus, 2013)

La Légende d'Henri IV, colloque du 25 Novembre 1994 (J & D Editions, 1995)

MacCulloch, Diarmaid, *Reformation – Europe's House Divided 1490–1700* (Penguin, 2004)

MacLeod, Catherine with Timothy Wilks, Malcom Smuts, and Rab MacGibbon, *The Lost Prince – the life and death of Henry Stuart* (National Portrait Gallery Publications, 2012)

Michel, Emile (trans. Elizabeth Lee), *Rubens, his Life, Work and Times* (William Heinemann, 1899)

Moore, Norman, *The History of the Study of Medicine in the British Isles* (Clarendon Press, 1908)

Morrah, Patrick, *A royal family – Charles I and his family* (Constable, 1982)

Nicholas, Donald, *Mr Secretary Nicholas 1593–1669: his life and letters* (Bodley Head, 1955)

Oman, Carola, *Henriette Maria* (Hodder and Stoughton, 1936)

Oxford Dictionary of National Biography

Page, Nick, *Lord Minimus – The Extraordinary Life of Britain's Smallest Man* (Harper Collins, 2001)

Pernot, Michel, *La Fronde* (de Fallois, 1994)

Petitfils, Jean-Christian, *Louis XIII* (Perrin, 2008)

Plowden, Alison, *Henrietta Maria – Charles I's Indomitable Queen* (Sutton, 2001)

Poisson, Georges, *La duchesse de Chevreuse* (Perrin, 1999)

Prawdin, Michael, *Marie de Rohan, Duchess de Chevreuse* (George, Allen, Unwin, 1971)

Reeve, L. J., *Charles I and the Road to Personal Rule* (CUP, 1989)

Russell, Conrad, *Parliaments and English Politics 1621–1629* (Clarendon Press, 1979)

Smuts, Malcolm R., 'Puritan Followers of Henrietta Maria in the 1630s', *English Historical Review*, XCIII (CCCLXVI) (1978)

Strickland, Agnes, *Lives of the Queens of England* vol. VIII (Henry Colburn, 1845)

Stevenson, *Revolution and Counter-revolution in Scotland 1644–1651* (John Donald, 2003)

Sharpe, Kevin, *Personal Rule of Charles I* (YUP, 1992)

Tabacchi, Stefano, *Maria de' Medici* (Salerno, 2012)

Treasure, Geoffrey, *The Huguenots* (YUP, 2013)

Trevor-Roper, Hugh, *Europe's Physician – the Various life of Sir Thomas Mayerne* (YUP, 2006)

Veevers, Erica, *Images of Love and Religion – Queen Henrietta Maria and Court Entertainments* (CUP, 1989)

Wedgwood, C. V., *The King's Peace 1637–1641* (Collins, 1955)

Wedgwood, C. V., *The King's War 1641–47* (Collins, 1958)

Wedgwood, C. V., *Strafford 1593–1641* (Jonathan Cape, 1935)

Wedgwood, C. V., *Thomas Wentworth, first Earl of Strafford 1593–1641 – a Revaluation* (Jonathan Cape, 1961)

Wilson, Peter H., *The Thirty Years War – Europe's tragedy* (Harvard University Press, 2011)

White, Michelle, *Henrietta Maria and the English Civil Wars* (Ashgate, 2006)

Whitaker, Katie, *A Royal Passion – the turbulent marriage of Charles I and Henrietta Maria* (Weidenfeld and Nicolson, 2010)

Wolfson, Sara, 'The Female Bedchamber of Queen Henrietta Maria: Politics of Familial Networks and Policy 1626–40', in Akkerman, N. and Houben, B. (eds), *The Politics of Female Households – Ladies-in-Waiting across Early Modern Europe* (Brill, 2014)

de Witt, Madame Henriette, *The Lady of Lathom* (London, 1869)

Worden, Blair, *The English Civil Wars 1640–1660* (Phoenix, 2009)

Wordsworth, Christopher, *The Manner of the Coronation of King Charles I of England* (London, 1892)

ACKNOWLEDGEMENTS

I am grateful to Nicola Gale, Christian Duck, Eleri Pipien, Sarah Kendall and Clare Owen of Amberley Publishing for their help in preparing my narrative. Nicola commissioned the book in the first place, giving me the opportunity to give my account of Henrietta Maria's life.

The British Library and the London Library were essential to this project. It would have been out of the question to write the book without them. I was lucky also to use the Lambeth Palace Library with its fascinating manuscript collection. Thank goodness there are libraries and librarians of this calibre. The breadth and depth of the collections is astonishing, as is the courtesy of the librarians. Considerable thanks also to the collections, with their open information policies, from which various illustrations come: the British Library, the National Gallery of Art, Washington DC, the Rijksmuseum, the Yale Center for British Art.

Caroline Hibbard helped me on Henrietta Maria's dowry, and Erin Griffey and Sara Wolfson gave moral support. These three brilliant experts on my subject were kind enough to give their time. Mark Bateson pointed the way to archives in Kent and also to Sara. Many thanks to all.

Without the enormously detailed work on the seventeenth century by academic historians I could not have tackled the book in the way I did. Although I have used primary sources as much as possible, the quality of the secondary sources makes them irresistible. It is on dedicated, demanding and often badly remunerated academic work that a reasoned understanding of our culture rests.

Michael and Daphne Dormer were kind enough to show me the lock of Princess Elizabeth Stuart's hair that they have in their keeping, and gave permission to use as illustrations pictures in their collection. It was through their daughter Leanda that I had an introduction to Amberley via Gareth Russell, who was enormously helpful. Many thanks to all.

Perhaps more than usually, mistakes are my own, since there was almost no time to canvas opinion or ask for comment before the text was submitted. I hope there are not too many.

LIST OF ILLUSTRATIONS

1. St. Germain-en-Laye, the fortress palace where Henrietta Maria lived as a child, in the royal nursery. (British Library)
2. The young Henrietta Maria. Engraving by Pieter Claesz. Soutman. (Rijksmuseum)
3. The Louvre, the Paris home of the kings of France. Etching by Jacques Callot, 1629. (National Gallery of Art, Washington DC)
4. The parents of Henrietta Maria, with their eldest son Louis. Henri IV is shown as Mars, Marie de Médicis as Pallas Athene. Gilt bronze medal by Guillaume Dupré 1603. (National Gallery of Art, Washington DC)
5. Charles I, when Prince of Wales. Miniature by Peter Oliver (Yale Center for British Art)
6. Dover Castle, where Henrietta Maria spent her first night on English soil. (Author's collection)
7. George Villiers, first Duke of Buckingham, famous for his beauty. (Private collection).
8. The Fyndon Gate, St Augustine's Canterbury. Henrietta Maria's wedding night was spent in the state bedroom above the entrance. (Author's collection)
9. Whitehall Palace. the royal headquarters in London. Engraving after Wenceslaus Hollar (Yale Center for British Art)
10. The Queen's Chapel, St James's Palace. One of Henrietta Maria's Catholic chapels in London, designed by Inigo Jones. (Author's collection)
11. The Queen's House, Greenwich. Another Inigo Jones building,

begun for Anna of Denmark and completed on Henrietta Maria's instructions in 1635. A number of changes were made under Charles II and in the nineteenth century, including the addition of flanking colonnades.(British Library)

12. Henrietta Maria and Charles I. Engraving by Robert van Voerst, 1634. (Rijksmuseum)

13. Henrietta Maria felt happiest at St James's Palace, when she gave birth. In 1638 the palace was placed at the disposal of her mother, Marie de Médicis. (Author's collection)

14. The Princess Royal Mary, with her husband William of Orange. Gerard van Honthorst, 1647. (Rijksmuseum)

15. The Diana Fountain, commissioned by Charles I for his wife, and originally placed in the garden at Somerset House. The statue is by the Huguenot Hubert le Sueur. The fountain is now in Bushy Park. (Author's collection)

16. Stadholder Frederick Henry, who did a good deal to help Henrietta Maria raise money and arms for Charles I in 1642–3. Dish, 1654. (Rijksmuseum)

17. Henrietta Maria with her adored Jeffrey Hudson. Next to him she seems rather tall. Anthony van Dyck, 1633. (National Gallery of Art, Washington DC)

18. Charles I – poised and withdrawn. Daniel Mytens. (Private collection)

19. Marie de Médicis visits Amsterdam in September 1638. Engraving by Salomon Savery. (Rijksmuseum)

20. Greyfriars Kirkyard, Edinburgh, where the National Covenant was first signed on 28 February 1638. (British Library)

21. Marie de Médicis at the time of her move to England. Engraving by Salomon Savery, 1638. (Rijksmuseum)

22. Charles I, at St Margaret's Westminster. (Author's collection)

23. Merton College, Oxford, where Henrietta Maria lived in 1643–4, and where she became pregnant with her last child, Henriette Anne. (Author's collection)

24. In Holland in 1642, Henrietta Maria makes a visit. Anonymous engraving. (Rijksmuseum)

25. The Beheading of Charles I in 1649. Anonymous engraving. (Rijksmuseum)

26. Oliver Cromwell closes down the Rump Parliament in 1653. Anonymous engraving. (Rijksmuseum)

27. Henrietta Maria as a widow. Miniature by David des Granges. (Yale Center for British Art)

28. Despite the defeat of the royalist cause in the civil wars, Charles II was restored as king in 1660. Silver medal by John Rhoettiers. (National Gallery of Art, Washington DC)

29. A view of Chaillot where Henrietta Maria set up a convent of the Order of the Visitation, and where she wanted to retire. Engraving by Rainer Nooms. (Rijksmuseum)

30. Maryland in the United States was named after Henrietta Maria, and founded as a place of religious tolerance. (British Library)

INDEX